Probing Experience

From Assessment of User Emotions and Behaviour to Development of Products

T0135100

Philips Research

VOLUME 8

Editor-in-Chief
Dr. Frank Toolenaar
Philips Research Laboratories Eindhoven The Netherlands

SCOPE TO THE *'PHILIPS RESEARCH BOOK SERIES'*

As one of the largest private sector research establishments in the world, Philips Research is shaping the future with technology inventions that meet peoples' needs and desires in the digital age. While the ultimate user benefits of these inventions end up on the high-streeet shelves, the often pioneering scientific and technological basis usually remains less visisble.

This 'Philips Research Book Series' has been set up as a way for Philips researchers to contribute to the scientific community by publishing their comprehensive results and theories in book form.

Dr. Rick Harwig

Probing Experience

From Assessment of User Emotions and Behaviour to Development of Products

Edited by

Joyce H.D.M. Westerink

Philips Research, Eindhoven
The Netherlands

Martin Ouwerkerk

Philips Research, Eindhoven
The Netherlands

Thérèse J.M. Overbeek

Philips Research, Eindhoven
The Netherlands

W. Frank Pasveer

Philips Research, Eindhoven
The Netherlands

and

Boris de Ruyter

Philips Research, Eindhoven
The Netherlands

 Springer

A C.I.P. Catalogue record for this book is available from the Library of Congress.

ISBN 978-90-481-7675-5
ISBN 978-1-4020-6593-4 (e-book)

Published by Springer,
P.O. Box 17, 3300 AA Dordrecht, The Netherlands.

www.springer.com

Printed on acid-free paper

Contents

Foreword by Fred Boekhorst vii

Contributors ix

Introduction: Probing Experience 1
Joyce Westerink, Martin Ouwerkerk, Thérèse Overbeek,
Frank Pasveer and Boris de Ruyter

1   Experience in Products 5
    Joyce Westerink

Part I   Probing In Order To Quantify

2   Inquiring About People's Affective Product Judgements 11
    Jettie Hoonhout

3   Atmosphere Metrics 25
    Ingrid Vogels

4   In Search of the X-factor to Develop
    Experience Measurement Tools 43
    Ingrid Mulder and Harry van Vliet

5   Probing Experiences: Logs, Traces, Self-report
    and a Sense of Wonder 57
    Erik Geelhoed, Josephine Reid, Richard Hull and Sharon Baurley

6   Objective Emotional Assessment of Industrial Products 69
    Wolfram Boucsein and Florian Schaefer

7   Measuring Experiences in Gaming and TV Applications 77
    Rosemarie J.E. Rajae-Joordens

8   Sensing Affective Experience   91
    Jennifer A. Healey

9   Brain, Skin and Cosmetics: Sensory Aspects Objectivated
    by Functional Magnetic Resonance Imaging..................... 101
    Bernard Querleux

10 The Assessment of Stress..................................... 109
    Ad Vingerhoets

11 Discovery of T-templates and Their Real-Time
    Interpretation using Theme 119
    Magnus S. Magnusson

Part II   Probing In Order To Feed Back

12 Where Will The User "drive" Future Technology?............... 129
    Antonio Maria Calvosa and Amedeo Visconti

13 A Wearable EMG Monitoring System for Emotions
    Assessment.. 139
    Cecilia Vera-Munoz, Laura Pastor-Sanz, Guiseppe Fico,
    Maria Teresa Arredondo, Francesca Benuzzi and Angel Blanco

14 Computing Emotion Awareness through Galvanic Skin
    Response and Facial Electromyography......................... 149
    Joyce H.D.M. Westerink, Egon L. van den Broek,
    Marleen H. Schut, Jan van Herk and Kees Tuinenbreijer

15 Unobtrusive Sensing of Psychophysiological Parameters 163
    Martin Ouwerkerk, Frank Pasveer and Geert Langereis

16 It's Heart Rhythm not Rate That Counts 195
    Deborah Rozman, Rollin McCraty and Dana Tomasino

17 Transformative Experience on the Home Computer 205
    Kurt R. Smith

18 The Emotional Computer Adaptive to Human Emotion 209
    Mincheol Whang

19 Using Physiological Measures for Task Adaptation 221
    Ben Mulder, Dick de Waard, Piet Hoogeboom,
    Lennart Quispel and Arjan Stuiver

20 The Usability of Cardiovascular and Electrodermal
    Measures for Adaptive Automation 235
    Florian Schaefer, Andrea Haarmann and Wolfram Boucsein

Foreword

Fred Boekhorst

Steady progress in Information and Communication technology has advanced the Internet, once merely a tool for exchange of scientific information between universities, to a platform that enables the transformation of our society. In this new, digital society, people can take more informed decisions because of new mechanisms for finding what you're looking for [Google], new mechanisms of accessing background knowledge [Wikipedia], new ways of engaging with one another [chat], new ways of trading goods [e-Bay] and many more. While these represent already profound changes in our lifestyle, the effects of digitizing society have just begun.

So far, the Internet has made information accessible through computer screens but the next wave will be "The Internet of Things". Environments will become smart and responsive to the presence of people and objects. The key underlying technology here is embedded sensor technology that allows sensors to monitor people and their environment and to communicate measurements. The combination of the Internet [representing Intelligence and pervasiveness] and sensor networks [representing Ambient probing] will unlock many new applications, for example in the field of optimized logistics, smart agriculture or more intelligent living environments. At Philips, we have set up three different laboratory environments that aim to research how an intelligent environment could help people. One of those environments is called "Care-Lab" in which we investigate how technology could help elderly maintain an independent lifestyle. Another example is our Shop-Lab, where we experiment with audio-, video-, lighting- and computer-vision technology to create a new shopping environment.

We have to realize ourselves that, while the enabling technologies have many fascinating aspects, the one thing that truly matters is the experience it creates in people's mind. Hence, while our Experience Labs [Home-Lab, Care-Lab, Shop-Lab] are packed with intelligent sensor technology to probe the environment, the Labs are also packed with observation technology to be able to start understanding how to create a desired experience, for example the experience of feeling safe and secure.

So, probing experiences, the theme of this book is a goal with multiple meanings: on the one hand, it relates to probing environments, deriving data from it to enable more informed support systems to aid the user in their goals; on the other hand, it relates to understanding and measuring the experience we try to evoke.

The book serves the purpose of bringing together experts in diverse fields. I hope that these proceedings serve the purpose of yielding new insights and stimulating further, original thinking.

Enjoy reading,

Fred M. Boekhorst.
Senior Vice President Philips Research
Program Manager Lifestyle

Contributors

Maria Teresa Arredondo
Life Supporting Technologies, Universidad Politécnica de Madrid (UPM)
Ramiro de Meztu 7, 28040 Madrid, Spain

Sharon Baurley
The University of the Arts London,
Central Saint Martins College of Art and Design
Southampton Row, London WC1B 4AP, UK

Francesca Benuzzi
Università di Modena e Reggio Emilia
Via Università 4, 41100 Modena (MO), Italy

Angel Blanco
SIEMENS S.A.
Spain

Fred M. Boekhorst
Philips Research
High Tech Campus 34, 5656 AE Eindhoven, The Netherlands

Wolfram Boucsein
Physiological Psychology
University of Wuppertal, D-42097 Wuppertal, Germany

Egon L. van den Broek
Center for Telematics and Information Technology (CTIT),
University of Twente
Postbus 217, 7500 AE Enschede, The Netherlands

Antonio Maria Calvosa
Innovation Team, Ferrari S.p.A, GT division
Via Abetone Inf. 4, 41053 Maranello, Italy

Guiseppe Fico
Life Supporting Technologies, Universidad Politécnica de Madrid (UPM)
Spain

Erik Geelhoed
Hewlett-Packard Laboratories
Filton Road, Stoke Gifford, Bristol BS34 8QZ, UK

Andrea Haarmann
Physiological Psychology, University of Wuppertal
D-42097 Wuppertal, Germany

Jennifer A. Healey
Intel Massachusetts, Inc., Advanced Technology Group, Digital Health
20 Ames St., Cambridge, MA 01239, Massachusetts, USA

Jan van Herk
Philips Research
High Tech Campus 34, 5656 AE Eindhoven, The Netherlands

Piet Hoogeboom
National Aerospace Laboratory (NLR)
Anthony Fokkerweg 2,1059 CM Amsterdam, The Netherlands

Jettie Hoonhout
Philips Research
High Tech Campus 34, 5656 AE Eindhoven, The Netherlands

Richard Hull
Hewlett-Packard Laboratories
Filton Road, Stoke Gifford, Bristol BS34 8QZ, UK

Geert Langereis
Philips Research
High Tech Campus 34, 5656 AE Eindhoven, The Netherlands

Magnus S. Magnusson,
Human Behavior Laboratory, University of Iceland and PatternVision Ltd
Reykjavik, Iceland

Rollin McCraty
Quantum Intech, Inc. and Institute of HeartMath
14700 W Park Ave, Boulder Creek, CA 95006, USA

Ingrid Mulder
Telematica Instituut
Brouwerijstraat 1, 7523 XC Enschede, The Netherlands

Ben Mulder
Department of Experimental and Work Psychology,
University of Groningen
The Netherlands

Martin Ouwerkerk
Philips Research
High Tech Campus 34, 5656 AE Eindhoven, The Netherlands

Thérèse Overbeek
Philips Research
High Tech Campus 34, 5656 AE Eindhoven, The Netherlands

Laura Pastor-Sanz
Life Supporting Technologies. Universidad Politécnica de Madrid (UPM)
Spain

Frank Pasveer
Philips Research
High Tech Campus 34, 5656 AE Eindhoven, The Netherlands

Bernard Querleux
L'OREAL Recherche
Aulnay-sous-bois, France

Lennart Quispel
Department of Experimental and Work Psychology,
University of Groningen
The Netherlands

Rosemarie J.E. Rajae-Joordens
Philips Research
High Tech Campus 34, 5656 AE Eindhoven, The Netherlands

Josephine Reid
Hewlett-Packard Laboratories
Filton Road, Stoke Gifford, Bristol BS34 8QZ, UK

Deborah Rozman
Quantum Intech, Inc. and Institute of HeartMath
14700 W Park Ave, Boulder Creek, CA 95006, USA

Boris de Ruyter
Philips Research
High Tech Campus 34, 5656 AE Eindhoven, The Netherlands

Florian Schaefer
Physiological Psychology, University of Wuppertal
D-42097 Wuppertal, Germany

Marleen H. Schut
Philips Consumer Electronics, The Innovation Laboratories
High Tech Campus 37, 5656 AE Eindhoven, The Netherlands

Kurt R. Smith
Healing Rhythms, The Wild Divine Project
P.O. Box 381, Eldorado Springs, CO 80025, USA

Arjan Stuiver
Department of Experimental and Work Psychology,
University of Groningen
The Netherlands

Dana Tomasino
Quantum Intech, Inc. and Institute of HeartMath
14700 W Park Ave, Boulder Creek, CA 95006, USA

Kees Tuinenbreijer
Philips Consumer Electronics, The Innovation Laboratories
High Tech Campus 37, 5656 AE Eindhoven, The Netherlands

Cecilia Vera-Munoz
Life Supporting Technologies, Universidad Politécnica de Madrid (UPM)
Spain

Ad J.J.M Vingerhoets
Department of Psychology and Health, Tilburg University
Room P 509, Postbus 90153, 5000 LE Tilburg, The Netherlands

Amedeo Visconti
Innovation Team, Ferrari S.p.A, GT division
Via Abetone Inf. 4, 41053 Maranello, Italy

Harry van Vliet
Telematica Instituut
Brouwerijstraat 1, 7523 XC Enschede, The Netherlands

Ingrid Vogels
Philips Research
High Tech Campus 34, 5656 AE Eindhoven, The Netherlands

Dick de Waard
Department of Experimental and Work Psychology,
University of Groningen
Grote Kruisstraat 2/1, 9712 TS Groningen, The Netherlands

Joyce H.D.M. Westerink
Philips Research
High Tech Campus 34, 5656 AE Eindhoven, The Netherlands

Mincheol Whang
Division of Media Technology, Sangmyung University
Seoul, Korea

INTRODUCTION: PROBING EXPERIENCE

Joyce Westerink, Martin Ouwerkerk, Thérèse Overbeek,
Frank Pasveer and Boris de Ruyter

There is no doubt, that in the future compelling user experiences will be key differentiating benefits of products and services. Probing the user experience plays a central role, not only during the design process, but also during regular usage: for instance a video recorder that recommends TV programs that fit your current mood, a product that measures your current level of relaxation and produces advice on how to balance your life, or a module that alerts a factory operator when he is getting drowsy.

Such systems are required to assess and interpret user experiences (almost) in real-time, and it is not yet clear how to achieve this. What are potential applications of psychophysiological measurements? Are real-time assessments based on monitoring of user behaviour possible? If so, which elements are critical? Are behavioural aspects important? Which technologies can be used? How important are intra-individual differences? What can we learn from products already on the market?

To answer these questions we brought together a group of experts that are known for their experience in a wide range of topics that are closely related to the above scope. On purpose, they come from different backgrounds, such as technology, academics and business. We share a basic understanding that there are various psychological processes that 'experience' derives from (perception, cognition, memory, emotion, behaviour, physiology), and that at least for products and services, the emotional qualities of these experiences are very important.

In pursuing our goal of enhancing positive and avoiding (unwanted) negative experiences, the capability of measuring them is important. Although experiences are subjective in nature, a variety of methods does exist that measures experiences in an objective manner. It is the intention of this book to further the use and development of such methods. Several standard procedures exist for measuring the experience-related processes outlined above:

- To get an overview of experiences in cognitive and memory-related processes descriptions and judgements are often elicited from

1

J.H.D.M. Westerink et al. (eds.), Probing Experience, 1–3.
© 2008 *Springer*.

the users (e.g. self-reports in the form of interviews or question-naires).

- To get an indication of the emotional aspects of the experience physiology recordings are often used. They are more pure in the sense that the user does not have to interpret or even recognize his emotions himself, since they take a physiological signal as basis. Extracting meaning from these data, however, is not always that simple or straightforward.

- Behavioural observations can serve to follow both emotional and cognitive processes (e.g. through facial expressions and button presses). Again the advantage of the pureness of the observations might be counterbalanced by the difficulty of interpreting the raw data.

Data like these serve the important goal of helping to know and understand the experiences certain products and services evoke. In this book a number of related articles are gathered in the first section of the book, entitled 'Probing in order to quantify': In their papers, Hoonhout and Vogels illustrate the importance of self-report measures to probe emotional aspects of products and surroundings. Mulder and Van Vliet and Geelhoed et al. similarly apply such self-reports to the emotional evaluation of prototypes, while using behavioural observations as additional tool. The goal of product evaluation is also served in the papers of Boucsein and Schaefer, Rajae-Joordens, Healey and Querleux, this time using psychophysiological measurements. Vingerhoets reports on the use of both types of methods to characterize stress, while Magnusson proposes a method that can aid in detecting recurring patterns in those behavioural and physiological measurements.

The above experience measurements can also be automated to a certain extent, each type requiring a certain time period to come to relevant interpretation: For judgements & questionnaires this period is estimated to be several minutes, while for behaviour observations, it is more likely to be in the order of seconds and for physiology recordings events might already get noticed over the time course of several milliseconds. When automated, the measurements deliver a continuous indication of the user's experiences. Incorporated in a product or system, such knowledge can be used to optimally adapt it in a closed loop to further the user's best interest.

A series of contributions is gathered around this theme in the second section of the book, entitled 'Probing in order to feed back'. The papers by Calvosa and Vera et al. present future views of how this might become relevant in the automotive and health care domains. Westerink et al. and Ouwerkerk et al. describe technology that will make these applications feasible and preferably unobtrusive. A few products and prototypes like this already exist, especially in the domain of stress detection, and they are presented in the contributions by Rozman et al.,

Smith and Whang. Also Mulder et al. and Schaefer et al. present research on such feedback systems, underlining their applicability with experimental data.

Most authors in this book were invited as speakers to a symposium, called "Probing Experience" like this book, which was held on June 7–8, 2006 in Eindhoven, the Netherlands. As a community, these authors discussed and exchanged ideas and started to develop a common understanding and working model of experience in products. A report on the outcome of the discussion on the nature and the role of experience in products as held during the Probing Experience symposium is therefore included in this issue.

1

EXPERIENCE IN PRODUCTS

Joyce Westerink

Abstract   We report on a discussion held at the Probing Experience Symposium on the topic of 'experience related to products'. It was underlined that there are various psychological processes that 'experience' derives from: perception, cognition, memory, emotion, behaviour, physiology. At least for products and services, the emotional qualities of these experiences were found to be very important. There is a distinction between products as tools, which are meant to save time, and typical leisure time products, which are meant to spend time on: for the first group positive experiences are an asset and negative experience should be avoided, whereas in the second group the explicit intention is to deliver emotions, positive and negative alike.

1   Introduction

This section is a report of a general discussion held at the Probing Experience Symposium. Not all symposium attendees chose to take part in the discussion, but a sufficiently large group of around 20 people did, and this group still contained representatives from industry, business and academia. The topic of the discussion was 'experience as related to products', when and how it plays a role. It was our explicit intention to create an open atmosphere in which contributions from the various backgrounds were approached in a constructive way. Therefore, the discussion session was deliberately planned after the symposium dinner and accompanied by an extra glass of wine. Also, it was preceded by a short group meditative session. The resulting discussion enjoyed the active participation of all present. Furthermore, it was appreciated by most, not only for its atmosphere but also for the gain in insight it brought.

2   Elements of experience

However important for products[1] and everyday life in general, defining what exactly is 'experience' is not an easy thing to do. As a first step one could realize that an experience can be seen as a perturbation of the normal

---

[1] Throughout the remainder of this chapter the word products is understood to include (physically not-embodied) services.

J.H.D.M. Westerink et al. (eds.), Probing Experience, 5–8.

state of affairs. This implies that there is a time course associated with the experience, a pattern of consecutive (re)actions. Both internal and external experience triggers are considered possible. Furthermore, a distinction can be made between passive and active experience: things that are inflicted upon you, and experiences that are part of your deliberate actions.

There are a range of psychological processes the experience could consist of, with some examples given:

- Perception.
  Fine arts, forest sounds were named as purely sensory, perceptive experiences.

- Cognition.
  Finding out the functionality or user interface of a new product involves various cognitive steps which constitute a significant part of the experience.

- Memory.
  Some experiences are remembered for life, and can be vividly re-lived.

- Emotion.
  The value of an emotion, either positive of negative, often plays an important role in an experience.

- Behaviour.
  Gestures, postures, facial expressions were mentioned as examples of behaviours that evolve in the course of an experience episode.

- Physiology.
  Intense (emotional) experiences are often accompanied by a range of psychophysiological changes in the human body.

Thus some experience elements are closely related to processes in the head, others to processes in the body.

3   The nature of experience in services and products

The importance of experience in present day products has already been sufficiently advocated (Pine and Gilmore, 1999), which directly begs the question what the nature of these experiences should be. In general, experiences can have more than only emotional qualities (see above), and it is definitely wrong to equate experience with only the emotional part of what is going on. However, in the case of products, the emotional feelings that accompany experiences are certainly very important. They will have a prime impact satisfaction and thus indirectly on sales.

One could ask whether these emotional experiences should always be positive? It appears to depend on the type of product:

- Some products are tools, things you need, but do not want to spend time on. Their goal is not to create experiences in itself. Nevertheless, they do. For these type of products a positive emotional engagement is an asset – probably for high-end products -, and negative experiences should be avoided.

- Other products are embraced with the explicit goal of spending part of one's leisure time on. Their task is to generate experiences, often positive in nature, but not necessarily so: some elements in movies or art deliberately evoke negative emotions.

The experiences a user has with a product build up over time: The novelty of the product and its complexity will determine how vivid these experiences are, and they will be retained in memory. The lessons derived might stick to the context of the product involved, but could also be integrated in a wider view of similar concepts. In the latter case such memories will influence expectations, not only of the present product, but also of similar products in the future.

4 How to make products that deliver a better experience?

In order to make products deliver better experiences, as a first step, it was considered important to conceive products that fulfil a real need of people. The experience of using these will be immediately recognized as a positive one. This doesn't necessarily imply, however, that people are really aware of what they need. Their view of what would be possible or worthwhile could be obscured by present-day conventions and lack of technical know-how. Thus people need help in analysing the needs of their situations. One potential user need put forward was for products that help us – individuality appreciating primates – to live as social insects in our overly populated world. Another enrichment would be if the products would create experiences that are transformative, in the sense that they have a positive, lasting influence in our daily lives.

Many products are helped in creating a positive experience if the cognitive effort needed to operate them is kept to a minimum. This holds for tool-like as well as for experience-generation products, since in both cases a reduction of cognitive effort will allow the user to direct more attention to what he/she really wants to spend time on. In order to generate a positive experience as far as the user interface is concerned, the cognitive effort needed should have been reduced beyond user expectations. These expectations will no doubt exist and will be based on experience with similar products and products with similar interfaces as they are accumulated in the user's memory. 'Making things simple' will thus be effective in counteracting negative experiences from the past, and for that reason only, in creating a positive experience in itself.

Needless to say, (unwanted) negative experiences should be avoided. According to stress research they are particularly harmful if they occur unpredictably and outside user control (Davis and Levine, 1982). Therefore full user control – of the product and possibly of the environment – is advocated as a safeguard.

5 Conclusions

The main understanding was that there are various psychological processes that 'experience' derives from: perception, cognition, memory, emotion, behaviour, physiology. It was believed that at least for products and services, the emotional qualities of these experiences are very important. For products as tools (which are meant to save time) positive experiences are seen as an asset, whereas negative experience should be avoided. Typical leisure time products (which are meant to spend time on), on the other hand, are often intended to deliver emotions, positive and negative alike.

Acknowledgements

We thank the participants of the discussion for their input: Antonio Calvosa, Janke Dittmer, Margot Franken, Erik Geelhoed, Elize Harmelink, Jennifer Healy, Jettie Hoonhout, Rob Lips, Evert van Loenen, Magnus Magnusson, Bettina Mueller, Ben Mulder, Ingrid Mulder, Martin Ouwerkerk, Therese Overbeek, Frank Pasveer, Privender Saini, Kurt Smith, Martijn Spit, Ad Vingerhoets.

References

Davis, H. and Levine, S. *Predictability, control and the pituitary-adrenal response in rats*, Journal of Comparative and Physiological Psychology 96, 1982, 393–404.
Pine, J. and Gilmore, J. *The experience economy*, 1999, Harvard Business School Press, Boston, USA.

Part I

PROBING IN ORDER TO QUANTIFY

2

INQUIRING ABOUT PEOPLE'S AFFECTIVE PRODUCT JUDGEMENTS

How was the Experience for You Just Now?

Jettie Hoonhout

Abstract   When developing products, considering only "classical" usability requirements is nowadays seen as no longer sufficient – using a product should result in an *experience* beyond usability and functionality. Although no consensus exists regarding what this precisely means in the context of product use, it is increasingly accepted that next to usability requirements, also emotional or affective aspects of product use, such as fun, enjoyment, pleasure, need to be considered. Taking such aspects into account implies that means need to be available to determine to what extent the interaction with a product is indeed an experience. This chapter presents an introduction in how this can be done using psychometric tools.

1 From Usability to User Experience

Traditionally, in Human Factors/Ergonomics, Human-Computer Interaction, and related domains, the main concern in the design of products and systems is usability, i.e., are the products easy and comfortable to use, safe, effective, efficient, and easy to learn how to use. Obviously, also for consumer products these performance criteria are important, especially in the case of safety, comfort, effectiveness and learnability. More and more it is recognised that particularly for consumer products other requirements should be considered as well: using such a device should be enjoyable, and engaging, the device should be appealing (e.g., Jordan, 2000; Helander, Khalid and Tam, 2001; Blythe, Overbeeke, Monk and Wright, 2003; Wensveen, 2005). One could say that next to performance related, classical usability requirements, affective aspects of product use are being taken into account. A buzz word used often now to capture such requirements is that using a product should be an *experience*.

The classical usability and utility requirements mainly come from a cognitive perspective, while generally *experience* is seen as a qualification that has to do with affect and emotion. Perceived enjoyment, playfulness, fun, flow, and

11

satisfaction are some examples of the labels that are often used. The claim that is being made is that products will be "more effective if they are more affective" (Norman, 2004).

However, fun, enjoyment, pleasure, and similar 'experience' labels are still ill-defined concepts (Hoonhout and Stienstra, 2003; Hassenzahl and Tractink-sky, 2006), and despite the growing interest in experience as a vital aspect in software and product design, a common understanding of what this is in the context of product use, and how products should be designed to achieve this objective, is still under development. After many years of research and practice of how to design usable products, it is much easier to give rules and guidelines for the design of usable products than for the design of pleasurable products.

In this chapter, a number of current ideas and views on user experience will be presented and discussed, followed by a presentation of how psychometric tools can be used to determine the affective response of the user to a product.

2   Ideas on What User Experience Entails

The shift from a focus on usability to a wider perspective that also takes into account the emotional appeal that products and product use might induce in users – something we might call *affectability* – cannot be more clearly embodied by Norman's book on emotional design (2004). In the past, Norman always had been one of the main advocates for considering ease of use in the design of products. His 1988 book *The Psychology of Everyday Things* is the clear testimony of that. However, in his 2004 book *Emotional Design; why we love (or hate) everyday things*, he presents a new view on the design and use of products. Norman states that "emotion, or 'affect,' can be seen as an information processing system, similar to but distinct from cognition. Cognition helps us to understand and interpret the world – however, this takes time. Emotion works much more quickly, and it plays an important role in making judgments, what is good, what is bad, and so on.

Norman distinguishes three levels of processing:

- Visceral: The most immediate level of processing, in which users react (automatically) to visual and other sensory aspects of a product that can be perceived before interaction with it occurs. Visceral processing helps to make rapid decisions about what is good or bad, safe, or dangerous.

- Behavioural: This level of processing is about managing most human behaviours. Norman states that interaction design and usability practices have primarily addressed this level of (cognitive) processing. Behavioural processing can enhance or inhibit the lower-level visceral reactions and it can be enhanced or inhibited by the reflective level.

- Reflective: This level involves conscious consideration and reflection on past experiences. This level is also about the personal stories and memories attached to a product, and how a product reflects on a person's image. Reflective processing can enhance or inhibit behavioural processing, but has no direct access to visceral reactions.

An example might be appropriate now. The author owns an old, but still working camera, of the no longer existing brand Miranda. At the visceral level it evokes positive emotions, due to the camera having a good, solid weight and grip, the surface feeling smooth to the touch, and the pleasant sounds the different controls make when being operated. At the behavioural level, it evokes positive emotions, as a result of the quality lenses available, the ease of operating the camera, clarity of the controls and displays. At the reflective level, the camera evokes positive emotions, on the basis of the memories attached to it, and how it came into possession, and the fact that it is a semi-professional camera, producing sharp, high-quality pictures, showing that the aim is to go beyond holiday snapshots.

In *Emotional Design*, Norman discusses the importance of this three-level model to design. This model is based on research in, among others, the domain of emotions, and it forms an interesting framework for thinking about the combination of cognitive and affective aspects of product use. However, he does not come with a method for systematically integrating this model of cognition and affect into the practice of user experience design. But one could say that in the design of a successful product all three aspects need to be addressed, the product should evoke positive affective feelings at all three levels: visceral design should address the first appearance of a product, how it feels to the touch, its first impression. Behavioural design then should address the product's utility, usability and performance; it is about the effectiveness of using the product. Reflective design, finally, is the most difficult and complex to realize. Where the other two levels address the immediate response of the product's users, the reflective level is taking it all in consideration, weighing appearance and performance, and then considering how it matches with ones image, how it makes one look. These considerations are heavily influenced by individual differences, individual histories, and culture.

Before Norman published his three-level model, a number of other authors published their ideas on what constitutes a pleasurable user experience, and in the next sections three of these ideas will be presented.

2.1 Four pleasures

Based on ideas from the sociologist Lionel Tiger, Jordan (2000) developed a model that distinguishes four different "pleasures" in the context of product use: physio-pleasure, socio-pleasure, psycho-pleasure, and ideo-pleasure.

- *Physio-pleasure* is about pleasures evoked by the senses. This includes pleasures connected with vision, hearing, touch, taste and smell. For example, tactile pleasures could come from holding and touching a product during interaction. Olfactory pleasures could come from, for example, the smell of the new product – think of the smell inside a new car.

- *Socio-pleasure* is about the enjoyment derived from interactions with others. Products can facilitate social interaction in various ways – e-mail and mobile phones, for example, facilitate communication between people. Social interaction can also be facilitated when products become a 'conversation piece'. Certain products even may be used to signal that one belongs to a particular group.

- *Psycho-pleasure* is about users' cognitive and emotional reactions. This could include issues relating to the cognitive demands of using the product or service and the emotional reactions brought about by the experience of using it. A product that allows one to complete tasks easily and quickly, will give more psycho-pleasure than a product that cannot be used without making many errors and problems.

- *Ideo-pleasure* is about users' tastes, values and aspirations. This could range from preferring one colour over another or preferring a particular type of styling, or about representing particular values important to the user. For example, a product made from biodegradable materials might be seen as embodying the value of environmental responsibility.

When comparing Jordan's four pleasures with Norman's three levels, it is clear that there are similarities: physio-pleasure seems similar to the visceral level, psycho-pleasure seems akin to the behavioural level, and both the socio-pleasure and ideo-pleasure appear to have commonalities with the reflective level. And like Norman's ideas, also Jordan's notions on pleasure do only provide guidance in product development at a general level.

2.2   Flow

Csikszentmihalyi (1975, 1990) conducted some of the earliest studies that attempted to understand enjoyment (albeit not in the context of product use). Csikszentmihalyi was the first to coin the term 'optimal experience' or *flow*, referring to feelings that his subjects reported to have experienced while involved in leisure and work activities. He postulated that an individual achieves a sense of *flow*, when he is "stretched to his limits" in a voluntary effort to accomplish something difficult and worthwhile. Flow is characterised by a feeling of being in control, by highly focused attention, and by an adequate match between challenge and skill, resulting in an intense state of joy, and emotional involvement in an activity for its own sake. Csikszentmihalyi also noted that happiness comes from creating new things and making discoveries.

Although the flow concept is frequently referred to in publications about enjoyable product interactions (e.g. Hassenzahl et al., 2000), Csikszentmihalyi looked at activities of people performed in the context of hobbies or work, rather than at product interactions. And again, the flow concept does not result in concrete specific guidance in product development.

2.3 Game heuristics

Triggered by the passion people display when they play games, several researchers have looked into what makes games so capturing and playing games so enjoyable, with the idea that findings from such studies could be applied in the design of e.g. software (Malone, 1982; Malone and Lepper, 1987; Rieber, 1996; Rieber et al., 1998). Malone postulates that users enjoy games when a number of conditions have been met. First of all, the game should offer the user appropriate *challenge*, i.e., the task difficulty should just match the user's current skill level, or rather be just a little bit demanding so the user is required to put extra effort into the game. Appropriate challenge also asks for the game to have a goal; attainment of the goal should be feasible, but also somewhat uncertain – goals that one will attain for certain are much less motivating to pursue. Of course, the users should get performance feedback in order to determine how far they are from reaching this goal.

Furthermore, the game should raise the user's *curiosity*, by not making all elements in the game obvious and explicit. For example, curiosity might be aroused by information that is surprising because it conflicts with the user's existing knowledge or expectations, or because it is in some way incomplete. The idea is that this will motivate the user to explore the game, and seek information to remedy this conflict.

Another important element is that of *control*. The willingness of the user to continue with the game is stimulated when the user has control over what is happening, and is for example allowed to influence the pacing or complexity level, or to control other aspects of the game that are meaningful and important to the user.

Fantasy has to do with the scene in which the activity is embedded. This should aim to intrigue the user, and provide an attractive setting. Fantasy elements should not only appeal to the emotional needs of the user (such as being able to identify with the characters in the game, or feel attracted to the characters and other elements in the game), but these elements should also provide relevant metaphors or analogies, that can help the user to figure out the important issues in the game.

Three more elements have to be considered according to Malone and Lepper when more than one player (or user) is involved. The first one is *co-operation*, which reflects the social desire to work with others. The second one is *competition*, the emotional desire to compete with others and compare ones performance with that of others. Finally, *recognition* is about the social need of being recognised and appreciated for one's skills, efforts, or knowledge.

These heuristics have been mainly applied in development of (educational) games (e.g., Rieber, 1996), although the idea to look at what makes games so appealing and apply that in the development of products has been brought up repeatedly (e.g. Hassenzahl et al., 2000; Hoonhout and Stienstra, 2003).

2.4   Some reflections on the presented ideas on product enjoyment

Although useful in developing a comprehensive theory about what makes interaction with products enjoyable, it is not easy to turn the current ideas described in the above paragraphs into concrete design guidelines. First of all, the various heuristics that can be distilled from the publications discussed cannot be generically applied to all types of experiences or situations. For example, challenge is not going to be a suitable or desirable criterion for all products: a coffee maker should not provide a challenge to its user, and operating a microwave oven might perhaps result in an enjoyable experience - the prepared meal, but the interaction with the device itself should primarily be functional and without much hassles, rather than being entertaining. On a different level, not all heuristics can be applied to the creation process of an enjoyable film - a leisure experience that does not require the viewer to be very active, at least not physically.

It is also not easy to translate the heuristics into concrete measures: for example, how much challenge is required, or how is ideo-pleasure going to be implemented. Also, the relative importance of the different heuristics is not clear: is challenge more important than say, for example, fantasy, and psycho-pleasure more or less important than socio-pleasure? Further studies should be able to shed more light on these questions.

And of course, the state of the user is likely to be important in the appreciation of interaction with a device or activity - what is seen as fun in the afternoon, might not at all be appreciated late at night. So, enjoyability, or for that matter any experience, is not solely a property or characteristic of a product, but depending also on personal characteristics and state of the user.

Finally, will the appreciation change with experience? That is, what is seen as fun to use in the beginning, will it still be considered to be enjoyable after having gained more experience with the device? From games it is known that one can promote from novice level to more expert levels, in order to keep the game challenging. But how is one going to implement something similar in regular consumer products?

3   How to measure experiences?

An important issue that will arise, when including affective aspects in the development of products and systems, is how to measure this experience. In Human Factors and related domains, determining the usability of a product in its classical meaning can be 'rather easily' achieved by observing users working with products, measuring countable parameters such as time-on-task, number of errors, time-to-repair, time-to-learn a task up to a certain level, et cetera. Effectiveness, efficiency, and learnability are all criteria related to perform-ance when using the device: how well is the user doing in terms of successful completion of tasks, how much time is involved in that, the number and nature of errors that are made. However, how does one 'count' the experience the user had? Of course, one could determine the frequency of use, or the dura-tion of use, but this will not be sufficient to determine the user's experience. This aspect is rather about the user's attitude and affective response towards the interaction with the device: in the opinion of the user, how appealing, entertain-ing or enjoyable is the interaction with the device. To collect this type of infor-mation about product use, researchers quite often apply instruments such as questionnaires and scales. Since experiences seem to be inherently subjective, it makes sense to use scales, asking the users about their experience (of course in a systematic, reliable and validated way): the psychometric approach.

Other means to study experiences are discussed elsewhere in this volume. For example, physiological measures also have been used to determine the affective response from users to product interactions. The advantage is that these methods give a real-time, continuous measurement of the emotional response of the user to interacting with a product, but drawbacks are that it is more invasive for the participant, working with these methods requires expertise and skill, and data analysis is not trivial.

Psychometrics is the scientific field that studies theory and techniques of psychological measurement, such as measurement of abilities and attitudes. One of the efforts in this field involves the construction of scales and questionnaires for measuring psychological phenomena. The use of such tools has a number of advantages:

-   It enables testing of large quantities of participants over a short period of time, and at relatively low cost, which is practical since time and financial resources to conduct user-studies are usually limited.

-   It is an easy to apply technique (although developing such scales is a rather more time-consuming, specialized and complex job).

-   Usually it is non-intrusive for participants.

And if designed well, scales and questionnaires are able to deliver reliable and valid data. Of course, respondents might reply to items in questionnaires and scales with incorrect or inaccurate answers. Reasons for this can be that respondents might not have the appropriate knowledge to answer correctly, or respondents might answer according to what they believe is a socially desirable answer, rather than answer truthfully. The risk that these and other biases may occur can be reduced by carefully designing the questionnaire or scale, by providing a proper introduction to it, and by ensuring that the respondents will indeed by able to provide a proper response to the items (see also Spector, 1992, Clark and Watson, 1995, and Bradburn et al., 2004).

When developing and applying scales, several requirements need to be taken into consideration:

- Validity: the extent to which a tool or method measures what it is intended to measure. It is the most important consideration in the selection of a tool. There are various ways to assess the validity of a tool, but it is beyond the scope of this paper to discuss these here. A detailed presentation is provided in Spector (1992) and Clark and Watson (1995).

- Reliability: the extent to which the tool provides stable and repeatable results across repeated administrations.

- Sensitivity: the capability of a tool to measure even small variations in what it is intended to measure.

- Intrusion: the degree of interference of a tool or method in the 'task' being performed: the degree to which it disturbs users or flow of user-system interaction.

- Acceptance: the extent to which people are willing to work with the measuring tool.

- Ease of Use: required expertise to apply the method. Methods should preferably be easy to use, easy to learn, not too cumbersome for the experimenter to work with, and easy to work with for the participant as well.

A detailed discussion of these requirements can be found in e.g. Spector (1992) and Clark and Watson (1995). Carefully following the steps described in the next section will increase the likelyhood that these requirements will be met.

3.1 Approach in developing rating scales

In developing rating scales the following steps are recommended (Spector, 1992; Clark and Watson, 1995):

- Test conceptualization: detailing the target construct that one wants to investigate using the scale. To this end, literature studies should be conducted, covering relevant published insights, knowledge, models and theories. Also, consultations with domain experts could provide relevant input. Furthermore, (exploratory) experiments to examine the construct could be carried out. And benchmarking of other, related scales could provide useful input as well. This step should also pay attention to factors such as how the test is going to be used, and by whom. Illustrative examples of what to do in this step are presented by Spector (1992) and Clark and Watson (1995).

- Draft item pool: Based on the input collected in the first step, one can now start with writing items. In this phase, conciseness is not an issue: the initial pool should be as broad and all-encompassing as possible. Each aspect of the construct should be covered – the previous step in the process should have provided input for this. The actual writing of the items should be treated with great care: the quality of the scale largely depends on this. Spector and Clark and Watson give some guidelines, but it is worthwhile to consult a handbook on questionnaire design (e.g., Bradburn et al., 2004). Scale construction is essentially an iterative process, of collecting input, item writing, testing, and rewriting.

- Part of this step is also choosing what format is going to be used: Likert-type formats, dichotomous formats (e.g. yes-no, true-false), semantic differentials, etc. Clark and Watson briefly discuss issues with the various formats – one cannot say that one type of format is better than the other, so pilot-testing could help to decide on a format.

- Test tryout and psychometric evaluation of the scale: Once the initial item pool has been written, the scale needs to be tested in an iterative process – evaluating the clarity of the items to begin with, adjusting formulation where needed. In subsequent tests the validity and reliability of the scale needs to be examined. Various methods and approaches exist to conduct such tests, but it is beyond the scope of this text to discuss these here. Spector and Clark and Watson discuss several of them.

3.2 Development of a scale on user experience: the Fun-Questionnaire

The so-called Fun-Questionnaire (or FunQ), is being developed by the author of this paper as a tool to determine the enjoyability of interacting with consumer devices. Early versions of the FunQ have been used in a couple of studies (Stienstra and Hoonhout, 2002; Bartneck, 2002), resulting already in valuable output for these studies. However, further testing, fine-tuning and validating of the scale is still continuing. In this section, the approach adopted in the initial development of the scale will be discussed.

From the discussion on experience and enjoyment in the introduction and in section 2 it will have become clear that it is not sufficient to simply ask users whether or not they enjoyed using a particular device. Enjoyability appears to be a concept that consists of multiple dimensions, and ideally a measurement instrument should reflect this. Also, one generic 'fun' measure will provide less informative feedback for redesign purposes. Furthermore, considering the context of use of this instrument – the development of consumer devices – several additional requirements had to be taken into account. A rating scale seemed to be an appropriate instrument for this purpose: it is easier to administer than, for example, physiological measurements – important when considering the iterative design and development approach of the consumer electronics industry. Also, it will be less invasive for participants in a test.

In developing the rating scale, the approach advocated by Spector (1992) has been adopted. Scale items were developed after a review of relevant literature about product evaluations (e.g. Jordan, 2000), and enjoyment in leisure activities and games (e.g. Malone, 1982; Malone and Lepper, 1987). Furthermore, interviews with users, usability experts and designers were conducted, to learn about their ideas on the concept of product interaction enjoyment. Aim of the interviews was to collect factors that according to them contribute to an enjoyable experience. These interview results were also used in the development of items for the scale. This resulted in a first version of the scale, with 59 items, covering the different aspects that were found in the literature and in the interviews. The draft scale was then evaluated with regard to the comprehensibility of the items in a test with 20 subjects. This led to further refinements (e.g. rewording) of the scale items. Also, some scale items were removed, resulting in a total of 45 items, divided over 7 dimensions, each in the format of a statement, that are to be rated on a 5-point scale by the respondents, indicating to what extent they agree or disagree with each item. The 7 dimensions are referring to main factors in product interaction enjoyment that were distilled from the literature review and expert interview sessions. The dimensions are overall appeal, motivating, challenging-exciting, curiosity, concentration-immersiveness, efficacy, and pride. In Table 1 a number of example items are listed.

Next, initial tests were conducted with three different electronic consumer applications, all three with some level of complexity in terms of functions and features, and all three expected to differ in enjoyability. To support this expectation before the actual tests would start, a number of colleagues were asked to give their impression of the enjoyability of the three devices – one was judged low on enjoyability (programmable thermostat), one medium (voice recording device), and one high on enjoyability (digital camera). Using devices with expected differences in 'funscores' in the test would help to get an impression on the sensitivity of the scale. In the test, the

Table 1. FunQ dimensions and some example items. In the items, 'this application' can be replaced by the name of the product that is tested. (Items translated from the Dutch).

Overall appeal

- This application looks very nice

Motivating

- Once you have started using this application, you simply want to continue using it

Challenging-exciting

- This application is far too difficult to use (reversely scored)

Curiosity

- I would like to try out what else one can do with this application

Concentration-immersiveness

- Time passed quickly while I was working with this application

Efficacy

- I was pretty good in using this application

Pride
- I believe that my friends will like this application

---

participants were asked to try out the three applications for a fixed amount of time. The applications were offered in balanced order to the participants, and after having used each application, the participants were asked to complete the FunQ scale. In addition, an exit interview was conducted to collect the participants' opinion about the applications and about the scale. Each application was used by 30 participants, who did not have any prior experience with the tested applications before the test. They were paid for their participation. This fact might have influenced their responses on the scale items, but since this was the case for all applications in the test, this was not considered to be a major problem with respect to evaluating the scale. The results of this test showed that the scale was able to demonstrate differences in enjoyment between the applications, and in the expected direction. But the test results also indicated that based on the distribution of the responses, and on the scores for internal consistency of the scale and its dimensions, some items could better be removed. Given the number of participants, and hence the amount of data, the underlying factor structure could not be reliably tested. Presently, the scale is being updated, based on the results of this test, and based on input collected in other tests (Stienstra and Hoon-hout, 2002; Bartneck, 2002). In a next, large study, the construct validity (Clark and Watson, 1995) of the scale will be extensively tested.

4 Discussion and Conclusion

Different products call for different experiences: a game console is expected to provide an immersive, compelling experience. A coffee maker, however, could suffice with a less exciting, but still satisfying and enjoyable experience. Operating a microwave oven should primarily be functional and without much hassles, rather than be entertaining. An MP3 player on the other hand might provide some surprising elements to its user e.g., by suggesting a playlist created by the device.

Given that different products call for different enjoyment 'profiles', a scale testing for enjoyment of product use should allow different profiles. Testing is not about comparing test scores to one overall high score, but matching a score pattern with the appropriate profiles of similar products. This implies that having a tool (a questionnaire, a scale) is not enough. Preferably, one would want to have a database with profiles of how different product categories score, indicating also the range of scores.

Furthermore, the test outcomes should preferably result in formative (i.e. diag-nostic) data, especially in the early phases of development of products, rather than in summative data (i.e. assessment). So, rather than obtain one overall measure of the affective quality of product interaction, test results should provide some indi-cation of which aspects in the interaction contributed to the score, and in which way, in order to offer information for the redesign of the application.

Since affective aspects of product use is a relatively new field (see also Childs et al., 2007), no large body of established methods and tools exist yet. A number of tools to be used in the design process of affective products have been published (e.g. ENGAGE, 2007). Several tools are available via the ENGAGE website (http://www.designandemotion.org/society/engage/). An example of such a tool is PrEmo (Desmet, 2003), which addresses the emotional response of product appearance, i.e. the first impression of how the product looks. Hassenzahl et al. (2000) attend with their questionnaire to novelty and the 'hedonic' appeal of software applications. The FunQ aims to determine a wide range of product aspects, to a large extent covering the factors that Jordan (2000) and Norman (2004) present as important in the appeal of products. Initial tests show that the FunQ appears to be a potentially useful instrument, providing test results that can help to fine tune different aspects of the product and the interaction, based on the score profile. However, more tests are needed to further validate this tool. For example, in a test both psycho-physiological measures and FunQ test scores could be obtained, and compared.

Of course, in order to determine the appeal of the product and of its use, one needs a prototype that allows at least some level of interaction. That means that the FunQ, and most other tools, can only be used at relatively late stages during the product development process – making it more difficult to change the product concept, if the scores suggest that this is necessary. To support guidance in the early phases of product development, theories around affective aspects of product use are essential. The ideas and heuristics as presented in section 2 are a starting point to guide further development of such theories, but more research is needed to build a comprehensive model of which aspects around human-product interaction result in an affective response in the user. This would support the development of products in the early stages in a more specific way than currently is possible.

References

Bartneck, C. (2002). eMuu. An embodied emotional character for the ambient intelligent home. PhD thesis. Eindhoven: Technical University.

Blythe, M.A., Overbeeke, K., Monk, A.F., & Wright P. C. (Eds.). (2003). *Funology: From usability to enjoyment*. Dordrecht, The Netherlands: Kluwer Academic Publishers.

Bradburn, N.M., Sudman, S., & Wansink, B. (2004). *Asking questions: the definitive guide to questionnaire design*. San Fransisco, CA: Jossey-Bass.

Childs, T., Rust, C., Wright, P., Ainsworth, P., & Nobbs, J. (eds.) (2007). Affective communications in design challenges for researchers. *CoDesign*, 3, supplement 1.

Clark, L.A., Watson, D. (1995). Constructing validity: basic issues in objective scale development. *Psychological assessment*, 7(3), 309–319.

Csikszentmihalyi, M. (1975). *Beyond boredom and anxiety*. San Francisco, CA: Jossy-Bass.

Csikszentmihalyi, M. (1990). *Flow: The Psychology of Optimal Experience*. New York: Harper & Row.

Desmet, P.M.A. (2003). Measuring emotion; development and application of an instrument to measure emotional responses to products. In: M.A. Blythe, A.F. Monk, K. Overbeeke, & P.C. Wright (Eds.), *Funology: from usability to enjoyment* (pp. 111–123). Dordrecht: Kluwer Academic Publishers.

ENGAGE (2007). Report on the evaluation of generative tools and methods for 'emotional design'. Deliverable D15.3. 2006. EU project Engage 520998.

Hassenzahl, M., Platz. A., Burmester, M., & Lehner, K. (2000). Hedonic and Ergonomic Quality Aspects Determine a Software's Appeal. In *Proceedings of CHI 2000*, the Hague. ACM, 201–208.

Hassenzahl, M, Tractinksy, N. (2006). User experience – a research agenda. *Behaviour and Information Technology*, 25(2), 91–97.

Helander, M.G., Khalid, H.K., & Tham, eds. (2001). *Proceedings of the International Conference on Affective Human Factors Design*. London: Asean Academic Press.

Hoonhout, H.C.M., Stienstra, M.A. (2003). Which factors in a consumer device make the user smile? In: D. de Waard, K. Brookhuis, S. Sommer, & W. Verwey (eds.), *Human Factors in the Age of Virtual Reality*. Maastricht: Shaker Publications.

Jordan, P.W. (2000). *Designing pleasurable products: an introduction to new human factors*. London: Taylor & Francis.

Malone, T.W. (1982). Heuristics for designing enjoyable user interfaces: Lessons from computer games, *Proceedings of the Conference on Human Factors in Computing Systems*, 63–68.

Malone, T. W., & Lepper, M. R. (1987). Making learning fun: A taxonomy of intrinsic motivation for learning. In R. E. Snow & M. J. Farr (Eds.). *Aptitude, learning and instruction. Volume 3: Conative and affective process analysis.* Hillsdale, NJ: Lawrence Erlbaum.

Norman, D.A. (1988). *The psychology of everyday things.* New York: Basic Books.

Norman, D.A. (2004). *Emotional design. Why we love (or hate) everyday things.* New York: Basic Books.

Rieber, L.P. (1996). Seriously considering play: designing interactive learning environments based on the blending of microworlds, simulations, and games. *Educational technology research and development* vol.44 (2), 43–58.

Rieber, L.P., Smith, L., & Noah, D. (1998). The value of serious play. *Educational Technology,* vol.38 (6), 29–37.

Spector, P.E. (1992). *Summated rating scale construction. An Introduction.* Newbury Park: Sage.

Stienstra, M.A., Hoonhout, H.C.M. (2002). TOONS Toys. Interaction toys as means to create a fun experience. In M. M. Bekker, P. Markopoulus, & Kersten-Tsikalkina (Eds.), *Interactive design and Children.*, p199–211. Maastricht: Shaker Publishing.

Wensveen, S.A.G. (ed.). (2005). *Designing pleasurable products and interfaces. Proceedings of the DPPI 2005 conference.* Eindhoven, the Netherlands: Technische Universiteit Eindhoven.

3

ATMOSPHERE METRICS

Development of a Tool to Quantify Experienced Atmosphere

Ingrid Vogels

Abstract   This paper presents a method to quantify the atmosphere of an environment as experienced by human observers. Atmosphere is defined as the experience of the surrounding in relation to ourselves, through the perception of external elements and internal sensations. An atmosphere does not necessarily give rise to a particular feeling, it only has the potency of changing people's affective state. Hence, methodologies to measure mood and emotion cannot be used. The new tool consists of a semantic differential rating scale for atmosphere perception in combination with a factor analysis. Two experiments are presented that demonstrate the usability and applicability of the method.

1   Introduction

Light has an immense effect on human beings. On sunny days people are usually more cheerful than during dark foggy days. Some people are extremely sensitive to light and experience fatigue and depression during prolonged periods of reduced daylight. Artificial light has also been found to affect people's mood, well-being and task performance (e.g. Flynn, 1992; Knez, 1995; Knez, 2001; Knez and Kers, 2000, McColl and Veitch, 2001). Hence, good lighting design is very important. But, what is 'good'? In the past, most researchers have focused on the effect of light on visual performance (e.g. Boyce, 2003). This has resulted in guidelines for the amount of illumination and tolerated glare for various situations and tasks. However, designers and researchers now realize that light should not only facilitate visibility but also accomplish an appropriate atmosphere and give people a pleasant feeling. In other words, research has shifted towards the biological and psychological effects of light.

In order to investigate the influence of light on mood and perceived atmosphere, a reliable method and metric is needed to measure and describe the experience of people, respectively. Various methodologies are used to

J.H.D.M. Westerink et al. (eds.), Probing Experience, 25–41.
© 2008 *Springer.*

measure affective states, such as emotions, moods, traits and sentiments. These methodologies can be classified into measurements of behavioural reactions (e.g. avoidance or approach), of expressive reactions (e.g. facial or vocal expressions), of physiological reactions (e.g. heart rate or galvanic skin response), or subjective assessments (e.g. semantic differential ratings or emotion pictures). Within the class of subjective assessments, various methods exist that are based on different emotional models. Some models assume that a number of emotions form the core of the repertoire of emotions and that all other -secondary- emotions can be derived from this set of basic emotions (e.g. Ekman, 1971; Izard, 1977; Plutchik, 1980; Tomkins, 1984). Other models assume that emotions can be described by a number (N) of underlying dimensions and that each emotion can be represented as a point in a N-dimensional space. An example of such a model is the PAD model, which is based on the observation that semantic differential ratings of diverse stimuli (e.g. paintings, gestures and adjectives describing emotions) have repeatedly identified evaluation, activity and potency as three basic dimensions of meaning. The PAD model uses pleasure-displeasure (P) as the emotional counterpart of positive-negative evaluation, arousal-nonarousal (A) as the correlate of stimulus activity, and, dominance-submissiveness (D) as the negative correlate of stimulus potency (Mehrabian and Russell, 1974). Another example is the PANAS model, which consists of two dimensions: positive affect (PA) and negative affect (NA) (Watson et al., 1988). Positive affect reflects the extent to which a person feels enthusiastic, active and alert, while negative affect includes aversive mood states as distress, anger, contempt, disgust, guilt and fear.

Atmosphere differs from emotion and mood in the sense that it is not an affective state, but it is the experience of the surrounding in relation to ourselves. The atmosphere of an environment is a subjective experience through the perception of external elements and internal sensations, but it does not necessarily give rise to a particular feeling. An environment only has the *potency* of changing people's mood in accordance with its atmosphere. If I am thinking of all the work I have to do, I would still feel pretty stressed in a relaxed environment. However, in a stressful environment I will never feel relaxed. Hence, the effect of environmental variables on mood will depend, among other things, on the initial affective state of the observer. On the other hand, the effect on perceived atmosphere is expected to be independent of people's mood. Nevertheless, people might have different opinions about the atmosphere of an environment depending on factors like age, culture and previous experience, but their opinion is expected to be stable over time (at least for a period of a few days).

Since atmosphere is presumably a more stable and less complicated variable than mood, our research aims at investigating how to create a particular atmosphere in a given environment with various light sources. Once this is fully understood, it might be interesting to study when and how an environment with a particular atmosphere changes people's mood. In contrast to mood, there is not much literature on methodologies for measuring atmosphere. Flynn (1977) has been one of the first to measure the subjective impression of environments for various lighting systems using semantic differential rating scales. He showed by means of factor analysis that there were three dominant categories of terms that discriminated between the lighting conditions. The categories were called: evaluative impression (e.g. pleasant-unpleasant), visual clarity (e.g. clear-hazy) and spaciousness (e.g. spacious-cramped). The last two categories describe how the environment is visually perceived, but not how the environment is *experienced*. Only the evaluative category contains a few atmosphere descriptors.

This paper presents a new measurement tool to quantify the atmosphere of an environment as experienced by human observers. Fist, a lexicon for describing atmosphere was collected and an atmosphere questionnaire was developed based on this lexicon. Then, the discriminative power of the atmosphere questionnaire was determined by testing the questionnaire for eleven different public spaces. Finally, the method was used to measure the perceived atmosphere in a simulated fashion shop for four different light settings.

2　Development of atmosphere questionnaire

This section describes a study that aimed at collecting terms that people use to describe the atmosphere of an environment. The terms were analysed, grouped and used to design a questionnaire that measures the experienced atmosphere.

2.1　Method

Around 200 people were asked to fill in a questionnaire about the phenomenon 'atmosphere'. Forty-three people responded within the time limit of one week. Thirty-three respondents were male and ten respondents were female. Their age ranged between 23 and 58 years, with an average of 41 years. People were asked to imagine a particular location (e.g. their living room, their favourite shop, the situation at their dentist) and to describe the atmosphere of the environment with as many terms as possible, e.g. 'knus' (cosy) or 'formeel' (formal). Next, they were asked to think of other terms that could be used to describe the atmosphere of an environment. The questionnaire was written in Dutch, since Dutch people were considered to be the most important target group at that moment in time.

2.2 Results

In total 184 different terms were collected. A close look revealed that the terms could be classified into three groups: (1) terms that are related to the emotion or mood evoked by the environment, (2) terms that are related to the atmosphere of the environment and (3) terms that give a more or less objective description of the environment. For emotion terms, such as 'angstig' (terrified), one can say: I feel '…'. For atmosphere terms, such as 'knus' (cosy), one can say: this environment is '…'. Most emotion terms can be changed into atmosphere terms, e.g. 'angstig' (terrified) becomes 'beangstigend' (terrifying). On the other hand, not all atmosphere terms can be changed into an emotion term, e.g. I cannot feel myself formal (although I can behave formally). The third class of terms are only related to the environment itself, such as 'schoon' (clean) and 'helder' (bright), and not to the feeling or association it might evoke.

The following procedure was applied to reduce the large list of terms. First, terms that fell into the third class were removed. Second, terms with

Table 1.   Final selection of atmosphere terms together with the English translation.

Atmosphere term	Translation	Atmosphere term	Translation
afstandelijk	*detached*	levendig	*lively*
beangstigend	*terrifying*	luxueus	*luxurious*
bedompt	*musty*	mysterieus	*mysterious*
bedreigend	*threatening*	ongedwongen	*uninhibited*
behaaglijk	*cosy*	ongemakkelijk	*uncomfortable*
beklemmend	*oppressive*	onrustig	*restless*
deprimerend	*depressed*	ontspannen	*relaxed*
enerverend	*exciting*	persoonlijk	*personal*
formeel	*formal*	romantisch	*romantic*
gastvrij	*hospitable*	ruimtelijk	*spatial*
geborgen	*safe*	rustgevend	*tranquil*
gemoedelijk	*pleasant*	saai	*boring*
gespannen	*tense*	sloom	*lethargic*
gezellig	*pleasant*	stimulerend	*stimulating*
inspirerend	*inspiring*	toegankelijk	*accessible*
intiem	*intimate*	vijandig	*hostile*
kil	*chilly*	vrolijk	*cheerful*
knus	*cosy*	warm	*warm*
koud	*cool*	zakelijk	*business*

Note: Please remind that it is not always possible to find a word with exactly the same meaning. Therefore, these translated words should only be used as an indication of the meaning and should certainly not be used to make an English version of the questionnaire.

a similar meaning were grouped, such as 'rustgevend' and 'ontspannen' (relaxed) or 'behaaglijk' and 'gemoedelijk' (pleasant). Next, from each group a few terms were selected in order to generate a practical list of 38 terms. Finally, we checked whether the list was sufficiently complete, i.e. whether we could think of other atmosphere terms with a completely different meaning than described by the list of terms. Table 1 shows the final list of 38 Dutch terms together with the best possible English translation.

The 38 atmosphere terms were used to develop an atmosphere questionnaire. The questionnaire contained a list of all the atmosphere terms. For each term, participants were asked to rate the applicability of this term with respect to the environment they were visiting, on a 5-point scale from 'not applicable at all' to 'very applicable'. In addition, participants could write down terms that were very applicable to the environment and not listed.

3 Usability of atmosphere questionnaire

This section describes an experiment to test whether the atmosphere questionnaire can be used to distinguish between the atmosphere of very different environments. A method is presented to analyse the responses to the questionnaire and to quantify the atmosphere of each environment along two dimensions.

3.1 Method

Eight persons participated in the experiment: five male and three female. All participants were native Dutch. Their age ranged between 32 and 58 years, with an average of 45 years. Participants were asked to visit eleven locations in the centre of Eindhoven. They were split into two groups of 4 people, each visiting the locations at a different day. The experiment took place at a sunny day between 10 and 12 in the morning. The locations were: a fashion shop (Men at Work), a sport shop (Perry Sport), a body shop (De Tuinen), a cell phone shop (Orange), a shoes shop (de Demer), a fast-food restaurant (Mac Donalds), a bank (ABN AMRO), a decoration shop (Valentino), a café (Queens), a casino (Toy-toy), an interior shop (Sfeervol Wonen). For each location, participants were asked to walk around and to pay attention to the atmosphere evoked by the environment. They had to take into account all aspects that contributed to the atmosphere, such as the building, the music and the people that were present. In the mean time, they had to fill in the atmosphere questionnaire. When all participants were ready, the group went to the next location.

3.2 Results

The responses of the participants were entered into a data sheet and analysed with a statistical program. Various analyses were performed (1) to test for differences between participants, (2) to test whether the atmosphere terms were suitable to discriminate between locations, (3) to find underlying factors of atmosphere perception and to test the reliability of these atmosphere factors and (4) to describe the experienced atmosphere of the locations in terms of the atmosphere factors.

3.2.1 Effect of participant   To test whether participants gave similar responses, Spearman's rho correlation coefficients were calculated between participants. Usually, correlations larger than about 0.8 are considered as being meaningful, although lower values can sometimes become significant. All correlations were found to be significant ($p < 0.05$). They ranged between 0.29 and 0.65 with an average of 0.45. Hence, correlations between participants were relatively small. A Pearson Chi-square test revealed a significant effect of participant on the distribution of the responses ($p < 0.001$), even after normalising the data per participant. This means that the number of times a participant used the ratings 1 to 5 varied between participants. The same analysis was performed per location and per atmosphere term. The effect of participant was significant for all locations and for 22 of the 38 atmosphere terms ($p < 0.05$). Hence, both the correlation and chi-square analyses indicate that not all participants evaluated the locations in the same way.

3.2.2 Effect of location   For each location the full scale was used. This means, that for each location some atmosphere terms were very applicable and other atmosphere terms were not applicable at all. Also, people did not come up with other terms they thought would be more appropriate to describe the experienced atmosphere. A Pearson Chi-square test revealed a significant effect of atmosphere term for each location ($p < 0.01$). Hence, the terms were suitable to describe the atmosphere of the locations and people could distinguish between terms.

To test whether the locations were evaluated differently, Spearman's rho correlation coefficients were calculated between locations. Correlation coefficients ranged between −0.29 and 0.78. Relatively high correlations were observed between the body shop and the decoration shop (0.61), the body shop and the café (0.70), the body shop and the interior shop (0.69), the decoration shop and the café (0.59), the decoration shop and the interior shop (0.62), and, the café and the interior shop (0.78). All other correlations were lower than 0.50. Hence, the experienced atmosphere of the body shop, decoration shop, café and interior shop were very similar, whereas the other locations were judged differently. The effect of location was confirmed by a Pearson Chi-square test for 32 of the 36 atmosphere terms ($p < 0.05$).

3.2.3 Atmosphere factors

The analyses described above demonstrate that people could distinguish between the atmosphere terms, i.e. they gave different responses for the different atmosphere terms. In addition, they could distinguish between the various locations. However, participants differed in their evaluation of the locations. This could mean that people interpreted the terms in a different way and, therefore, correlations between terms would be very low. On the other hand, participants could have interpreted the terms in a similar way but just have different opinions about the evoked atmospheres of the locations. In this case, terms with similar (or opposite) meaning would be highly correlated.

The Spearman's rho correlation coefficient between atmosphere terms ranged between -0.61 and 0.82. The observation that some terms were positively or negatively correlated, suggests that participants did use these terms in a similar way. For instance, when participants evaluated the term 'behaaglijk' as very appropriate, they also found the term 'geborgen' very appropriate and the term 'kil' not appropriate. However, not all participants found the term 'behaaglijk' appropriate for the same location. One participant could say 'behaaglijk' whereas another participant could say 'kil'.

In order to get more insight into the relation between terms and to find out whether the 38 atmosphere terms could be described in terms of a few underlying dimensions, a principal component analysis (PCA) was performed. This statistical analysis generates linear transformations of the independent variables, called factors, such that the first factor accounts for a large part of the variance of the data and the contribution of each successive factor is lower than the previous one. In this experiment, the independent variables are the 38 atmosphere terms and the PCA generates 38 factors that together explain 100% of the variance of the data. For each factor, an eigenvalue is calculated, that represents the importance of the factor and a list of factor loadings, which indicates to what extent each variable contributes to this factor. In order to simplify the interpretation of the factors, an orthogonal rotation method (Varimax) is often used to minimize the number of variables that have high loadings on more than one factor.

There are several criteria used in the literature to decide how many factors should be extracted. One method is to take all factors with eigenvalues larger than 1. A second method is to take those factors that explain 90% of the variance of the data. Another frequently used method is to take those factors with an eigenvalue that is clearly distinct from that of the successive factor. This can be visualised by plotting the eigenvalues as a function of the successive factors (a scree-plot) and taking the factors before the first 'elbow' of the curve. According to these criteria, the number of atmosphere factors would be seven, sixteen and two for the first, second and third method, respectively. Since a large number of factors is not what we aim at, it was decided to use the third method and to continue with two factors. After a Varimax rotation, these factors explained 30% and 19% of the variance of the data.

Figure 1 shows the factor loadings of each atmosphere term for the two factors. Some terms have high factor loadings on the first factor and low loadings on the second factor (e.g. 'intiem'), whereas other terms have high loadings on the second factor and low loading on the fist factor (e.g. 'stimulerend'). Other terms have relatively low loadings on both factors (e.g. 'formeel'). Therefore, the atmosphere terms were divided into three groups, based on the *absolute* values of the factor loadings. The first group contains terms with loadings larger than 0.5 for the first factor and smaller than 0.5 for the second factor. The second group contains terms with loadings larger than 0.5 for the second factor and smaller than 0.5 for the first factor. And the third group consists of all other terms, i.e. terms with loadings smaller than 0.5 for both factors.

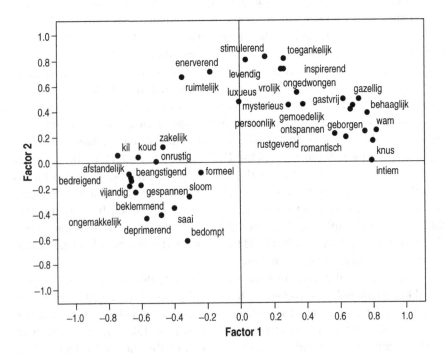

Figure 1. Factor loadings of all atmosphere terms.

Within the first two groups, two subgroups are created, with either positive or negative loadings on the primary factor. A reliability test was used to calculate for each subgroup the proportion of the variability in the responses that is the result of differences between the participants. That is, answers to a reliable questionnaire will differ because participants have different opinions, not because the questionnaire is confusing or has multiple interpretations. Cronbach's alpha was 0.89, 0.89 and 0.88 for the terms with positive loadings on factor 1, terms with negative loadings on factor 1 and terms with positive loadings on factor 2, respectively. As the analysis requires at least two terms, the reliability could not be determined for the negative part of factor 2. As expected, low reliability was obtained for the terms with low loadings on both factors (alpha = 0.34). The high reliability values demonstrate that participants used the terms within each subgroup in a similar way. Therefore, one may conclude that the atmosphere questionnaire is a reliable method to distinguish at least two dimensions of atmosphere perception.

The two atmosphere factors can be interpreted by reviewing the meaning of the terms that contribute to each factor. The terms of the first factor can be described as different degrees of 'behaaglijkheid' (hereafter referred to as 'cosiness') and the terms of factor two can be described as different degrees of 'levendigheid' (hereafter referred to as 'liveliness'). Interestingly, these dimensions are comparable to the evaluation (positive versus negative affect) and activity (arousal versus nonarousal) dimensions that have been found in many other studies.

3.2.4 Atmosphere of locations Now that the dimensions underlying atmosphere perception have been extracted, the responses of the participants for each location can be expressed in terms of these dimensions. For each participant and each location a 'cosiness' score and 'liveliness' score was computed by weighting the response to each atmosphere term by the factor loadings of the PCA, as described in equation 1:

$$F_j = \frac{\sum_{i=1}^{38} R_i \times L\_pos_{ij}}{\sum_{i=1}^{38} L\_pos_{ij}} + \frac{\sum_{i=1}^{38} R_i \times L\_neg_{ij}}{\sum_{i=1}^{38} L\_neg_{ij}} \qquad (1)$$

where F_j corresponds to the weighted score for factor 1 or factor 2, R_i is the rating of term i (scaled between 0 and 1), L_pos_{ij} and L_neg_{ij} are the positive and negative loadings of term i on factor j. First, a weighted score was computed for the positive loadings and for the negative loadings, respectively. Then the positive and negative scores were added. This was done because the sum of the positive loadings could be different than the sum of the negative loadings. If the ratings were weighted with the sum of the absolute value of the loadings, the weighted score would be biased towards positive (or negative) when most terms would have a positive (or negative) loading.

Figure 2 shows the 'cosiness' score and 'liveliness' score for each location averaged across participants. The crosses correspond to the standard error of the mean. The figure clearly shows that the experienced atmosphere depends on location. This was confirmed by an ANOVA that revealed a significant main effect of location and participant both for 'cosiness' and 'liveliness' ($p < 0.001$). The atmospheres of the locations are very plausible. For example, the interior shop, decoration shop, body shop and café should give the consumers a pleasant and comfortable feeling. This corresponds well to the cosy and a bit lively atmosphere. The sport shop should motivate consumers to become active, which corresponds to the very lively atmosphere. The shoes shop was a very cheap and badly illuminated shop that evoked a boring atmosphere. And also the casino (Toy-Toy) was experienced to be boring according to the (non-gambling) participants.

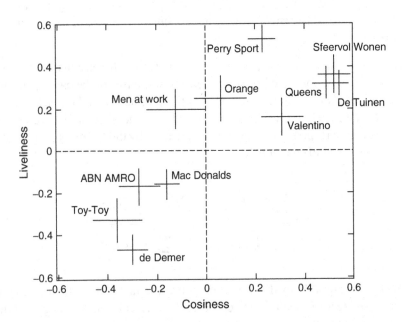

Figure 2. Experienced atmosphere of the eleven locations expressed in terms of the two atmosphere factors 'cosiness' and 'liveliness'.

4 Influence of light on atmosphere

The previous experiment has demonstrated that the atmosphere questionnaire in combination with a factor analysis is a very useful tool to quantify how people experience a particular environment. The method is very well able to distinguish between different environments. The same method was used to determine the experienced atmosphere of a fashion shop under different illumination conditions.

4.1 Method

The experiment took place in a room of about 3 × 5 meters that resembled a fashion shop. The shop contained three shelves with cloths in different colours and two displays with cloths, shoes and bags. Moreover it had more than 300 light sources. A light architect was given the assignment to created four different light settings that people would associate with the seasons spring, summer, autumn and winter, respectively. The goal was to show retailers that they can create a 'spring atmosphere' and bring people in the mood for buying spring cloths while it is still winter. Figure 3 gives an impression of the different light settings in the shop.

Sixteen people participated in the experiment: eight male and eight female. Their age ranged between 26 and 52 years, with an average of 39 years. All people were native Dutch. The participants were split into four groups of 4 people, each visiting the shop at a different day. Participants entered the shop with one of the light settings on. They were asked to walk around and to pay attention to the atmosphere evoked by the shop. As soon as they had obtained a good impression of the shop, they started to fill in a questionnaire. When all participants were ready, they left the room. The experimental leader changed the light setting and asked the participants to fill in the same questionnaire for this situation. The procedure was repeated till all four light settings were evaluated.

The presentation order of the four light settings was balanced between groups of participants in order to diminish a possible effect of order. Since participants saw the light settings one after each other, they could not compare

SPRING   SUMMER   AUTUMN   WINTER

Figure 3. Impression of the four light settings in the simulated shop.

Table 2. Factor loadings of the bipolar visual appearance terms on the three factors.

Visual appearance	Translation	F1	F2	F3
helder-donker	bright-dim	−0.13	**0.82**	−0.06
niet uniform-uniform	nonuniform-uniform	**0.69**	−0.10	−0.14
interessant-eentonig	interesting-monotonous	0.62	0.39	−0.57
theatraal-diffuus	dramatic-diffuse	**0.80**	−0.07	0.21
complex-eenvoudig	complex-simple	**0.83**	0.04	0.00
kleurrijk-kleurloos	colourful-colourless	0.61	0.29	−0.53
heldere gezichten- duistere gezichten	faces clear-faces obscure	0.20	**0.75**	0.26
verblindend-niet verblindend	glaring-not glaring	0.10	0.27	**0.85**
helder-wazig	clear-hazy	0.10	**0.81**	−0.02

Note: The bold numbers indicate that the loadings are high on one factor and low on the other factors.

all light settings with each other. Hence, the evaluation of the first light setting might have been different when it was presented later during the experiment. This could have been solved by presenting all light settings before filling in the questionnaires. However, we wanted to simulate a practical situation. Normally, people visit a shop with only one light setting and they experience a certain atmosphere without being able to compare it with other light settings.

The questionnaire consisted of two parts. First, participants had to evaluate the atmosphere of the shop using the atmosphere questionnaire. Second, they had to evaluate the visual appearance of the light effect on a 5-point scale for each of the bipolar terms of Table 2.

4.2   Results

The responses of the participants were entered into a data sheet and analysed with SPSS. The following sections describe the analyses that were performed to (1) determine the effect of participant, (2) to find underlying factors of atmosphere perception, (3) to find underlying factors of visual appearance, and, (4) to describe the experienced atmosphere of the light settings in terms of the atmosphere factors.

4.2.1   Effect of participant To test whether participants gave similar responses, Spearman's rho correlation coefficients were calculated between participants for each of the two questionnaires. The correlation ranged between −0.17 and 0.65 for 'atmosphere' and between −0.37 and 0.62 for 'visual appearance'. A Pearson Chi-square test revealed a significant effect of participant on the distribution of the responses for each questionnaire ($p < 0.001$).

The effect of participant was significant for all light settings, 7 atmosphere terms and 4 visual appearance terms ($p < 0.05$). Hence, both the correlation and chi-square analyses indicate that there were large differences between the responses of the participants.

4.2.2 Atmosphere factors The same procedure as describe in section 3.2.3 was used to determine the factors underlying atmosphere perception. A scree plot analysis showed an 'elbow' at the third factor. This suggests that there are at least two underlying factors. After a Varimax rotation, the first two factors explained 22% and 21% of the variance in the data.

Figure 4 shows the factor loadings of each atmosphere term for the two factors. The atmosphere terms were divided into three groups as described in section 3.2.3. Within the first two groups, two subgroups were created, with either positive or negative loadings on the primary factor. A reliability test revealed high values of Cronbach's alpha: 0.91, 0.86, 0.87 and 0.83 for the terms with positive loadings on factor 1, terms with negative loadings on factor 1, terms with positive loadings on factor 2 and terms with negative loadings on factor 2, respectively. As expected, low reliability was obtained for the terms with low loadings on both factors (alpha = 0.45).

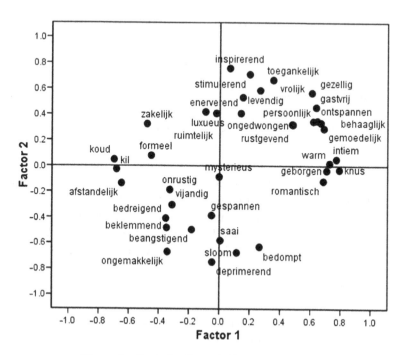

Figure 4. Factor loadings of all atmosphere terms.

The distribution of the terms over the factors can be compared with the results of the previous experiment. There are many similarities between the two experiments, i.e. many terms with high loadings on the primary factors of Figure 1 have also high loadings on the primary factors of Figure 4. However, the following differences can be observed:

- The terms 'gezellig' and 'rustgevend' had high positive loadings on factor 1, but move to the group with low loadings, while the opposite holds for the terms 'gastvrij' and 'persoonlijk'.

- The terms 'beangstigend', 'bedreigend', 'gespannen', 'onrustig' and 'vijandig' had high negative loadings on factor 1, but move to the group with low loadings.

- The terms 'enerverend', 'ongedwongen', and 'ruimtelijk' had high positive loadings on factor 2, but move to the group with low loadings.

- The terms 'saai' and 'sloom' had low loadings, but move to the group with high negative loadings on factor 2.

- The terms 'deprimerend' and 'ongemakkelijk' had high loadings on factor 1, but moves to the group with high loadings on factor 2.

In short, most terms have high loadings on the same factors for the two experiments, some terms are added from or move to the group with low loadings and only two terms change from factor 1 to factor 2. In spite of these changes, the factors can still be interpreted as 'cosiness' and 'liveliness'.

4.2.3 Visual appearance factors   A PCA analysis on the bipolar visual appearance terms revealed three factors. After a Varimax rotation, the first three factors explained 27%, 25% and 17% of the variance in the data. Table 2 shows the loadings of the visual appearance terms on the three factors. Terms with high loadings on the first factor and low loadings on the other factors are: 'niet uniform – uniform', 'theatraal-diffuus' and 'complex-eenvoudig'. These terms are related to the spatial complexity of the light distribution. Terms with high loadings on the second factor and low loadings on the other factors are: 'helder-donker', 'heldere gezichten-donkere gezichten' and 'helder-wazig'. These terms are related to visual clarity. There is only one term with a high loading on the third factor, namely 'verblindend-niet verblindend', which is related to the amount of glare.

4.2.4 Perception of light settings   The responses of the participants can be expressed in terms of the factors underlying atmosphere perception and visual appearance, respectively. The same procedure as described in 3.2.4 was used. For

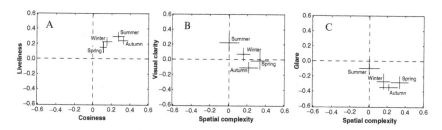

Figure 5. Experience of the four light settings expressed in terms of the atmosphere factors 'cosiness' and 'liveliness' and the visual appearance factors 'spatial complexity', 'visual clarity' and 'glare'.

each participant and each light setting a score was computed on each factor by weighting the responses to the atmosphere and visual appearance terms by the factor loadings of the PCA.

Figure 5 shows the score averaged across participants on the atmosphere and visual appearance factors per light setting. The crosses correspond to the standard error of the mean. ANOVA and post-hoc analyses were performed to test for significant effects of light setting and participant. For the factor 'cosiness', the light settings 'winter' and 'spring' were significantly different from 'summer' and 'autumn' ($p < 0.01$). The effect of participant was not significant ($p = 0.37$). For the factor 'liveliness', there was a significant effect of participant ($p < 0.05$) but not of light setting ($p = 0.32$). For 'spatial complexity', the light setting 'summer' was significantly different from 'spring' and 'autumn' ($p < 0.05$) and the effect of participant was significant ($p < 0.01$). For 'visual clarity', the light setting 'summer' was significantly different from 'spring' and 'autumn' ($p < 0.05$), but there was no significant effect of participant ($p = 0.51$). Finally, for 'glare' there was no significant effect of light setting ($p = 0.17$) and participant ($p = 0.16$).

The graphs and statistical analyses show that the differences between light settings are in fact relatively small. The only significant and consistent difference was found between the light settings 'summer' and 'spring'. The 'summer' setting was evaluated lower on the 'spatial complexity' scale, higher on the 'visual clarity' scale and equal on the 'glare' scale compared to the 'spring' setting. This is in agreement with the intension of the light designer, who wanted to have a bright and white light setting for the 'summer', to get the impression of a sunny day, and a more colourful light setting for the 'spring', to create an association with the colours of blossom and flowers.

The finding that the 'summer' setting was evaluated higher on the 'cosiness' scale compared to the light setting 'spring', suggests that the amount of 'cosiness' decreases with 'spatial complexity' and increases with 'visual clarity'. However, the two visual appearance factors were not varied independently, as can be seen in Figure 5. Therefore, it is not clear whether both 'spatial complexity' and 'visual clarity' or only one of them actually contributes to 'cosiness'. At this moment, it is not possible to draw any conclusion about the relation between atmosphere factors and visual appearance factors. In order to get more insight into the relation between light variables, visual appearance and experienced atmosphere, the same methodology could be used, but a more diverse and well defined set of light settings should be presented.

5   Discussion

This paper presents a new measurement tool to quantify the atmosphere of an environment as experienced by human observers. In the first study, a lexicon for describing atmosphere was collected and an atmosphere questionnaire was developed based on this lexicon. The second study demonstrated by means of a factor analysis that atmosphere can be described by at least two factors: 'behaaglijkheid' (cosiness) and 'levendigheid' (liveliness). A reliability test showed that the variability in the responses was mainly the result of differences between participants and not because the atmosphere terms had multiple interpretations. The last experiment showed that the atmosphere factors are reproducible.

Although the method appears to be valuable, it should be tested more extensively. More terms could be included to test the robustness of the factor analysis. When the method is used for different applications (e.g. offices or medical environments) more factors might emerge. Since the evaluation of the environment takes considerable time, it might be interesting for some applications to shorten the questionnaire, for instance, by using only those terms with high loading on one of the factors. Finally, the whole procedure described in this paper could be repeated for different languages and the underlying factors could be compared.

In summary, the atmosphere questionnaire in combination with a factor analysis seems to be a useful tool to facilitate the design of products that allow people to create the appropriate atmosphere. As our focus is on lighting design, the method will be used to investigate which light variables (e.g. mean luminance, color variation, shadows) are important for creating various atmospheres.

References

Boyce, P. (2003). Human Factors in Lighting. London: Taylor & Francis.

Ekman, P. (1971). Universals and cultural differences in facial expressions of emotions. In J.K. Cole (Ed.), *Nebraska Symposium on motivation 1971* (pp 207–283). Lincoln: University of Nebraska Press.

Flynn, J.E. (1977). A study of subjective responses to low energy and nonuniform lighting systems. *Lighting Design and Application*, 167–179.

Flynn, J.E. (1992). Lighting-design decisions as interventions in human visual space. In J.L. Nasar (Ed.), *Environmental Aesthetics: Theory, Research and Applications* (pp 156–170). New York: Cambridge University Press.

Izard, C.E. (1977). *Human Emotions*. New York: Plenum.

Knez, I. (1995). Effects of indoor lighting on mood and cognition. *Journal of Environmental Psychology*, 15, 39–51.

Knez, I. (2001) Effects of colour of light on nonvisual psychological processes. *Journal of Environmental Psychology*, 21, 201–208.

Knez, I. and Kers, C. (2000). Effects of indoor lighting, gender and age on mood and cognitive performance. *Environment and Behavior*, 32, 817–831.

McColl, S.L. and Veitch, J.A. (2001). Full-spectrum fluorescent lighting: a review on its effect on physiology and health. *Psychological Medicine*, 31, 949–964.

Mehrebian, A. and Russell, J.A. (1974). *An Approach to Environmental Psychology*. Cambridge, MA: MIT Press.

Plutchik, R. (1980). *Emotions: A psychoevolutionary synthesis*. New York: Harper and Row.

Tomkins, S.S. (1984). Affect theory. In K.R. Scherer and P. Ekman (Eds.) *Approaches to Emotion* (pp 163–196). Hillsdale NJ: Erlbaum.

Watson, D., Clark, L.A. and Tellegen, A. (1988). Development and validation of brief measures of positve and negative affect: The PANAS scales. *Journal of Personality and Social Psychology*, 54, 1063–1070.

4

IN SEARCH OF THE X-FACTOR TO DEVELOP EXPERIENCE MEASUREMENT TOOLS

Ingrid Mulder and Harry van Vliet

Abstract   User experience as a concept is increasingly studied. Although most authors agree that several factors influence experience some way or another, it is still unclear which factors are part of the user experience, how these factors relate to one another, and how these factors can be assessed in order to help design for experiences. In the X-factors project critical factors that determine user experience of new ICT products and services were searched for. An experience framework including the experience factors presence, aesthetics, and mood was leading in our research on the relationship between design principles and user experience. Additionally, possible pitfalls and obstacles that might hinder experience research being beneficial have been explored in the context of the design and development process of new ICT products and services. In the final section, theoretical and methodological issues for the development of experience measurement tools are reflected upon.

1   Introduction

Over the last years, the fields of Human-Computer Interaction, Interaction Design and Usability Engineering have adopted a wider interpretation of quality than just usability. Interactive products not only become more useful and usable tools, they also have other quality attributes to be (commercially) more distinctive. In the last decade it has become apparent that usability alone does not offer the end-users of services everything they need. People want products and services to deliver added value in their daily life contexts of work and leisure. The word 'user experience' has been used increasingly to signify these 'extra' qualities, such as empathy, fun, trust and emotion, see for example the ISTAG report (ISTAG Report on Experience and Application Research, 2004), p. 51. The fact that user experiences now have been spotted by among others marketeers and designers, does not mean experiences have not always been around. Consumers, businesses, and economists lumped them into the service sector along with such uneventful activities as dry cleaning, auto repair, wholesale distribution, and telephone access (Pine and Gilmore, 1999). Even before, philosophers and artists have tried for centuries

43

J.H.D.M. Westerink et al. (eds.), Probing Experience, 43–56.
© 2008 *Springer.*

to capture the essence of human experience. All these ideas have found their way into the *sensus communis* of what we regard as experiences: experience is about personal involvement, about holistic engagement with a product or service across a span of time; an experience is subjective, it implies values; it is also something that sticks with you (bad or good); and finally, it is here and now, but leaves a trace in memory.

Existing work on user experience is oriented towards its multidimensional meaning (e.g. McCarthy and Wright, 2004; Shedroff, 2001), defining experience (also often termed as customer experience) more from a marketing and management perspective (e.g. Pine and Gilmore, 1999; Tscheligi, 2005) or developing first approaches to models and frameworks of user experience. In a first approach to diversify existing approaches we could distinguish product-centred models (define experience as a construct which can be treated more or less independently from the context, from the user and from the time frame in which a product is used, e.g. Marcus, 2004), process-centred models as user experience is changing over time (e.g. Kankainen, 2003), interaction-centred models which try to explain the user experience of a particular moment in time (e.g. De Ruyter, 2004), and empirically grounded models (e.g. Kidd, 2002). Most of the models are first iterations and introduce different factors of "their" experience approach, but a solid overall framework is missing which leads to an operational level of assessment methodology (see also Mulder and van Vliet, 2006; van Vliet and Mulder, 2006).

Future compelling user experiences will be key differentiating benefits of products and services. However, what are these X-factors that determine the user experience? What are the right ingredients for designing killer applications? Many businessmen and marketeers are keen on getting these answers. In the X-factors project we searched for the X-factors and how these factors could be assessed. The goal of the project was to develop reliable and validated instruments to assess the expected experiences of targeted users of new mobile and home services. This has been done by a preliminary selection of underlying factors that determine user experience. These factors in turn have been used to provide an easy-to-use instrument that supports the assessment of the user experience to be expected given a certain new service. The reliability and validity of this assessment were methodologically researched by comparing the expected user experience to the actual (observed) user experience (see Figure 1). The model used in this figure represents that the selected experience factors are also related.

In the first phase of the project we determined the feasibility of experience research in the context of the design and development process of new ICT products and services. As a first stage a quick scan based on a preliminary framework was conducted and possible pitfalls and obstacles that might hinder the experience research being beneficial were identified.

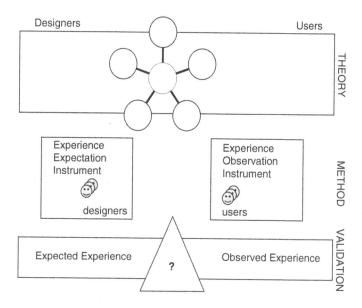

Figure 1. Experience research framework.

First, experience models and factors were selected to determine the contextual framework. Then, these experience factors were made operational to develop experience instruments. We distinguished between an Experience Expectation Instrument and an Experience Observation Instrument. The Experience Expectation Instrument can be seen as an instrument for designers, all involved in the design process, to assess the expected user experience. The Experience Observation Instrument is an instrument to assess the actual user experience, and will be used together with users preferable in in-situ research; however lab evaluation fits as well.

2 In search of the X-factor

As said before, research of experiences in the context of new product and service development has gained a lot of attention over the last few years. There seems to be agreement that user experience is an important concept to understand. In various fields (e.g. consumer behaviour, service marketing) various thoughts and ideas exist on how to model user experiences. Also, introspective techniques are potentially able to assess user experience perceptions, like in the early days of experimental psychology. On the other hand, it is still an open question if and how user experience models, methods, and techniques map to the domain of ICT products and services. In the next sections we look for experience factors applicable in the context of the design and development process of new ICT products and services.

Although most authors agree that several factors influence experience some way or another, there is no agreed upon list of experience factors that explain the user experience. What's more, it is still unclear how experience factors relate to one another, and how these factors can be assessed. We define experience as beyond usability; focussing on the whole, not on the ingredients. In other words, we look at the forest, not at a single tree. Although, functionality is part of experience as a broad concept, experience is foremost subjective. The same product or service can be experienced in different ways from different users, on sensorial, cognitive, and especially emotional levels. We therefore try to get more insight in these emotional levels. Although this defines our scope of experience research, it does not answer what we take into account in our experience model. Figure 2 shows some order in the wholeness of experience by distinguishing between physical, social, and personal context, and zeroth-, first-, and second-order factors of experiences. Zeroth-order refers to every possible influence that is not directly related and too general to be part of an explanatory model. First-order factors are related but do not belong to the scope of our research, the second-order factors are the explanatory constructs that are taken into account in the hypotheses of the research. Put differently, zeroth-order factors are taken care of by randomization in

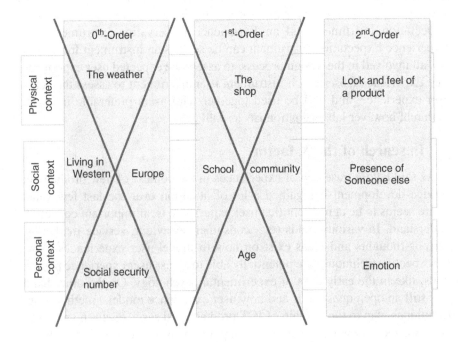

Figure 2. Some order in the experience of everything.

experimentation, first-order factors are deliberately not taken into account, and the second-order factors are controlled by the experimental design.

We started the project with a quick scan through all steps of the experience research model (Figure 1). Thus, instead of first defining an experience theory in an elaborate way, we defined a preliminary experience framework, developed experience measurement tools, and validated this in the context of a specific ICT product. Hence, our main goal was to reveal possible pitfalls and obstacles that might hinder experience research. In order to define the second-order experience factors to be included in the preliminary framework we used as a starting point the Aesthetics and Immersion quadrants in Philips' perspective on the origin of the experience (see e.g., De Ruyter, 2004) to have a critical discussion and reflection on factors that are explaining experience. In our initial model we included three factors trying to explain and assess experience, namely presence (being there), aesthetics (beauty), and the role of mood.

Presence or the sense of 'being there' has been discussed in literature as an essential, defining aspect of virtual environments, and has often been associated with immersion. Presence is a psychological state in which the illusion of non-mediation is perceived, even though the person always knows that the experience is mediated (Witmer and Singer, 1998). Presence is continuously changing and dynamic, influenced by physiological self perceptions, cognitive self descriptions, and recursive interactions of these variables with the environment. Presence need to be studied by evaluation of physiology, behaviour, and cognition as the three states do not necessarily correlate to one another for any particular environmental stimulus (Huang and Alessi, 1999).

Aesthetic pleasure is in many discussions equivalent to the experience of beauty and the most prototypical aesthetic judgments are those of beauty. Beauty is regarded as a pleasurable experience (positive valence), not related to any expected utility, is immediate, without intermediate reasoning, and is objectified: it lies in the object. As an example consider this definition of aesthetic response: 'a state of intense enjoyment characterized by feelings of personal wholeness, a sense of discovery, and a sense of human connectedness' (Csikszentmihalyi and Robinson, 1990). There are three main views on beauty: 1) the objectivist's view which regards 'beauty' is a property of an object that produces a pleasurable experience in any suitable perceiver. Typical object features contributing to 'beauty' are: balance and proportion, symmetry, informational content and complexity, (figure-ground) contrast and clarity, and of course the 'golden section'; 2) the subjectivist's view which regards 'beauty' as a function of idiosyncratic qualities of the perceiver: "beauty is in the eye of the beholder". A typical argument is the social constructivist's emphasis on the historically changing and culturally relative nature of beauty; 3) and thirdly the interactionist's view: 'beauty' emerges from patterns in the way people and objects relate.

Mood is almost always theoretically discussed in the context of emotional experience. Although a complex field of study in itself some characteristics though come easily to the fore:

1. Emotions are 'immediate': you become angry in an instance and then it fades away.

2. Emotions are intense: we are deeply frustrated or in love, blind of jealously or we want to disappear completely because of shame.

3. Emotions are disruptive: we shake like a leaf, we get into a blind panic, we break out in tears and freeze of fear.

4. Emotions are subjective: it is *you* who feels depressed, elevated or jealous.

5. Emotions have something to do with bodily sensation: sweating, trembling, 'butterfly'-feeling.

6. Emotions relate to certain action readiness: to hit or embrace someone, you want to jump of joy, make yourself very small because of shame.

7. Emotions are 'triggered' by something or someone: a memory of a lost love, someone offending you, a missed train.

Moods are similar to emotions in that they are affective states, but differ from emotions in several respects. Moods have a longer duration (hours, days, months) than emotion. 'Extreme' long durations are regarded as psychopathologic: e.g., depression and manic, phobias, anxiety states. Moods are not elicited by an external event or outlasting such an event, or disproportionate to such an event in intensity or duration (you are angry at someone, but when you are irritated, miserable or cheerful this isn't reducible to a specific event). Moods are global and diffuse (not directed at specific objects or events but 'surroundings'): everything is irritating; everything is open and attainable (moods 'colour' the surrounding). This is also referred to as 'background states' or 'vagueness', that is largely unaffected by external stimuli, and finally moods have lower intensity than emotions. In addition, moods do have an influence on the performance of cognitive tasks such as problem solving, and on memory and concentration. It is reasonable to assume they also relate in some way to user experiences.

3   Measuring experience factors

First, we selected literature and empirical research in which the concepts presence, aesthetics and mood were made operational, and searched for validated experience assessments instruments. For example, the concept presence has been studied largely in virtual environments, often referred to as physical presence or telepresence. Related presence factors are 'spatial presence', the sense of being there in the virtual environment, 'involvement', attention to the real and virtual environment, and 'realness', reality judgement of the virtual environment. In other words, the experience factor presence can be defined as the feeling of being here or being there. We looked into over 20 questionnaires to assess the concept presence, the number of items varied from 2 to 77 (http://www.presence-research.org/AppendixA.html). Each item was scored for applicability in the context of the design and development process of new ICT products and services by two independent raters. Two presence questionnaires containing 8 and 6 items (Kim and Biocca, 1997; Slater et al., 1994) appeared to be rated 100% applicable, and also appeared to be 'easy-to-use'.

Measurement of aesthetics can be divided along the lines of the views described earlier on: the measurement of visual product aesthetics, the measurement of aesthetic preferences and the measurement of aesthetic judgement. Guided by the circumstances of the experimental setting (introduction of a new product that tries to enhance the 'aesthetics') we choose to pick a questionnaire aimed at measuring the user experience that related to visual aesthetics of products (Bloch et al., 2003).

The background of empirical mood research is mainly to measure the effects of certain kinds of treatment in psychopharmacology and psychotherapy. This is mostly done by 'mood adjective check lists': subjects rate how they feel at the moment of asking by checking a list with adjectives (cheerful, anxious, tense, timid, and so on). This is followed by an analysis through the method of dimensional analysis. The main discussion in this field is 'unipolar vs. bipolar'. The unipolar view states that there are several factors that are (nearly) orthogonal, factors like aggression, fatigue, vigor and so on. The bipolar view states that there are several dimensions with contrasting 'ends' on which different moods can be plotted. Overall there seems to be consensus on two bipolar dimensions, which correspond closely to ideas by Wundt: pleasantness – unpleasantness, and activation – deactivation (arousal – calm) (e.g., Watson, 1978; Wundt, 1902). Based on this discussion we selected the Brief Mood Introspection Scale (BMIS; Marcus, 2004) – 6 adjectives, 2 selected from each of eight mood states: happy, calm, energetic, tired) and changed the 21-point Likert scale into a 5-point scale. Next to that, we added a second overall moodscale: aroused – calm.

In sum, we searched for validated instruments to assess the concepts of our experience framework. The next step is to use these instruments for the development of an Experience Observation Instrument and an Experience Expectation Instrument as well. For the development of the Experience Observation Instrument we used the selected (validated) instruments with some little adjustments. However, for the development of the Experience Expectation

Instrument this is not so straightforward. As one might expect, designers think more in functionalities and how the assessed experience might relate to a certain adjustment of 'buttons'. We used the Experience Observation Instrument for presence, mood, and aesthetics, and reformulated the questions into an operationalisation from a designers' perspective. We asked to what extent designers did take the experience items into account in their design, and asked for actual design decisions. The models and techniques that can be used to determine the experience factors 'presence', 'mood', and 'aesthetics' are used in the development of an Experience Observation Instrument. In the remainder of this article we present an initial study in which the experience measurement tools are validated, and possible pitfalls and obstacles that might hinder experience research have been explored.

4   Initial study: Personal content watching experience

In order to validate the Experience Observation Instruments we conducted a small-scale test. The goal was to study whether it was possible to assess the experience factors in a minimally obtrusive way with easy to use instruments. The experience measurement instruments described above were used to develop an Experience Observation Instrument. Besides the questionnaires for aesthetics, presence and mood, additional measurements of heartbeat and estimated time were used. More specifically, for presence we used the concepts 'engage in a story (being there)', 'forget environment (not being here)', and asked (afterwards) for time estimations of the durations of the viewing. In order to assess mood we used a rating scale to assess 'pleasant-unpleasant' and 'calm-aroused', and measured the heartbeat, and finally, to assess aesthetics we used a validated scale to get insight in concepts as beauty, personal value, sensibility, and purchase behaviour. Based on these inputs a visualisation of experience factors was constructed and used to get feedback from the respondents on our assessment (see Figure 3).

In a small-scale test in which we looked at the effect of AmbiLight on the experience of watching personal content the Experience Observation Instrument was validated. The aim was to test whether our instruments and the resulting visualisation made sense to the respondents, and whether they were easy to use. It was definitely not aimed to test whether the intervention of AmbiLight was strong enough to affect experiences. The experimental setting was made as realistic as possible. We intend to concentrate more on the subjective experience than on the intervening new technology. For that reason, an out-of-the-way room in the office building was transferred into a common living room. We deliberately furnished a room in the office building in order to avoid association with lab environments, such as the Philips HomeLab. An underlying assumption was that we expected that people

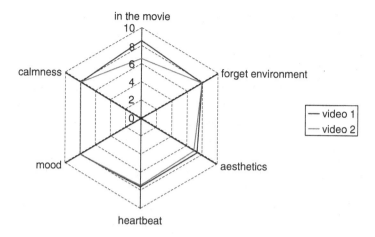

Figure 3. Visualisation of the results.

invited to the HomeLab might be more focussed on technology. Respondents were asked to hand in some personal content, for instance a video of their holiday or children, and to invite someone with whom they like to watch the video. A selection of 10 minutes of their personal home video was used in the experimental setting. The new ICT product we used in all our experiments was an AmbiLight 1 TV, the similar television for all experiments. We used a within-subjects design to make a comparison of two designs (with and without AmbiLight). Thus, each respondent tried each design, except for the control groups (with – with and without – without). We counterbalanced the study, having two respondents started watching their personal content with AmbiLight and two other respondents without AmbiLight in order to avoid having the order effects give an advantage to one design.

Eight respondents and their partners participated in the small-scale test, and were randomly assigned to the four conditions beforehand. Upon arrival, participants were greeted by the experimenter and seated at a table next to the experimental living room to get a short introduction and time to fill in the questionnaires before first watching. Heartbeat was measured and participants were asked to remove their watch (in order to avoid checking the duration of the watching time. Participants were guided to the living room for their first watching of 5 minutes (the duration was not mentioned). After the first watching condition participants returned to the intake table to repeat the measurements, and one of the experimenters was able to change the AmbiLight condition, if necessary, unnoticeably. After the second watching condition one of the experimenters joined the participants in the living room, switched the television off, and asked them to fill in the questionnaires and to measure the heartbeat one extra time. In addition, their estimations of the duration of their watching experience were asked. One experimenter started with an exit interview, while the other experimenter came up with the visualisation based on the experience measurements.

Some illustrative findings from the interviews are that respondents indicated that the personal content is more distinctive for experience than the influence of AmbiLight. Interestingly, respondents having the condition 'AmbiLight on' put too low a value of (estimated) watching time. Another respondent indicate: 'It was my own video, therefore I was pretty fast engaged in the story ('being there'); there is a whole story behind (memories)'. Another interesting aspect was that remembering experiences distinguishes personal content from commercial content (movie). A final comment to the visualisation referring to the score of calmness 'watching TV in a lab is more relaxed than at home (with the whole family walking around)'.

5   Lessons learned and reflections

The major result was that the participants acknowledged the visualisation of experiences as a good means to discuss experience. However, as most experimental studies it also raises new questions and issues to take into account in our future research. For instance, the experimental setting, including the presence of (familiar) others, and the selection of content (in relation to AmbiLight) require more attention. The heartbeat measurement was not considered intrusive, which support the idea of using more physiological data acquisition tools.

In order to come up with statistical analyses that reveal something about the effect of the new ICT products and services, we should extend the number of subjects, and relate this to the choice of the experimental design. The development of easy-to-use questionnaires, translation problems, scales, interpretation and the number of questions need more in-depth research. In the current test, we used an existing product and were therefore able to assess experiences while using the product. Different Experience Observation Instruments might be applicable to assess experiences of new concepts.

6   Towards an experience expectation instrument

As said before, the development of an Experience Expectation Instrument is not so straightforward. In order to relate the assessed experience factors to design guidelines we need to understand how the experience factors relate to functionalities and characteristics of the new ICT products and services. We deliberately chose for a structured interview instead of a similar experimental setup as for the validation of the Experience Observation Instrument. The Experience Observation Instruments used in the experimental study with users were used, and some questions were reformatted into operationalisations from a designers' perspective.

Three members of the AmbiLight design team (including researchers, designers and developers) were interviewed. After a brief introduction we asked them about their role in the AmbiLight design trajectory, and what they consider as an (AmbiLight TV watching) experience? Next, we asked them to fill out the Experience Observation Instrument's items for mood, presence, aesthetics, thus the same questions as the participants in the user study did. However, with the difference that we asked them to fill out the questionnaire twice: one estimating AmbiLight on, and one questionnaire estimating AmbiLight off. We asked to what extent designers did take the experience factors into account in their design, and asked for actual design decisions. We concluded the interview by asking the designers for needs and wishes they had regarding an Experience Expectation Instrument.

For the interviews with designers we gained several insights for the development of an Experience Expectation Instrument in general, but also for understanding our initial study of the quick scan. Presence was the main experience factor AmbiLight was designed for. However, AmbiLight was not designed to improve the experience of watching personal content (together). Rather, it had been designed for improving the experience of watching commercial content (movies). Moreover, the designers indicated their doubts regarding the needs and desires of an Experience Expectation Instrument. They actually believe that a proper user centred design process in which users were involved early on and in an iterative way in the design trajectory is crucial, as was the case in the AmbiLight design trajectory, and doubt whether Experience Expectation Instruments can add value to such an iterative user-centred design approach. Relevant experience factors or at least the translations into functionalities that can be fine-tuned may very well be application specific, and therefore, doubts are expressed whether appropriate Experience Expectation Instruments are feasible in practice. However, what might help a design team is better understanding of experience factors, a better or more explaining theory or model of experience. In addition, the designers indicated that better Experience Observation Instruments were welcomed as well.

7 Appraisal of feasibility

The major goal of the first stage of this project was a feasibility study of experience research in the context of the design and development process of new ICT products and services. A quick scan based on a preliminary framework was conducted and possible pitfalls and obstacles that might hinder the experience research being beneficial are identified. Below the appraisal of feasibility in terms of respectively theory, method, and validation is summarised.

7.1   From (the right) X-factors to (falsifiable but usable) models

There are indeed several theories and models on experience; however we found some pitfalls with these theories and models. The theories are mostly descriptive and not explanatory. They are quite diverse and not well integrated, and seldom used in the context of new ICT products. Moreover, they are more often than not, holistic, taking everything into account: physical surroundings, social space, personal history, and are not directed to changing and enhancing the experience. Another interesting question is how to deal with shared experiences?

7.2   From the theory-methodology 'link' to (practical) expectation and observation instruments

Indeed, for every concept in the quick scan (validated) surveys were found. However, are surveys the only and the right instrument to 'capture' experiences? And, is it possible to capture the 'wholeness' of the experience? Spatio-temporal and compositional aspects were recognized but not taken into account. What kind of design is preferred for experience research? An 'in-situ' approach might be more appropriate to study experiences in real-life situations. How does an Experience Instrument for designers relate to proper knowledge about experience factors with a user centered design process?

7.3   From instrument validation to validating delta between both experience instruments

There are several valid experimental design possibilities in which users and designers can be involved. However, some problems with the validations are found. For example, which designer should be involved? A product manager, an engineer, or both. Should different instruments be used in each step of the design process? Can the 'delta' between expected and observed be determined and interpreted?

8   In short

In this methodology-oriented project models and techniques that can determine X-factors are searched for and reflected upon. Experience measurement tools for 'presence', 'mood', and 'aesthetics' have been validated on a small scale test. In our future work we aim to extend the current X-factors model with new experience factors such as 'social context' and 'connectedness' into an explanatory model, and to optimize existing methods for experience design and analysis.

Acknowledgements

The work described here is based on team work of Hans Nelissen (Vodafone Group R&D), Gerard Hollemans and Karin Nieuwenhuizen (Philips Research), Ingrid Mulder, Henri ter Hofte, Harry van Vliet, Johan de Heer, Henk de Poot, and Wouter Teeuw (Telematica Instituut) in the X-factors project. Discussions in this project have been inspired by earlier work in the Freeband FRUX project (www.freeband.nl).

References

Bloch, P.H., Brunel, F.F., & Arnold, T.J. (2003). Individual differences in the centrality of visual product aesthetics: concept and measurement. *Journal of Consumer Research, 29*, March 2003, pp. 551–565.

Csikszentmihalyi, M. & Robinson, R.E. (1990). *The Art of Seeing: An Interpretation of the Aesthetic Encounter.* J. Paul Getty Museum, Los Angeles.

De Ruyter, B. (2004, May 19). Invited talk at Telematica Instituut, Enschede, The Netherlands.

Forlizzi, J. & Ford, S. (2000). The building blocks of experience: an early framework for interaction designers, Proceedings of the conference on Designing interactive systems: processes, practices, methods, and techniques, ACM Press, New York.

http://www.presence-research.org/AppendixA.html

Huang, M.P. & Alessi, N.E. (1999). Presence as an Emotional Experience. In J.D. Westwood, H.M. Hoffman, R.A. Robb, & D. Stredney (eds). Medicine Meets Virtual Reality: The Convergence of Physical and Informational Technologies Options for a New Era in Healthcare, Amsterdam: IOS Press, pp. 148–153.

ISTAG Report on Experience and Application Research. Involving Users in the Developments of Ambient Intelligence. Available online: http://www.cordis.lu/ist/istag2004.htm

Kankainen, A. (2003). UCPCD: user-centered product concept design, Proceedings of the 2003 conference on Designing for user experiences, ACM Press, San Francisco, California.

Kidd, A. (2002). *Technology Experiences: What makes them Compelling?* HP Laboratories Bristol.

Kim, T. & Biocca, F. (1997). Telepresence via television: Two dimensions of telepresence may have different connections to memory and persuasion. *Journal of Computer-Mediated Communication, 3* (2).

Marcus, A. (2004). Six Degrees of User Spaces, *User Experience, 2* (6).

Mayer, J.D. & Gaschke, Y.N. (1988). The experience and meta-experience of mood. *Journal of Personality and Social Psychology, 55*, 102–111.

McCarthy, J. & Wright, P. (2004). *Technology as Experience*, MIT Press.

Mulder, I. & van Vliet, H. (2006). Experience in all its beauty. Paper presented at CHI2006 workshop on Theory and Method for Experience Centred Design. CHI 2006, April 22–27, 2006, Montreal, Canada. Available online: http://www-users.cs.york.ac.uk/~mblythe/index_files/Page907.html

Pine, B.J. & Gilmore, J.H. (1999). *The Experience Economy*, Harvard Business School Press.

Shedroff, N. (2001). Experience Design, New Riders Publishing 1.

Slater, M., Usoh, M., & Steed, A. (1994). Depth of presence in virtual environments. *Presence: Teleoperators and Virtual Environments*, 3, 130–144.

Tscheligi, M. (2005). More experiences: Other sides of the profession story, ACM *Interactions*, 12, 3.

van Vliet, H. & Mulder, I. (2006). Experience and Design: Trojan Horse or Holy Grail? In: E.L.C. Law, E.T. Hvannberg, M. Hassenzahl (eds.), User Experience – Towards a Unified View, COST294, pp. 58–62. Proceedings of the The Second COST294-MAUSE International Open Workshop: User Experience – Towards a Unified View held in conjunction with The fourth Nordic conference on Human-Computer Interaction (NordiCHI 2006), October 14–18, 2006, Oslo, Norway.

Watson, Sr., R.I. (1978). *The Great Psychologists*. (4th edition). New York: J.B. Lippincott Co.

Wundt, W. (1902). Principles of Physiological Psychology. Translated by Edward Bradford Titchener (1904): http://psychclassics.asu.edu/Wundt/Physio/

Witmer, B. & Singer, M. (1998). Measuring presence in virtual environments: A Presence Questionnaire, *Presence: Teleoperators and Virtual Environments, 7*, pp. 225–240.

5

PROBING EXPERIENCES: LOGS, TRACES, SELF-REPORT AND A SENSE OF WONDER

Erik Geelhoed, Josephine Reid, Richard Hull and Sharon Baurley

Abstract   Two studies are described in which logging electronic data in conjunction with self-report provided a deeper insight into user experiences. During a field trial, interaction with a "visual" radio was electronically logged throughout and shed light on subjects' daily diaries. In a location-based audio play, users' tracks and traces were used in conjunction with interview data. In a third study, participants wore fashionable communicating garments; Galvanic Skin Response data triggered a sense of wonder. The studies highlight the ad-hoc nature of our use of electronic data to probe experiences and the need for a more rigid theoretical framework.

1   Introduction

The starting point for this paper is the first paragraph of the introduction to this book:

There is no doubt that in the future compelling user experiences will be key differentiating benefits of products and services. Evaluating the user experience plays a central role, not only during the design process, but also during regular usage: for instance a video recorder that recommends TV programs that fit your current mood, a product that measures your current level of relaxation and produces advice on how to balance your life.

Thus, if a (mobile) computer system could accurately determine what my mood is, it could then for instance provide me with media (music, film or a digital photograph on the wall in a digital photo frame) that will suit my mood. This value proposition is one that over the last decade or so has surfaced in a great many brainstorms and this book lists some impressive advances in psycho-physiological measurements, a consistent framework for defining different classes of moods as well as some early applications.

However, is there compelling evidence, in this day and age of moral panic about invasion of privacy, that people would *want* their mood sensed? Secondly, do consumers want a system that automatically delivers media or makes lifestyle recommendations based on a particular mood? A third issue revolves

57

J.H.D.M. Westerink et al. (eds.), Probing Experience, 57–68.
© 2008 *Springer.*

around the balance between the chances of a system getting it right and getting it wrong. It is entirely possible that a certain class of people would be very tolerant about a system sensing their mood wrongly or making unwanted media recommendations whereas for others the system only needs to get it wrong once and they will never use it again. To shed light on optimising the accurate detection rate of such a system (and its decisions or recommendations) the framework of Signal Detection Theory (SDT) might be of benefit.

SDT (e.g. Swets, 1964) provides a mathematical and statistical framework to weigh off the benefit of getting it right Vs. the cost of getting it wrong and has been used for over 50 years in diverse settings, e.g. identifying enemy submarines, breast cancer screening etc. In all its simplicity, the diagram below (Figure 1) captures the point of departure for this approach.

On the left hand side we see the possible stimulus events that an observer tries to evaluate: The lower case **n** signifies that there is noise only (e.g. there is no enemy submarine) and (lower case) **s** signifies that (amongst some level of noise) there is a signal (e.g. somewhere in the deep dark murky waters there lurks an enemy submarine). An observer (a person on the look-out or a radar system) can then make the judgement upper case **S**, yes there is a signal (an enemy submarine) or **N**, no there is only noise. In the first case (S) where the observer correctly identifies the enemy submarine or the cancer, this is referred to as a **Hit**. Similarly when the observer's response is no, there is noise only (N) and this is correct, then this is called a **Correct Rejection**. However if there was no signal and the system (or observer) responds with an "S" response (yes there is a submarine), this is called a **False Alarm** and lastly if there is a signal but the observer responds with an "N" (noise only) then this defined as a **Miss**.

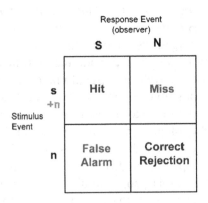

Figure 1. SDT Framework.

An observer can be strict or lax in their judgement with different consequences. In simple terms: In the first (strict) case there will be few false alarms but also few hits. In the latter (lax) case there will be more hits but also more false alarms. SDT then models the consequences of the Receiver Operating Characteristics (the observer's strict or lax approach). In the literature on emotion sensing, there is seldom (or no) mention of Signal Detection Theory; regularly reports focus entirely on the benefit of getting it right.

The papers in this book show that measurement of physiological correlates of emotion is very precise in highly controlled laboratory environments and this regularly involves a considerable battery of measures. In addition researchers use fairly consistent frameworks for defining emotions. However, the interpretation of the physiological data resulting in objectively and accurately defining which emotion a subject currently experiences is still some way off. Applying a similar range of measures into mobile contexts is still problematic although measurement of heart-rate variability has already produced commercially available applications.

Thus, because of the problematic nature of correctly interpreting sensing data (i.e. there might be a considerable cost in getting it wrong) we have tended to use sensing data in a different way. Here we present small sections of three studies from the Mobile Bristol Program, where we have used log data, location sensing and galvanic skin response sensors; in the first two studies as a complement to psychological data and in the third without any interpretation at all. In this way we have avoided the issues but our approach might be valuable for the theme of this book nonetheless.

Study 1: Augmented Digital Audio Broadcast Home Trial [Geelhoed et al., 2005].

2   Quick overview

We explored the potential of Digital Audio Broadcasting (DAB) through a series of user trials. Our iPAQ-based prototype allows listeners to a local Bristol radio station to interact with a set of web pages broadcast alongside the digital audio stream and displayed on a small colour display via a wireless backchannel, for example to vote or buy a tune they hear on the radio. We conducted a field trial, where nine households used the radio for a week. We saw a consistent use throughout the period of the trial and the prototype seemed to be quickly integrated into people's lifestyles. For the participants, the DAB radio has value because the information, at a glance, comes to you, effortlessly as part of the broadcast, without having to spend time booting up a computer. An enhanced DAB radio will benefit the radio station by extending its brand, through branded free services, as well as offering commercial opportunities, such as selling music. Critical success factors for a successful product that incorporates an enhanced DAB relate to having a backchannel, good interface design, providing information at a glance, where the frequency of updating the information will be important to keep users interested. The popularity of Digital Multimedia Broadcast (DMB) implemented in mobile phones in Korea, indicates that there are opportunities in the mobile arena.

Below we report in more detail how logging the interaction in conjunction with diary report data provided a deeper insight into how the visual radio was quite rapidly integrated into people's lifestyles.

In Figure 2, we show how for household 5 we derived a time line across eight days, from Friday to Friday, with the various categories of interactions – buy, movies, news, weather, events and competition – per day and per time of day. The height of the bars indicates the duration of the interaction in seconds.

From this example (typical for the rest of the group), it is clear that the use of the prototype across the week is constant. This in itself is an important finding as in field trials there is always the possibility of a drop off in usage after the initial novelty effect has worn off. For most weekdays there is a short usage in the mornings (e.g. on Mondays the five day weather forecast was checked quickly and then the user cast the "vote of the day") and somewhat longer in the evenings, when people come home from work, sit down with a cup of tea and check the visual radio more extensively.

The analysis of the diary forms questionnaire yielded interesting results. We evaluated a six day period. In the shared households more than one person kept a diary. As a result we analysed 11 diary forms.

In one of the questions, participants were asked: "Did you use the prototype to look up information you would otherwise have looked up elsewhere (e.g. on the internet or in the newspaper?)"

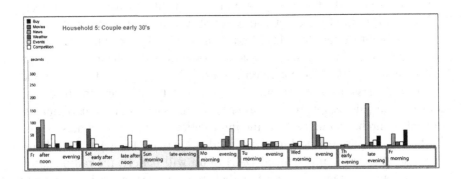

Figure 2.   Use of prototype across a week for household 5.

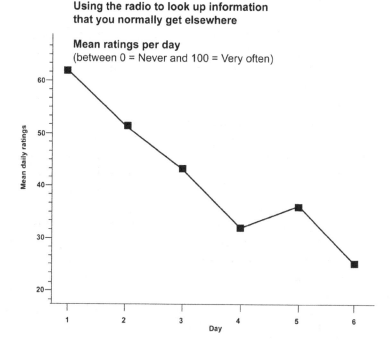

Figure 3. The radio coming into its own.

ANOVA (Repeated Measures) across all six days yielded an unexpectedly significant "day" effect for how participants rated this question: p=.03. Figure 3 shows a consistent lowering of the (mean) ratings. ANOVA comparing the first and the sixth day was even more significant: p=.002. So, by the end of the trial and day by day in its progress(ion) people judged that they used the radio less and less to look up information that they would normally get elsewhere.

This could indicate that people used the radio less and less, i.e. the novelty value had quickly worn off. However the log files revealed a consistent usage. In addition, in their interviews there were no indications of a lessened enthusiasm or of a slowly declining interest.

As we observe consistent usage coupled to positive feedback, there is the suggestion that DAB services such as the ones we incorporated in the field trial quickly become part of people's sets of daily behaviours, activities, in other words it becomes integrated into people's lifestyles. They no longer look up the five day weather forecast on the internet, or cast the vote of the day on the GWR website, but use the radio instead.

In this manner the three data sets, log-files, diary forms and interview data, proved to be complementary and gave us a deeper insight.

Study 2: Parallel worlds: Immersion in location-based experiences. [Reid et al., 2005]

3   Quick overview

In experience design the notion of immersion plays an important role. We analysed the stages and circumstances for immersion based on quantitative and qualitative feedback from 700 people who took part in a three week long public trial of a location-based audio drama.

We commissioned two writers to write an interactive play called Riot! 1831 which was staged for public consumption in Queens Square, Bristol, England for a period of three weeks in spring 2004. The interactive play is based on the actual riots that occurred there in 1831. Walking round the square triggered a variety of sound-files, each one a short vignette based on real events that took place in the square. For example you could hear the rioters' voices as they plundered the surrounding buildings, the flames as buildings burn, the merchants as they flee for their lives and the Dragoon Guards as they sabre-charge through the crowds cutting the rioters down.

Thirty-four regions covered the 150 m wide square and associated with each region were three different sound files. In general moving into a region would trigger one of the sound files to start playing and moving out of the region would cause it to stop. Visitors could sign up and receive the loan of a small back-pack containing an iPAQ PDA, GPS receiver and headphones with which they strolled around the square.

The wider research is about the stages of immersion in this location-aware situated mobile experience and the implications for future designs. However, for the purpose of this book, we describe the experience of a father and son, aged 10, as an illustration of how the findings from the interview data and the system-trace files of movement provided a deeper insight. The following extract shows how the son in particular initially experiments with the system to discover the effect of being on a region boundary. This is similar to the engagement stage of immersion in computer games. He enjoys the process of discovery and engages with the interaction style.

> Father: ... We took a while to familiarise ourselves. I think we must have crossed over a few times because sometimes we would say, "What's this" and then it would drop out. Yeh I got used to it and then I was fine. Did you get used to it?

> Son: Yeh I always find that I stand at the edge of the zones and sometimes it turns off and then turns back on the sound.

> I: And how did you work out where to go?

> Son: I just tried going each way and if it stayed for a while then I knew I was nearer the middle.

Father: I could see you were going like a crab at times. You were going two paces that way then that way

Figure 4 shows the map of the regions in the square and the thick line punctuated by dots shows the path that the son took around the square and it is not hard to identify the points at which the son stood at the edges of the zones. Each dot indicates a sound file starting up or stopping. Figure 4 also shows the amount of content heard in each of the regions. There are three files that can be played in each region and so to hear all of the content each region would have had to be entered three times and the whole of the sound file listened to each time. The son listened to a large proportion of the content and often revisited regions. Both father and son spent over an hour in the square and listened to sixty-two different sound files. The time that they invested listening and exploring the square shows that they were engaged in the content. The son also shows some emotional engagement with the play *"You could also see – like picture what was actually happening because you could actually know what it would have been like and you could actually*

Figure 4. Son's route walked and amount of content heard.

picture the people who were in the riot". Their interview also indicates that they may have become totally immersed at times.

I: How about other people in the square?

Father: I paid no attention to them whatsoever I must confess

Son: I was more listening than looking really

Father: We were well absorbed

While both father and son report feelings of immersion they also describe talking to each other and swapping headphones to share their experience. In addition, the path in Figure 4 shows that their experience was not smooth. The long "V" shapes indicate a large GPS bounce, where the person has not actually moved but GPS has reported an erroneous reading.

These discontinuities suggest that throughout the experience episodes of deep immersion are interspersed with episodes of navigation, searching and communication. This implies that fleeting or sporadic periods of deep immersion are so powerful that they can make the overall experience feel really compelling despite system problems. In the bigger report, based on the complete quantitative and qualitative data set, a model is then proposed for immersion as a cycle of transient states triggered by events in the overall experience. Again, the combination of self-report and location sensing data proved to be a powerful way to gain deeper insight.

Study 3: Communication-Wear: User evaluation of two prototypes, [Baurley et al., 2006]

4   Quick overview

Communication-wear is a clothing concept that seeks to augment mobile communications by enabling expressive or inferred emotional messages to be exchanged remotely between people who are relationally close, by conveying a sense/experience of touch, and presence. We gauged user perceptions on such smart textiles in two user trials. Young participants in the study responded positively to the concept of being connected through their clothing. In particular the ability to exchange sensory messages seems to bring out deeply emotional comments. Subjects said that the fact that the other person could affect their clothing in some way, made them feel closer to that person, thereby providing a sense of presence. The research is multi-disciplinary, drawing on expertise from fashion and textile design, wearable computing, and psychology.

In our experiment participants "worked" in pairs; they could communicate with their partner in a number of "affective" ways. A tactile actuator that attempted to simulate a stroking sensation was engineered using shape memory alloy wire and a pleated fabric insert. This pleated insert was located on the inside of the lower part of the sleeve so that it would slide against the top of the lower arm. Skin galvanic response sensors were also introduced, which were integrated into the lining of the garment looping around the index and second finger on the left hand. Fibre-optics were engineered into the garment on the inside of the arms. A subject, by hugging themselves and stretching mechanical stretch sensors was able to deliver a warming sensation (through heat pads) in the shoulders of the partner. An arm stroke by the sender was received as pleated fabric being drawn up the arm. In addition, physiological arousal, as sensed by the GSR sensors, was relayed to the partner by light being emitted from the fibre optics (Figures 5 and 6).

The latter, the GSR-activation, evoked a sense of wonder. Subjects experienced it as a kind of subliminal messaging. Some articulated that this was preferable to other types of actuation as it is not something we would normally have access to. Most thought that seeing what was happening to the other person made them feel closer to that person.

"The reason why I like the lights is because it's about how someone is feeling, excited … it's more than a physical reaction."

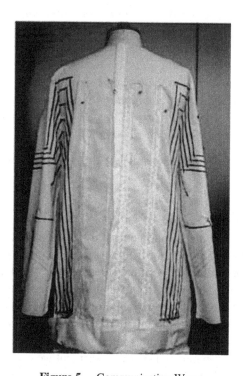

Figure 5. Communication Wear.

Figure 6.   Lighting up.

"What was most intriguing was the fact that she's having a reaction; maybe it's not to me, that doesn't matter, it's the fact that it is very personal to see someone's sweat is represented by light. It is a personal or intimate thing."

"...it's because it's something that you would never know; you can't read people's reactions in that way; you would never know someone's personal reaction and then suddenly you can read it, it lights up, it's really in your face, the glow. I think it's that contrast between not knowing and then suddenly knowing; and you are the only one who knows."

In short, we used a bio-sensor but left the interpretation up to the users themselves.

5   Discussion

Given the subjective nature and general difficulty of interpreting bio-sensor and contextual data stemming from a (mobile) computer system with an acceptable level of accuracy, we have steered away from emotion-sensing. In the three examples, in order to probe users' experiences, we used more traditional psychological self-report techniques in conjunction with bio-sensing, location sensing and logging interaction. For the visual DAB-radio study and the location based audio play our interpretations were made in an ad-hoc manner and in the communication-wear experiment we made no interpretation at all (a very lazy option). So the question then is: What sort of lessons can we learn from our own more applied research in relation to the other papers in this book?

Firstly it shows the value of such time-series data in conjunction with self-report data and we can expect more and more of this type of data analysis in the future. As Fred Boekhorst (Vice President Philips Research) states in his foreword: "We are just starting to understand". Since research is just coming off the ground, any experiments that have successfully made use of sensor data, even in an ad-hoc fashion, are worth considering for subsequent developments.

In this book there are papers about the current state of the art in bio sensing, the use of fairly consistent frameworks for classifying emotion and the way physiological correlates of emotion might lead to developing experience measurement tools. Furthermore we read about applied research in gaming, the perfume industry and as an aid in the growing market of "well-being". It seems therefore that, whilst applications are finding their way into the market, in parallel components for a more theoretical framework are getting into place, even though for sometime to come we will still make use of ad-hoc interpretations. This book provides high value in bringing the different research strands (and stakeholders) together.

Interestingly in the communication-wear experiments, we highlight a consumer (fashion) application where bio-sensing without interpretation seems, all the same, to evoke deeply emotional experiences. There are other applications of using bio-sensor data without them being tied to an experiential interpretation. For instance, in a recent location based game "Ere be Dragons", heart-rate was used in a very playful manner.

Where a theoretical framework is concerned, we would strongly advocate using psycho-physics techniques to complement psycho-physiological approach. In particular Signal Detection Theory might be a valuable addition to the developing theoretical framework. Furthermore the theoretical (although not yet applied) work on real time interpretation via T-templates holds promise.

Acknowledgement

The CommunicationWear research is supported by the Arts and Humanities Research Council through the AHRC's Fellowships in the Creative and Performing Arts scheme, UK.

References

Baurley, S., Geelhoed, E., and Moore, A. Communication-Wear: user evaluation of two prototypes, Paper submitted to the IEEE International Symposium on Wearable Computers, 2006 (http://www-static.cc.gatech.edu/gvu/ccg/iswc06/), Montreux, Switzerland October 11–14.

'Ere be Dragons': www.i-am-ai.net/erebedragons/video

Geelhoed, E., Barfield, L., De Bruine, A., Hull, R., and Jeffries, H. Augmented Digital Audio Broadcast Home Trial., HP Labs external technical report, 2005: http://www.hpl.hp.com/techreports/2005/HPL-2005-203.html

Mobile Bristol: http://www.mobilebristol.co.uk/publications.html

Reid, J., Geelhoed, E., Hull, R., Cater, K., and Clayton, B. Parallel worlds: Immersion in location-based experiences. In Gerrit van der Veer (ed.), CHI2005: Conference On human Factors in Computing Systems, April 2005.

Swets, J.A. (ed.) 1964, Signal Detection and recognition by human observers, New York, Wiley.

6

OBJECTIVE EMOTIONAL ASSESSMENT OF INDUSTRIAL PRODUCTS

Wolfram Boucsein and Florian Schaefer

Abstract   We developed an objective emotional assessment to detect subtle emotion-eliciting properties of products. Electrodermal activity, electrocardiogram, peripheral blood volume, and the activity of three facial muscles (zygomaticus, levator labii, corrugator) are continuously recorded, amended by subjective ratings of various emotional properties induced by interactions with the product. Among the physiological measures, finger pulse volume, skin conductance, and facial muscular activity were most sensitive in revealing tactile effects and their interactions with product worlds being introduced to generate a positive emotional experience. In particular, multivariate evaluation techniques were most successful in revealing subtle differences in products that could not be detected by a traditional sensory assessment.

1 Introduction

The application of psychophysiology in product testing is most popular for advertising. Using psychophysiological concepts and methods in the process of designing industrial products is much less known to the Western industry. While having contact with colleagues in Japan and Korea, we learned about an intriguing concept that is called "kansei" in Japan and "kamsung" in Korea. Its lexical meaning is intuitional mental activities related to feeling and desire. Originally, kansei or kamsung referred to a personal ability to discriminate and evaluate the quality of art or the purity of the natural environment. In the field of engineering, kansei or kamsung is used for sensitivity and feeling of a person being in contact with a product. As the final goal, engineers wish to control such qualities as beauty, desirability, comfort, and pleasantness manifested in an industrial product. Therefore, engineers attempt to measure a person's kansei or kamsung by using psychophysiological methods in the process of designing products (Yagi, 2000). Our laboratory has now more than nine years experience with the use of psychophysiology in product testing.

J.H.D.M. Westerink et al. (eds.), Probing Experience, 69–76.
© 2008 *Springer.*

Our field of application is to assess subtle emotion-eliciting properties of cosmetic products. Tactile and olfactory properties of cosmetics constitute relative weak stimuli. In addition, because of the high quality of today's cosmetic products, differences between products are very hard to detect. Therefore, the assessment of their emotion-eliciting properties can not be performed by a traditional sensory assessment using subjective comparisons only but requires rather subtle methods. During the last five years, we developed an objective emotional assessment (OEA) in our laboratory, during which skin conductance, electrocardiogram, peripheral blood volume, and the activity of three facial muscles (see Figure 1) are continuously recorded, followed by a subjective rating of various emotional properties of the product. Heart rate deceleration, finger pulse volume modulation, skin conductance, and facial muscular activity were most sensitive in revealing tactile and olfactory effects and their interactions with optical and acoustical cues being introduced to generate a positive emotional imagination. Especially, multivariate evaluation techniques were most successful in revealing subtle differences in cosmetic products that could not have been detected by a traditional sensory assessment.

This paper summarizes the results of three experiments performed by our group, evaluating emotional qualities of tactile and olfactory characteristics of cosmetic products. Other than by means of a traditional sensory assessment (Busch and Gassenmeier, 1997), our newly developed technique called objective emotional assessment (OEA) is not only able to differentiate the physical properties of the products but also reveal their emotion-inducing properties

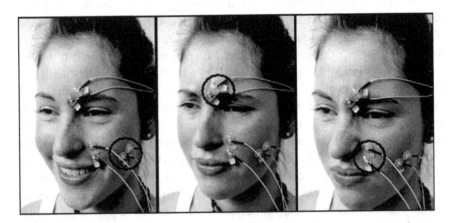

Figure 1. Facial electromyogram: (left) zygomaticus "pleasure"; (middle) corrugator supercilii "critical evaluation"; (right) levator labii superioris "disgust".

that could not be assessed by traditional techniques. The use of OEA comprises both subjective and physiological measures. Psychophysiological responses (e. g., changes in heart activity, peripheral pulse volume, skin conductance, and facial muscular activity) are largely controlled by phylogenetically old parts of the human brain, especially the limbic system.

The detection of these prior-to-consciousness, emotional driven responses is of great interest for a proper understanding of the acceptance or refusal of products by consumers. In many instances, decisions to buy or not to buy a product are not rationally based. Instead, they originate from non-conscious images in our brain.

Psychophysiological measures cannot only reflect an immediate emotional response to a product during an initial contact or a manipulation phase. Their additional advantage over verbal descriptions such as used in the traditional sensory assessment is that they cannot be easily faked. Thus, they constitute an objective measure of what is taking place during the interaction of the tactile or olfactory stimulation by a product and the inner images in the customer's mind.

2 Experiment 1

Foams play an important role in the consumer's experience of cosmetic products such as shampoos. Therefore, in our first study, the OEA technique has been used to differentiate the emotional qualities of four well described industrial tensides (foams) in 12 highly trained female panelists (Boucsein et al., 1999). Each subject received the four tensides in counterbalanced order, split into two sessions, each one preceded by a standard foam as a reference.

The following physiological measures were recorded throughout a 30 sec contact phase and a subsequent 30 sec handling phase: electrocardiogram, skin conductance, finger pulse volume amplitude and electromyographic activity of three facial muscles (zygomaticus major, levator labii superius, and corrugator supercilii; see Figure 1). After each foam presentation, a 21-item Likert scale was used to obtain subjective ratings of the foam's hedonic qualities. In order to directly compare the OEA results with those from traditional product testing, a sensory assessment of each foam was subsequently performed by the same subjects, followed by a two weeks home use test. Thereafter, the OEA was completely repeated.

In general, there was a very good correspondence between the results of the OEA and the traditional sensory assessment that was complemented by a free hedonic description of the foams. Orienting-eliciting qualities of the foams were best reflected in heart rate deceleration and increased skin conductance responses, while stimulus complexity elicited a decrease in heart rate variability. A variation coefficient of the finger pulse volume amplitude revealed specific differences in a tactile orientation towards the foams. Each of the facial muscles reflected different emotional and cognitive processes following the contact and/or manipulation with the foams: the zygomaticus major reflected pleasantness, the levator labii unpleasantness, and the corrugator supercilii a critical evaluation of the stimulus in question. In general, the foams could be differentiated more fine-grained with the OEA technique and could better predict the outcome of the home use tests compared to the traditional sensory assessment.

3   Experiment 2

Since tactile properties of cosmetic products constitute weak stimuli, they can be expected to be easily modified by mental images. In order to enhance an intended positive emotion-inducing effect of such a product, its experience can be embedded in a certain "world" that generates a positive emotional imagination. The second study tested such an influence in 12 males and 12 females, half of each being laymen and experts in sensory assessment (Boucsein et al., 2002). Two product worlds (emotional and technical) and three different hair samples, two of them treated with different shampoos, and an untreated hair sample as control, were presented to each subject in counterbalanced order of all six combinations. The same kind of OEA as used in the first experiment was applied and compared with a traditional sensory assessment.

Among the physiological measures, finger pulse volume and facial muscular activity were most sensitive in revealing effects of and interactions between product worlds and hair samples. A multivariate evaluation of the physiological data revealed three discriminant functions that explained 78% of the total variance and enabled a re-classification considerably better than chance. The first discriminant function clearly separated the treated from the untreated hair samples which was not possible by subjective ratings or traditional sensory assessment. The two other discriminant functions comprised a hedonic and a product world factor (Figure 2).

The emotional product world exerted the largest influence in case of the weakest tactile differences between the hair samples, and its influence was larger in laymen than in experts. Gender effects were most prominent in the subjective domain where females responded more favourable to the emotional world compared to males. Again, the multivariate psychophysiological methodology of OEA used here was superior to traditional sensory assessment in revealing subtle differences in the tactile perception of cosmetic products.

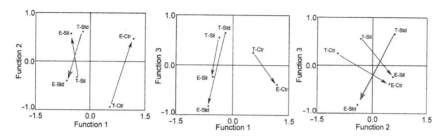

Figure 2. Projections of the group centroids for the six experimental conditions on the three possible combinations of discriminant functions. Abbreviations: E: emotional product world, T: technical product world. Ctr: control, Std: standard shampoo, Sil: silicate shampoo hair samples. For each hair sample, changes from the technical to the emotional product world are indicated by arrows (Boucsein et al., 2002, Figure 6, reprinted with permission).

4 Experiment 3

The third study extended the use of OEA to typical fragrances as applied in cosmetic products. Lavender was used as a relaxing odor and jasmine as an activating one. Since females are generally better than males in odor perception, 24 female subjects that proved to be good smellers in an olfactory discrimination test were chosen for the study. Each fragrance was presented twice to each subject in a counterbalanced order. Special care was taken to generate an exact trigger point for the physiological recording: a constant air flow of 8 liter per minute passed through a glass tube with two holes under the subject's nostrils (Figure 3). The time and amount of fragrance injected in the air stream were exactly controlled, avoiding to generate additional acoustic stimuli for the subject. The same kind of OEA as in the two earlier experiments was applied. In addition, respiratory activity was recorded to ensure the fragrance presentation during inspiration.

As in the second study, a multivariate analysis of the physiological data was performed, revealing three discriminant functions. Although showing weaker effects compared to the ones found in our second experiment, the multivariate evaluation revealed a sensitive pattern of the two fragrance's shifts from trial 1 (lav1 and jas1) to trial 2 (lav2 and jas2), as shown in Figures 4 and 5.

Discriminant function 1 clearly separated the two trials, while function 2 separated the two fragrances from each other (Figure 4). As can be inferred from Figure 5, the centroids for the two fragrances moved in a different direction from trial 1 to trial 2 on discriminant function 3. Using the weights as shown in Table 1 and the results of the univariate analyses, this contrasting move can be interpreted as follows: The initially greater interest in and the more positive emotion induced by jasmine declined during its repeated presentation,

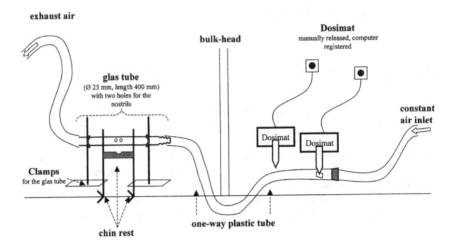

Figure 3. Apparatus for the presentation of fragrances.

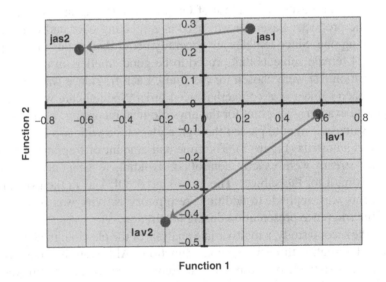

Figure 4. Discriminant functions 1 & 2.

whereas the initially negative touch of lavender disappeared and its greater relaxing properties intensified in the second trial.

The subjective evaluation confirmed the objectively measured emotional and arousing properties of the two fragrances: Lavender was perceived as more intense with a negative touch in the first instance but as relaxing when presented repeatedly. Jasmine was experienced as more exciting with a positive emotional touch and required a higher subjective concentration when presented first, but

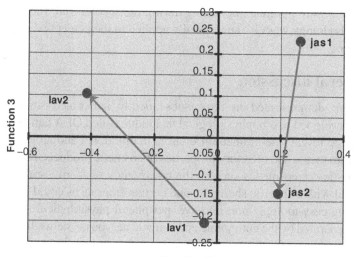

Figure 5. Discriminant functions 2 & 3.

Table 1. Weights of the physiological parameters for the three discriminant functions.

Physiological parameter	Discriminant function		
	1	*2*	*3*
EMG, levator labii, maximum amplitude	−0.292	−0.182	−0.250
EMG levator labii, sum of amplitudes	−0.175	0.107	−0.175
IBI standard deviation	−0.128	−0.014	0.112
SCR sum of amplitudes	−0.119	0.064	−0.080
PVA modulation	−0.046	0.362	0.316
IBI minimum	0.106	−0.277	0.240
EMG corrugator, maximum amplitude	0.039	0.261	−0.230
NS.SCR frequency	0.153	0.038	−0.375
IBI maximum	−0.078	−0.119	0.310
EMG corrugator, number of responses	−0.007	−0.258	0.294
Heart rate	0.098	0.282	−0.286
Heart rate variability	−0.058	0.193	0.280
Mean IBI	0.027	−0.252	0.268
EMG zygomaticus, number of responses	0.008	−0.035	0.254
EMG levator labii, number of responses	0.041	0.050	0.144

EMG = electromyogram, IBI = interbeat interval from the electrocardiogram, SCR = skin conductance response, NS.SCR = non-specific SCRs, PVA = puls volume amplitude.

these effects were not much persisting during the second trial. In general, our OEA-methodology was also successfully applied to the perception of cosmetic fragrances.

5 General discussion

We have demonstrated in three subsequently performed studies that a recently developed psychophysiological technique called OEA can be successfully used to reveal fine-grained differences in emotional and arousing effects arising from tactile and olfactory properties of cosmetic products. Rather subtle characteristics of cosmetics such as the consistency of foams, smoothness of hair treated with a specific shampoo, and certain fragrances could be differentiated using easy-to-apply non-invasive, peripheral physiological measures of changes generated by the autonomic and somatic nervous systems. In particular, OEA allowed more fine-grained analyses as compared to classical techniques used in the cosmetics industry such as sensory assessment and even home use tests, in predicting emotion-inducing properties of cosmetic products in the customer. The OEA methodology is suitable for being applied to designing other products as well (Eisfeld et al., 2005, 2006).

References

Boucsein, W., Schaefer, F., Schwerdtfeger, A., Busch, P., & Eisfeld, W. (1999). Objective emotional assessment of foam. *SÖFW-Journal*, 125, 2–17.

Boucsein, W., Schaefer, F., Kefel, M., Busch, P., & Eisfeld, W. (2002). Objective emotional assessment of tactile hair properties and their modulation by different product worlds. *International Journal of Cosmetic Science*, 24, 135–150.

Busch, P., & Gassenmeier, T. (1997). Sensory assessment in the cosmetic field. *Parfümerie und Kosmetik*, 78, 16–21.

Eisfeld, W., Schaefer, F., Boucsein, W., & Stolz, C. (2005). Tracking intersensory properties of cosmetic products via psycho-physiological assessment. *International Federation Societies of Cosmetic Chemists (IFSCC)*, 8, 25–30.

Eisfeld, W., Wachter, R., Stürmer, R., Schaefer, F., & Boucsein, W. (2006). Perceivable wellness effects via a new liposome concept for fabric care. *SÖFW-Journal*, 132, 84–92.

Yagi, A. (2000). Engineering Psychophysiology in Japan. In: Backs, R., Boucsein, W. (Eds.), Engineering Psychophysiology (pp. 361–368). Lawrence Erlbaum Ass. London: Plenum Press.

7

MEASURING EXPERIENCES IN GAMING AND TV APPLICATIONS

Investigating the Added Value of a Multi-View Auto-Stereoscopic 3D Display

Rosemarie J.E. Rajae-Joordens

Abstract   The longer-term use of multi-view 3D displays in gaming and TV applications was investigated in two experiments. Participants played a video game on a 20″ 3D monitor (experiment 1) or watched a movie on a 42″ 3D display for 90 minutes (experiment 2); half of the time in 3D, the other half in 2D with the same temporal and spatial resolution as the 3D mode. Meanwhile, galvanic skin response and heart rate were measured (both assumed to assess emotions and presence), followed by questionnaires at the end of each session. Gaming performance (experiment 1) and memory performance (experiment 2) were also measured. The results show that 3D displays provoke significantly higher positive emotions and stronger feelings of presence than 2D displays in the gaming application, and are highly preferred by a large majority (85%) of the participants. Watching TV on a 3D display does not significantly evoke more emotions than on 2D displays, although a trend towards an increase in emotions is found, and 3D is preferred above 2D, or at least not found to be annoying by 95% of the participants. In conclusion, 3D displays have added value in gaming applications, and to a lesser extent to TV applications with a relatively low amount of depth added.

1   Introduction

Philips has developed a multi-view auto-stereoscopic 3D display. The technology used in this display is based on a 9-views lenticular screen, placed in front of a standard LCD monitor. In this way, different images are displayed at different horizontal viewing directions. As a consequence, a viewer sees a different image with his left eye and right eye, independent of his position (see Figure 1). Hence, the viewer can move in front of the screen and still experience stereoscopic depth and motion parallax without using special glasses. During demonstrations, such as conferences, viewers looking at a 3D display are in general very positively surprised (WOW-effect) and mention an increased sense of reality, or in other words, a stronger feeling of presence as

77

J.H.D.M. Westerink et al. (eds.), Probing Experience, 77–90.

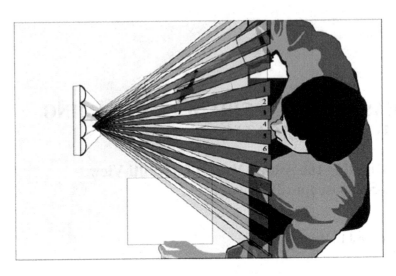

Figure 1.   Principle behind a multi-view auto-stereoscopic lenticular 3D display as designed by Philips.

compared to 2D. So far, it was not clear how these 3D displays are experienced after longer-term exposure. Hence, it was the aim of this study to evaluate the longer-term use of such a 3D display for both gaming and TV applications.

To investigate the longer-term experience on 3D displays, techniques known from virtual reality research were studied. In a number of studies (Wiederhold et al., 2001; Meehan et al., 2002), feelings of presence have been examined using psychophysiological measures, e.g. skin conductance and heart rate (HR), both associated with arousal. Skin conductance is also referred to as electrodermal activity or galvanic skin response (GSR). The latter term is used in this study. A change in arousal affects the activity of the sympathetic nervous system, which in turn results in a series of bodily changes including altered skin conductivity and heart rate. Emotions as joy and anger, attention and sexual feelings all cause higher arousal and a rise in GSR and HR. Withdrawal and relaxation, on the other hand, are characterized by a decrease in arousal and a fall in GSR and HR. It has been demonstrated that feelings of presence increase when the screen size of the television increases from 12 to 46 inch, and that a higher GSR accompanies this increased feeling of presence (Lombard et al., 2000). Another study showed that an increase in GSR in a multi-player game as compared to the single-user version is accompanied by stronger feelings of engagement, excitement and fun (Mandryk and Inkpen, 2004), i.e. factors that can facilitate presence. Thus, both GSR and HR seem to be useful parameters to establish the longer-term experience on 3D displays.

Besides these autonomic psychophysiological responses, that generally happen without awareness of the person involved, it is interesting to investigate the conscious experiences using different types of subjective measures, such as questionnaires, interviews and thinking-aloud protocols. With respect to the investigation of the longer-term experience on 3D displays, four aspects seem to be of main importance, namely feelings of presence, engagement, visual eyestrain, and symptoms of simulator sickness.

Especially visual eyestrain is an important phenomenon to be considered in the light of this study. Firstly, looking at objects appearing in front of a 3D display evokes a conflict between the accommodation and convergence process of the eye (Wann et al., 1995). This accommodation-convergence mismatch is expected to be one of the main causes of visual eyestrain induced by looking at a 3D display. Secondly, the occurrence of cross talk of information between the right and left eye is also mentioned to cause visual eyestrain (Pastoor, 1995). Because lenticular multi-view 3D displays in general show a considerable amount of cross talk and because also the accommodation-convergence mismatches occur, multi-view 3D displays are expected to induce at least some visual eyestrain after longer-term exposure.

Additional to the questionnaires, it might be useful to investigate the performance of the viewer. During a game, events can be logged. Relevant scores for the gamer, such as the number of enemies killed and the number of times the participant lost a live, might provide interesting information about the performance of the gamer in the 2D and 3D mode. With regard to the TV application, the amount of attention might be a good candidate because the allocation of sufficient attentional resources to the mediated environment is proposed to be an important component of presence (Ijsselsteijn et al., 2000). Attention, however, can only be indirectly measured by memory tests; the premise is that accurately directed allocation of attention increases the recall of details. Therefore, the Temporal Order Judgment task (Jasowoski and Verlger, 2000) and the Two-Alternative Forced-Choice Recognition test (Pezdek and Greene, 1993) might be useful to investigate memory performance when watching 2D and 3D TV.

The present study consists of two experiments. Both focus on the longer-term use of multi-view 3D displays in gaming and TV applications, respectively. Therefore, 20 experienced gamers were invited to play Quake III Arena game twice; once with the display set to the 3D mode, and once to the 2D mode. Another 20 participants were asked to watch the movie *"Lord of the Rings: Fellowship of the Ring"*; half with the display set to the 3D mode, half in the 2D mode. In both experiments, the 2D and 3D mode had the same spatial and temporal resolution. For the 3D mode 9 different views were displayed to create an experience of depth, while in the 2D mode 9 identical views were shown. During the gaming and TV watching sessions, the psychophysiological measures GSR and HR were monitored. At the end of each session, a number of subjective measures were taken. Therefore, the participants had to fill in three questionnaires to investigate feelings of presence and engagement, visual eyestrain and symptoms of simulator sickness. Performance, i.e. gaming performance in the gaming application and memory performance in the TV application, was also measured. Assuming that the initially positive effect of the 3D display as seen after short-term exposure remains over a longer period, stronger emotions, reflected by higher GSR and HR values, stronger feelings of presence and better performance are expected when playing a game or watching a movie in the 3D mode as compared to the 2D mode.

2   Material and methods

2.1   Experiment 1: Gaming application

In total, 20 experienced gamers (19 males and 1 female with an age varying between 22 and 44 years) participated in this experiment. They were asked to take place in front of a Philips 20″ 3D Monitor (9 view lenticular, resolution of 1600×1200 and an optimal viewing distance of 40 cm). Electrodes (Porti system, TMS International BV, the Netherlands) were attached to the participant's body: two passive ones on the torso for ECG, two active ones on the left hand palm for the GSR and another passive electrode on the calf of the right leg as a reference.

Next, the light in the test room was lowered to 5 lux measured at the screen in the direction of the viewer, and the procedure depicted in Figure 2 was followed. The subject started a 10-minutes Windows Memory Game (in 2D) in order to get stabilized electrical contact between the electrodes and the skin. Meanwhile, the test leader was able to check the psychophysiological signals. During the final 3 minutes of this 10-minutes adaptation period, HR and GSR were measured in order to establish a baseline value. Subsequently, subjects were asked to play Quake III Arena for 45 minutes. Half of the subjects played the first session in the 2D mode, the other half started in the 3D mode. By means of a remote control unit, the display could easily be switched from 2D (9 identical views) to 3D (9 slightly different views) and vice versa. There were no restrictions for the game; participants were free to choose the difficulty level and other settings. Before each session, the game was reset to its initial settings in order to prevent start-up differences. Gaming scores and losses were logged. After 45 minutes gaming, a spot light was turned on to allow the subjects to fill in three questionnaires: a Presence and Engagement Questionnaire, followed by a Visual Symptoms Questionnaire and Simulator Sickness Questionnaire (Häkkinen et al., 2002).

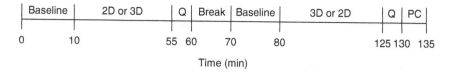

Figure 2. Time planning of the experimental procedure (Q = three questionnaires on presence and engagement, visual symptoms and simulator sickness; PC = paired comparison) with time expressed in minutes. Half of the participants first played in the 2D mode (9 identical views), the other half started in the 3D mode (9 slightly different views).

After a 10-minute break, in which the electrodes were disconnected in order to leave the test room, the procedure described above was repeated. The display was set to the mode (2D or 3D), which the participant had not played yet. After filling in the questionnaires for the second time, subjects were asked to compare the 2D and 3D mode and indicate which mode they liked the most.

2.2 Experiment 2: TV application

In total, 20 subjects (19 males and 1 female with an age varying between 24 and 58 years) participated in this experiment. They were asked to take place in front of a Philips 42″ 3D TV (9 view lenticular, resolution of 1920 × 1080, and an optimal viewing distance of 200 cm) in a living room like setting with the light lowered to 18 lux measured at the screen in the direction of the viewer.

The procedure followed in this experiment was similar to that of Experiment 1. Instead of playing a 10-minutes Windows Memory Game, the subject had to watch a 10-minute nature documentary on dolphins (in 2D) in order to get the electrodes adapted to skin temperature and to establish a baseline measure. Further, the Quake III Arena game was replaced by 90 minutes of the movie "*The Lord of the Rings: Fellowship of the Ring*" with a resolution of 760 × 540 pixels in RGB format with an additional depth map. Half of the subjects saw the first 45 min of the movie in the 2D mode, the other half started in the 3D mode. Note that the 2D and 3D mode had the same spatial and temporal resolution. They only differed with regard to the amount of depth present.

For the performance analysis, two memory tests were used. In the Temporal Order Judgment test, participants had to indicate 20 times the order of appearance in time of two still images, i.e. frames that were separated in the movie by about 30 seconds. In the Two-Alternative Forced-Choice Recognition test, participants had to indicate 12 times which image out of two was taken from the movie they just had seen. The images not taken from the movie were all frames from other Lord of the Ring movies.

3   Results

3.1   Experiment 1: Gaming application

3.1.1   Psychophysiological measures   Mean GSR and HR were calculated for 15 blocks of 3 minutes plus one additional block of 3 minutes for the baseline measurements. The HR data of 3 subjects and GSR data of 4 subjects were useless due to large disturbances in the recorded signal and were therefore omitted from the analyses. Mean GSR as a function of time is depicted in Figure 3.

An analysis of variance with repeated measures on GSR with Display (two levels: 2D and 3D) and Time (15 levels: 15 × 3 minutes) showed a significant main effect of Display [$F(1,15)=4.773$; $p=.045$], whereas the main effect of Time [$F(14,2)=1.395$; $p=.495$] and the interaction effect Display × Time [$F(14,2)=0.181$; $p=.983$] were found not to be significant. This finding suggests that the GSR in the 3D mode is significantly higher than in the 2D mode, and that this effect is sustainable over a period of 45 min, whereas GSR in the 2D mode soon returns to baseline values.

A second analysis of variance with repeated measures on GSR with Display (two levels: 2D and 3D) and Time (2 levels: block 0 and 1) revealed that GSR increased directly after starting the game [$F(1,15) = 15.635$; $p = .001$] as compared to the baseline value. Also a significant interaction between Display

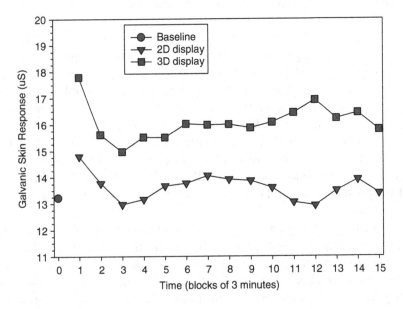

Figure 3.   Mean GSR in μSiemens as function of time for both gaming on the 2D and 3D display as compared to playing memory in a 2D mode (baseline).

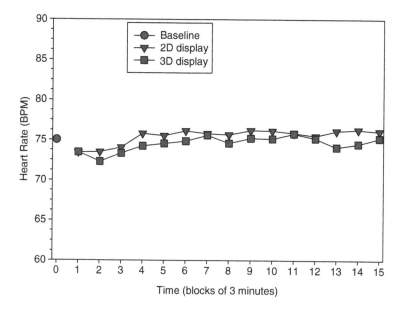

Figure 4.   Mean HR in beats per minute as function of time for both gaming on the 2D and 3D display as compared to playing memory in a 2D mode (baseline).

and Time was found [$F(1,15) = 7.694$; $p = .014$], indicating that the WOW-effect in the 3D mode is significantly higher than in the 2D mode.

Figure 4 shows mean HR as a function of time. An analysis of variance with repeated measures revealed no significant main effect of Display [$F(1,16) = 1.172$; $p = .295$] and Time [$F(14,3) = 6.096$; $p = .081$], neither a significant interaction effect between Display and Time [$F(14,3) = 1.915$; $p = .326$]. In other words, HR is not affected during the experiment at all.

3.1.2 Subjective measures   Table 1 shows the results of the Presence and Engagement Questionnaire for the 2D and 3D mode. By means of the non-parametric Wilcoxon's matched pairs test, it was tested whether the Feeling of Presence scores and Engagement scores as experienced in the 2D mode were significantly different from those in the 3D mode. Post hoc Wilcoxon's matched pairs tests were performed to identify which items were responsible for the significant overall effects. As can be seen, 3D has a significantly higher overall presence ($p < 0.001$) and engagement score ($p = .006$) than 2D. 3D scored significantly higher than 2D on all 5 presence-related and on half of the engagement related items.

The Visual Symptoms Questionnaire ($p = .085$) and Simulator Sickness Questionnaire ($p = .183$), on the other hand, revealed no significant differ-

Table 1. Mean Presence and Engagement Questionnaire scores for the 2D and 3D mode.

Presence and Engagement Questionnaire (n = 20)	2D	3D	P
Feeling of Presence	2.88	3.68	.000
I had a sense of being in the gaming scenes	3.45	4.05	.008
I felt I could have reached out and touch things	2.40	3.70	.003
I felt that all my senses were stimulated at the same time	2.45	3.10	.012
It felt realistic to move in the gaming environment	3.05	3.90	.004
I had a strong sense that characters and objects were solid	3.05	3.65	.038
Engagement	3.77	4.18	.006
I would have liked this game to continue	3.70	4.10	.021
I vividly remember some parts of this game	3.65	3.95	.190
I'd recommend this game to my friends	3.60	4.10	.031
I felt myself being 'drawn in'	3.65	4.30	.014
I lost track of time	3.90	4.25	.177
I enjoyed myself	4.25	4.50	.132
My experience was intense	3.95	4.40	.033
I responded emotionally	3.45	3.85	.083

ences between 2D and 3D. Finally, at the end of the experiment, 85% of the participants indicated to prefer the 3D mode to the 2D mode.

3.1.3 Gaming performance   Mean SCORE (total number of enemies killed) and LOSS (total number of times being killed) for the 2D and 3D mode is depicted in Figure 5. A two-way mixed model ANOVA on SCORE with Display (two levels: 2D and 3D) as a within-subject factor and Order (two levels: 2D first and 3D first) as a between-subject factor showed a significant interaction effect between Display and Order [$F(1,15) = 11.10$; $p = .005$], whereas the main effect of Display [$F(1,15) = .733$; $p = .405$] was found not to be significant. In other words, participants initially eliminate the enemies more effectively in the 3D mode, but that this effect disappears after prolonged use. Finally, a two-way mixed model ANOVA on LOSS showed neither a significant main effect of Display [$F(1,15) = .751$; $p = .400$], nor an interaction effect between Display and Order [$F(1,15) = .577$; $p = .459$].

3.2   Experiment 2: TV application

3.2.1 Psychophysiological measures   Mean GSR and HR were calculated for the first 13 blocks of 3 minutes plus one additional block of 3 minutes for the baseline measurements. The last 2 blocks (6 minutes) as well as all

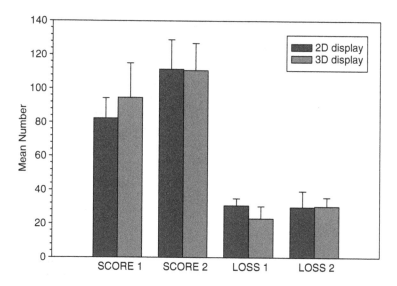

Figure 5. Mean SCORE and LOSS (+S.E.M.) for the 2D and 3D mode in session 1 and 2.

HR data of 5 subjects and all GSR data of 3 subjects were useless due to large disturbances in the recorded signal and were therefore omitted from the analyses. Mean GSR as a function of time is depicted in Figure 6.

An analysis of variance with repeated measures on GSR with Display (two levels: 2D and 3D) and Time (13 levels: 13 × 3 minutes) as within-subject factors showed that neither the main effect of Display [$F(1,16) = 3.462$; $p = .081$] and Time [$F(12,5) = 3.985$; $p = .069$] nor the interaction effect between Display and Time [$F(12,5) = 0.571$; $p = .802$] were found to be significant. For both the main effect of Time and Display, however, a trend is seen, suggesting that GSR in the 3D mode tends to be higher than in the 2D mode, and tends to increase in both modes equally over time.

A second analysis of variance with repeated measures with Display (two levels: 2D and 3D) and Time (2 levels: block 0 and 1) revealed that the main effect of Time [$F(1,14) = 0.083$; $p = .778$] and Display [$F(1,14) = 0.156$; $p = .699$] as well as the interaction effect between Display and Time [$F(1,14) = 0.156$; $p = .699$] were not significant. These findings indicate that starting to watch the movie in the 2D and 3D mode does not evoke a WOW-effect on GSR.

Figure 7 shows the mean HR data as a function of time. An analysis of variance with repeated measures on HR revealed that neither the main effect of Display [$F(1,14) = 0.161$; $p = .694$] and Time [$F(12,3) = 0.444$; $p = .865$] nor the interaction between Display and Time [$F(12,3) = 1.418$; $p = .433$]

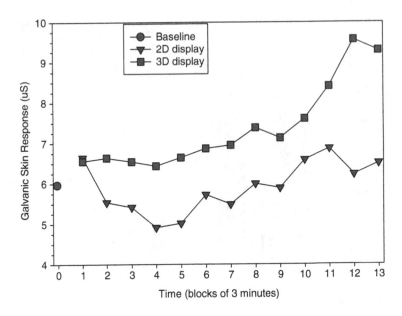

Figure 6. Mean GSR in μSiemens as function of time for both watching "Lord of the Rings" on the 2D and 3D display as compared to watching a nature documentary in the 2D mode (baseline).

were found to be significant, indicating that HR is not affected during the experiment at all.

3.2.2 Subjective measures Table 2 shows the results of the Presence and Engagement Questionnaire for the 2D and 3D mode. As can be seen, no significant differences are found on the overall presence (p = .850) and engagement score (p = .343). A Post hoc Wilcoxon's matched pairs test showed that 3D only has a significantly higher score on realism of the movie (p = .014) than 2D. Further, the Visual Symptoms Questionnaire (p = .0234) and Simulator Sickness Questionnaire (p = .277) revealed no significant differences between 2D and 3D either.

At the end of the experiment, 50% of the participants indicated to prefer the 3D mode above the 2D mode, while 45% of the participants mentioned to have no preference at all.

3.2.3 Memory performance Table 3 shows the mean number of right answers for Session 1 and 2 for both the Temporal Order Judgment memory test (TOJ) and the Two-Alternative Forced-Choice Recognition test (2AFC). The Mann-Whitney U-tests on the TOJ score of Session 1 and 2, and the 2AFC

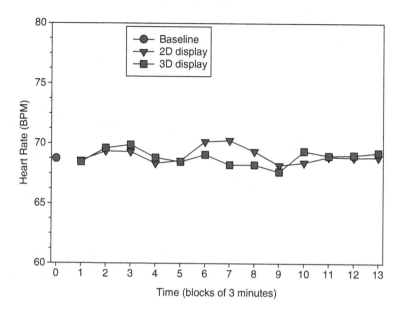

Figure 7. Mean HR in beats per minute as function of time for both watching "Lord of the Rings" on the 2D and 3D display as compared to watching a nature documentary in the 2D mode (baseline).

Table 2. Mean Presence and Engagement Questionnaire scores for the 2D and 3D mode.

Presence and Engagement Questionnaire (n = 20)	*2D*	*3D*	*P*
Feeling of Presence	2.86	2.93	.850
I had a sense of being in the movie scenes	2.95	2.80	.429
I felt I could have reached out and touch things	2.35	2.45	.747
I felt that all my senses were stimulated at the same time	2.65	2.80	.453
It felt that the movie environment seemed realistic	3.20	3.50	.014
I had a strong sense that characters and objects were solid	3.15	3.10	.941
Engagement	3.83	3.75	.343
I would have liked this movie to continue	4.25	4.10	.559
I vividly remember some parts of this movie	4.15	4.20	.564
I'd recommend this movie to my friends	4.25	4.15	.157
I felt myself being 'drawn in'	3.60	3.70	.527
I lost track of time	3.50	3.30	.206
I enjoyed myself	4.25	4.15	.414
My experience was intense	3.35	3.25	.480
I responded emotionally	3.30	3.15	.480

Table 3. Mean Temporal Order Judgment memory test (TOJ) and the Two-Alternative Forced-Choice Recognition test (2AFC) scores for the 2D and 3D mode.

Memory tests (n = 20)	*2D*	*SEM*	*3D*	*SEM*	*Z*	*P*
TOJ						
Session 1	5.40	1.51	5.80	1.03	−.699	.485
Session 2	4.40	1.51	4.70	1.06	−.394	.693
2AFC						
Session 1	4.90	1.29	5.50	.707	−.958	.338
Session 2	5.40	.843	4.40	1.26	−1.84	.065

score of Session 1 and 2 with Display (two levels: 2D and 3D) as between-subject factor showed no significant effects, although a trend towards a better memory for 2D is seen for the latter test in the second session.

4 Discussion

In the present study, the longer-term experience with 3D displays in gaming and TV applications has been investigated by means of GSR and HR measurements, three questionnaires and performance analyses. In line with the expectations, gaming in the 3D mode evokes a higher GSR and higher scores on the Presence and Engagement Questionnaire than the 2D mode. A closer look to the results shows that both in the 2D and 3D mode a significantly higher GSR is measured directly after starting the game as compared to the baseline measurement. The effect in the 3D mode, however, is considerably stronger than in the 2D mode, indicating that starting playing evokes a psychophysiological effect with a larger WOW-effect for the 3D mode than the 2D mode. Moreover, from the fact that the difference in GSR between 2D and 3D remains the same over time, it can be concluded that the 3D effect does not disappear after longer-term exposure.

Watching *"Lord of the Rings: The Fellowship of the Ring"* on TV in the 3D mode, on the other hand, does not significantly affect GSR as compared to the 2D mode. No significant differences between the 2D and 3D mode are found in the Presence and Engagement Questionnaire either, although a significant increase is found for 3D on the sub-item "realism of the movie environment". A closer look to the results reveals that GSR tends to be higher in the 3D mode than in the 2D mode, but that this effect is just not significant(note that this effect would have been significant incase an one-sided instead of two-sided statistical test had been used). The absence of an effect might be attributed to a difference in attitude between passively watching

TV (lean-backward application) and actively playing a game (lean-forward application). Also the difference in the source of the image material might have influenced the amount of involvement. In the TV application, the video material used was not available in 3D format, and thus 2D material had to be converted to 3D material. In the gaming application, perfectly rendered 3D graphics was used. Since the conversion of image material from 2D to 3D inherently creates some artifacts, smaller depth ranges are usually used, decreasing the perceived depth. Hence, we can conclude that in the TV application the GSR behaves more or less in the same manner as in the gaming application, although the responses are less pronounced due to experimental design choices and the nature of the TV application.

With regard to HR, no significant effects are found at all; even not in the gaming experiment, where a significant effect of GSR is found. An explanation for the absence of a display effect might be that HR is less sensitive than GSR. The studies in which an effect of HR is found, are all using a virtual environment by means of head mounted displays, so it might be that gaming on a desktop monitor is not immersive enough to measure an effect on HR.

Although visual eyestrain was expected to be a possible issue in 3D displays due to the accommodation-convergence mismatch and cross talk of information between the right and left eye, no significant differences between the 2D and 3D mode on the Visual Symptoms and Simulator Sickness Questionnaire are found, even not after 45 minutes of intense gaming and watching a movie. These findings indicate that the expected eyestrain seems not to be crucial.

Performance analyses show that in the beginning of the game, participants eliminate enemies more effectively in the 3D mode as compared to the 2D mode, but this effect disappears after prolonged gaming as the gamer becomes accustomed to the gaming environment. This finding that the experience on the 3D display seems to be more natural is in line with the results of a recent study in which 3D images are judged more natural than their 2D versions when presented on a 9-view auto-stereoscopic 3D display (Seuntiens et al., 2005). On the other hand, the two memory tests at the end of the TV experiment show no significant effects. Again, as with the GSR results, this effect might be due to the amount of depth added and the lay-back nature of the TV application.

Finally, the 3D display is found to be preferred above 2D by 85% of the participants in the gaming application, and by 50% of the participants in the TV application. Another 45% of the subjects in the TV experiment indicated to have no preference between the 2D and 3D mode at all.

In conclusion, 3D displays provoke significantly higher positive emotions and stronger feelings of presence than 2D displays in the gaming application, and is highly preferred by a large majority of the participants. Watching TV on a 3D display does not significantly evoke more emotions than 2D displays, although a trend towards an increase in emotions is found, and 3D is preferred above 2D, or at least not found to be annoying by 95% of the participants. Thus, 3D displays have added value in gaming applications, and to a lesser extent to TV applications with a relatively low amount of depth added. Further research is needed to investigate the effect of real 3D video material, allowing larger depth ranges, on presence and engagement.

Acknowledgements

The author wants to thank Tinuke Oluyomi from the University of Toronto in Canada for preparing and performing the second experiment in an excellent way.

References

Häkkinen, J. Vuori, T., and Puhakka, M. Postural Stability and Sickness Symptoms after HMD Use. *Proc SMC Symp*, 147–152 (2002).

Ijsselsteijn, W.J., De Ridder, H., Freeman, J., and Avons, S.E. Presence: Concept, determinants and measurements. *Proc SPIE Symp*, 3959–3976 (2000).

Jasowoski, P. and Verlger, R. Attentional bias towards low intensity stimuli: an explanation of the intensity dissociation between reaction time and temporal order judgments? *Consciousness and Cognition* 9, 435–456 (2000).

Lombard, M., Reich, R.D., Grabe, M.E., Bracken, C.C., and Ditton, T.B. Presence and television: The role of screen size. *Human Communication Research* 26, 75–98 (2000).

Mandryk, R.L. and Inkpen, K.M. Physiological indicators for the evaluation of co-located collaborative play. *Proc CSCW Symp*, 102–111 (2004).

Meehan, M., Insko, B., Whitton, M., and Brooks, F.P. Physiological measures of presence in stressful virtual environments, *ACM Transactions on Graphics* 21, 645–652 (2002).

Pastoor, S. Human factors of 3D imaging: results of recent research at Heinrich-Hertz-Institute Berlin. *Proc IDW Symp*, 69–72 (1995).

Pezdek, K. and Greene, J. Testing Eyewitness Memory: Developing a measure that is more resistant to suggestibility. *Law and Human Behaviour* 17, 361–369 (1993).

Seuntiens, P., Heynderickx, I., and Ijsselstein, W. Viewing experience and naturalness of 3D images. *Proc SPIE Symp*, 43–49 (2005).

Wann, J.P., Rushton, S.K., and Mon-Williams, M. Natural problems for stereoscopic depth perception in Virtual Environments. *Vision Research* 19, 2731–2736 (1995).

Wiederhold, B.K., Jang, D.P., Kaneda, M., Cabral, I., Lurie, Y., May, T., Kim, I.Y., Wiederhold, M.D., and Kim, S.I. An investigation into physiological responses in virtual environments: an objective measurement of presence, in: *Toward cyberpsychology: Mind, cognition and society in the internet age*, edited by G. Riva, and C. Calimberti (IOS Press, Amsterdam, 2001), pp. 175–183.

8

SENSING AFFECTIVE EXPERIENCE

Jennifer A. Healey

Abstract   Recording affective experience through psychophysiological measures presents many challenges. In the laboratory setting, where conditions can be controlled it is often difficult to generate the range and magnitude of emotional response that might want to be studied. In the ambulatory environment, physiological responses to motion and daily activities often confound physiological responses to affect and affective experience is difficult to record. This paper reviews the methods used to stimulate and assess affective experience in different environments and compares data collected using ECG, EMG, GSR, BVP and respiration and from in laboratory experiments, free ambulatory experiments and automobile driving experiments. In addition, two real-time systems for ambulatory assessment are presented: "StartleCam" a wearable image recording system that triggers off the slope of the GSR and the "Stress Tachometer" a metric of driver stress based on the LF/HF ratio of Heart Rate Variability calculated based on the last 100 seconds of ECG data.

1 Introduction

The paper presents various methods for recording affective experience in three types of environments: in a laboratory setting, in an ambulatory setting and in an automobile. Each of these environments presents a different set of challenges for eliciting affective responses, documenting these affective responses and synchronizing these annotations with a physiological record. The main challenge with measuring affective response in the laboratory is generating authentic affective responses within the short time the subjects participate and within the ethical guidelines of most oversight committees on the use of human subjects. The two greatest challenges in the ambulatory environment are differentiating affective physiological responses from other physiological responses and accurately capturing affective ground truth. The automobile provides a compromise situation where the subject has restrained movement and where the situational ground truth can be recorded but where the subject can also face genuinely dangerous and unexpected situations. Although the range of emotions experienced while driving can be limited, the strength of feeling is often genuine and strong. Sensing affective experience

91

J.H.D.M. Westerink et al. (eds.), Probing Experience, 91–100.
© 2008 *Springer.*

each of these environments has two components, measuring the variables that reflect underlying physiological change associated with changes in affect and accurately labeling affective experience.

2   Labeling affective experience

Labeling affective experience is challenging for two reasons, a framework describing the range of affective experience you wish to capture must be well defined and there must be a reliable way to measure the subject's affective experience with respect to this framework. Emotion theorists have proposed several sets of basic emotions (Ortony et al., 1988) many of which are tailored to the particular forms of expression that they wish to study. For example, the basic emotion set proposed by Paul Ekman (1993), who studies universal facial expressions includes anger, fear, disgust, sadness, enjoyment and surprise all of which are expressed in the face. In contrast, pianist Manfred Clynes (1978) proposed a basic set of emotions that includes: no emotion, anger, hate, joy, sex, love, and reverence, emotions that he found to have unique finger pressure expressions that could be expressed through piano music. An alternative to labeling emotion according to a basic named set is to quantify affective experience along continuous axes of affective qualities. Examples of affective frameworks include two-dimensional arousal-valence space used by Lang (1993), where affective experience is rated according to the level of arousal (high to low excitement) and valence (the positive or negative aspect of the emotion). Another model is the Russell's (1964) circumplex model of emotion that labels affect in a radial space with opposing affect pairs: arousal and sleepiness, excitement and depression, pleasure and misery and contentment and distress.

Once a model is created or chosen to define the experience, a reliable method of recording the experience must be established. The assumed gold standard for reporting is subject self report, although this has been found to be unreliable because either the subject must be interrupted during the experience to record it or must remember a past experience. Alternatively, subject's reactions can be assumed from experimental conditions or judged from third party observers.

3   Physiological affect metrics

Several physiological metrics have been known to reflect affective response. These include heart rate and heart rate variability, blood volume pressure, skin conductance or galvanic skin response (SCR/GSR), and electromyogram (EMG). High arousal emotions will cause increases in heart rate, increases in sympathetic tone that can be detected through heart rate variability (McCraty et al., 1995), higher levels of skin conductivity and more orienting response activity. Heart rate can be sensed either through an electrocardiogram signal (ECG) or through a blood volume pulse monitor (BVP, photoplethysmograph). Heart rate variability is generally only calculated using the more precise ECG reading, however BVP also contains information regarding vasoconstriction which has been used to differentiate defensive reactions such as fear from offensive reactions such as anger (Ekman et al., 1983; Kahneman, 1973; Levenson, 1992). The positive and negative aspects of emotion are less reflected in physiological variables and are more easily distinguished in facial expression and voice analysis.

4 Sensing affect in the laboratory

The laboratory setting provides the ideal situation for observing subject behavior. In the laboratory, the experimenter has control of the environment of the experiment, including scripting how people interact with the subject, using a room without external distractions, and limiting the stimuli to those wishing to be studied. The subject can be asked to sit still in a chair and be asked to engage in tasks that do not involve physical activity. If the subject is stationary and not moving his or her arms, it is possible to use sensors that are normally disturbed by motion artifacts such as a pulse oximeter or photoplethysmograph to measure heart rate. It is also possible to measure facial expression through EMG if the subject is reacting primarily to the planned stimuli and not changes in lighting or conversational interaction with other people.

The main challenge with sensing affect in the laboratory is stimulating authentic affective response. Common methods of inducing responses include: looking at pictures and video, listening to music, performing mental math problems, listening to stories and interacting with computer games. An alternative approach, frequently used in voice and facial expression analysis is using acting-out emotions. We tested two approaches. In the first experiment, a motivated person authentically tried to feel and express emotion using a visualization-driven acting method and in the second experiment physiological reactions to music were used to drive music selection.

4.1 Eight emotion experiment

The first experiment was based on the Sentic Cycle experiment proposed by Manfred Clyne (1978). In this experiment, the subject is asked to feel each of the eight basic emotions that Clynes proposed: No Emotion, Anger, Hate, Grief, Platonic Love, Romantic/Sexual Love, Joy, Reverence, while pressing a button that measured horizontal and vertical finger pressure. In addition the subject wore a BVP and GSR sensor on the opposite hand as well as a respiration sensor that measured chest cavity expansion and an EMG that measured jaw clenching. The same subject repeated experiment for 30 days, generating 20 complete data sets. The preliminary results of this experiment showed (Healey and Picard, 1998a) anger could be differentiated from other states with 100% sensitivity and 98% specificity and that high arousal emotions (anger, grief, sex, joy) could be differentiated form low arousal emotions with 86% sensitivity and 88% specificity, while positive states (love, sex, joy) could be distinguished form negative states (anger, hate, grief) with 82% sensitivity and 50% specificity. Improved results were also found using more sophisticated statistical procedures in further publications (Picard et al., 2001), however both sets of analyses take advantage of the particular structure of the data (in the Sentic cycle experiment emotion states occur in sequence, in typical psychological experiments the order would be randomized) and the fact that the single subject used the same visualization sequence for each emotion and the same affectations for emotion expression, perhaps generating only a narrow range of feeling and expression within the possible range of interpretation for each emotion. Figure 1 shows an example of data collected during the experiment.

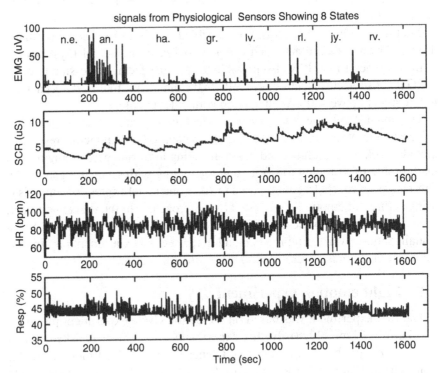

Figure 1. Raw signals from the eight emotion experiment showing readings from EMG, skin conductance, heart rate from BVP and the respiration sensor throughout the Sentic cycle of no emotion (ne), anger (an), hate (ha), grief(gr), platonic love (lv), romantic love/sex (rl), joy (jy) and reverence (rv). In this typical example, anger (200–400 seconds) shows the most EMG activity and the slope of the skin conductance increases during high arousal states and decreases during low arousal states.

4.2 Personalized music selection

An application for personalized music selections was based on the findings that the slope of the skin conductance increased during high arousal states and decreased during low arousal states (Healey et al., 1998). In this application, the goal was to play music to keep the listener at a constant overall arousal level. Songs were pre-classified into different arousal level categories and stored on a computer. A beginning song was selected at random. If the users' average skin conductance increased during the song, a song was selected at random from the next lower arousal level category. Similarly, if the user's skin conductance decreased a song from the next higher arousal level category was chosen.

5 Sensing affect in the field

Ideally authentic emotional experience could be captured in the uncontrolled ambulatory environment by continuous physiological monitoring. If an unobtrusive system could be worn constantly, all physiological reflections of authentic affective state could be captured, recorded and studied.

5.1 Wearable monitoring

A wearable system designed to capture affect was designed using a wearable computer with EMG, BVP, respiration, and skin conductance sensor (Healey and Picard, 1997). This system was worn by several different subjects who were familiar with using wearable computers and by one user for several hours a day. From these experiments, only anecdotal results could be extracted. The reasons for this were twofold: physical activity and the movement effects of daily activities on the sensors in general overwhelmed affective readings, secondly, subjects were allowed to freely report their affective state and rarely did any subject use emotion words proposed by any of the emotion theorists. Instead of reporting "anger," "fear," "joy" or "sadness" subjects often reported feeling "fine," "tired," "hungry," "overwhelmed" or "bored." This may have been a result of social masking or that the subjects were not "in touch" with their emotional state or it may be that the basic emotions that theorists propose do not happen frequently and that physical (tired/hungry) and mental (overwhelmed/bored) states dominate people's perception of "feelings."

5.2 StartleCam

One of the interesting anecdotal results that did arise from the wearable monitoring experiments was that when a wearer was suddenly surprised by an unexpected event, a very large orienting response occurred in the skin conductance reading. This is not an unexpected finding as these responses have been reported to occur with surprise, "orienting," and attention

(Boucsein, 1992). The idea behind StartleCam was to create a system to capture events that caused the startle reaction through a series of images and then send those images back to a central server and perhaps alert one of the friends or family of the wearer if they could not be contacted after such an event (Healey and Picard, 1998b). The StartleCam system consisted of a wearable computer with a skin conductance sensor, a digital webcam and a wireless internet connection. The webcam continuously recorded images and saves them in memory. After a few minutes the oldest images would be discarded to make room for new images. Simultaneously, skin conductance was constantly monitored. If a significant orienting response was detected, the series of images from several seconds preceding the detection were sent back to the server. The reason for this is that the skin conductance startle response is sometimes delayed by 1–5 seconds after the stimulating

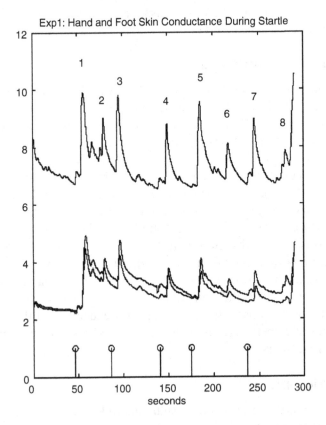

Figure 2. Examples of the skin conductance orienting response. A white noise stimulus was used at each of the times marked by the lollipop markers along the bottom. The orienting response is often delayed by several seconds.

event as shown in Figure 2. In the original startle detection algorithm (Healey and Picard 1998b), the signal convolved with startle template, a derivative of the convolved signal was taken and a threshold was applied that found areas of high slope. This method was effective even though it did not detect the onset of the startle because the camera data for several preceding seconds was saved and transmitted. This algorithm had the drawback of triggering on startle responses that had the greatest slope, but not necessarily the greatest magnitude. Later this algorithm was improved. A much shorter low-pass filter was used on the signal, and after the difference threshold was triggered, a search was performed on the original signal to find the minimum preceding and the maximum following the point of highest slope (which was always on the rising edge of the response; Healey, 2002). With these additional points the size of the response could be calculated. The magnitude of the response could then be used as to make the decision on whether or not to send the images back to the server, where only images associated with very large responses would be sent. This allowed for greater robustness in the system and less dependency on the derivative threshold. Previously the derivative threshold had to be carefully set for each individual and would often send too few or too many images.

6   Affect in an automobile

The automotive environment offers a compromise between the overly constrained laboratory and the unconstrained ambulatory environment. The automobile driver is constrained to be seated, the only movement that occurs is arm motion turning the wheel, head and neck motion to navigate and leg and foot motion to control the acceleration and braking. These motions are far less disruptive to overall physiological response than walking, talking or stair climbing. The car environment also allowed several cameras to be installed to record the road conditions, the driver's facial expression and a series of note card annotations made by the observer. A video stream showing the data from the driver's physiological signals was synchronized with the camera video streams using a quad-splitter. An example of the composite video captured during the drive is shown in Figure 3. The goal of this experiment was to capture the affective state of stress. Stress was induced by the driving task, and a drive was designed to take the subject through city roads that were likely to cause high levels of stress and highway segments that were assumed to cause low levels of stress.

Both questionnaire analysis and an analysis of the video by third party observers were performed to judge the occurrence of stress (Healey, 2002; Healey and Picard, 2005). An example of a typical drive is shown in Figure 4. The figure is divided up into six major segments, an initial rest period, a city driving, then a highway driving period followed by the reverse trip on the highway, the city

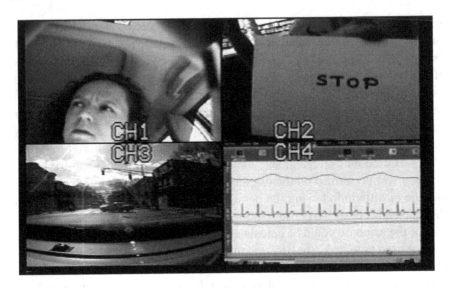

Figure 3. An example of video captured during the drive. Clockwise from the upper left: the driver's facial expression, annotations made by the observer, the driver's physiological signals and the road conditions.

and a final rest period. The diagram shows the first rest period in white, the first city period in gray, a thin area of darker gray representing the toll booth onto the highway, then the first highway period in white, an exit, roundabout and re-entry period in grey, followed by the return highway trip in white, a dark gray toll period, a gray city driving period and a white final rest period. During both rest periods it can be seen that the skin conductance (GSR) is virtually flat and that the GSR during both highway driving periods is far lower and has far fewer orienting responses than the city driving periods. Heart rate can be seen to increase at each of the tolls. The autonomic balance measure (the ratio of the low frequency to high frequency energy in the heart rate power spectrum; Healey, 2002; McCraty et al., 1995) is slightly delayed with respect to the timeline because it uses a window of heart beats that occurred one to three minutes previously. The results of the experiments showed that the skin conductance, heart rate and heart rate variability were the variables most correlated with moment to moment driver stress. This inspired a demonstration where the driving video was played alongside two "tachometers" one showing skin conductance and one showing the autonomic balance variable. If implemented in the vehicle in real-time the tachometers would allow a driver to monitor the status of their personal stress in the same way that the cars tachometer allows the car's engine to be monitored.

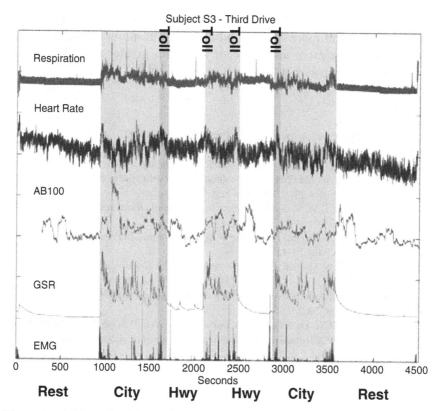

Figure 4. An example of data collected during one of the drives is shown. The top signal shows the respiration sensor, next is the heart rate signal, the autonomic balance signal, the skin conductance signal (GSR) and along the bottom is the EMG signal.

7 Conclusions

Measuring affect through physiological signals is a challenging process. First physical variables must be controlled or accounted for since physical responses almost always overwhelm affective responses in physiology. Second, the space of emotions is sufficiently vast and ill defined so that it is difficult to study all possible emotions, and the amount of data necessary to fill such a complex model is difficult to obtain and annotate. A smaller study focused on a particular subset of emotions will allow a more focused set of sensors to be used and make the challenge of annotating data less complex. Finally, an automatic documentation method such as image or video recording can provide vital ground truth for annotating physiological signals. As the sensors and computers used for monitoring become smaller and more mobile and the software tools for analysis and annotation become more automatic, it opens up greater possibilities for sensing affective experience.

References

Boucsein, W. *Electrodermal Activity.* Plenum Press, New York, 1992.

Clynes, M. *Sentics: The Touch of Emotions.* Doubleday, New York, 1978.

Ekman, P. Facial Expressions and Emotion. *American Psychologist* 48(4):384–392, 1993.

Ekman, P., Levenson, R.W. and Friesen, W.V. Autonomic nervous system activity distinguishes among emotions. *Science* 221:1208–1210, Sep. 1983.

Healey, J and Picard, R.W. Affective Wearables, *Personal Technologies* Vol 1, No. 4, pp. 231–240, 1997.

Healey, J and Picard, R.W. *Digital Processing of Affective Signals*, in Proceedings of ICASSP, Seattle, Washington, May 12–15, 1998a.

Healey, J and Picard, R.W. StartleCam: *A Cybernetic Wearable Camera*, in Proceedings ISWC, Pittsburgh, PA, 1998b.

Healey, J. Wearable and Automotive Systems for the Recognition of Affect from Physiology, MIT PhD Thesis May 2002.

Healey, J. and Picard, R.W. Detecting Stress During Real-World Driving Tasks Using Physiological Sensors. *IEEE Transactions on Intelligent Transportation Systems* 6(2): 156–166, 2005.

Healey, J., Picard, R.W. and Dabek, F. A New Affect-Perceiving Interface and Its Application to Personalized Music Selection, in Proceedings of the 1998 Workshop on Perceptual User Interfaces, San Fransisco, CA, November 4–6, 1998.

Kahneman, D. Arousal and Attention, *Attention and Effort.* Prentice-Hall, Englewood Cliffs, N.J. pp. 28–49, 1973.

Lang, P.J., Greenwald, M.K., Bradley, M.M. and Hamm, A.O. Looking at pictures: Affective, facial, viseral and behavioral reactions. *Psychophysiology* 30:261–273, 1993.

Levenson, R.W. Autonomic nervous system differences among emotions, *American Psychological Society* 3(1):23–27, Jan. 1992.

McCraty, R., Atkinson, M., Tiller, W.A. and Rein, G. The effects of emotions on short-term power spectrum analysis of heart rate variability, *American Journal of Cardiology* 76:1089–1093, 1995.

Ortony, A., Clore, G. and Collins, A. The *Cognitive Structure of Emotions.* University Press, Cambridge, 1988.

Picard, R.W., Vyzas, E. and Healey, J. Toward Machine Emotional Intelligence: Analysis of Affective Physiological State. *IEEE Transactions Pattern Analysis and Machine Intelligence* 23(10), October 2001.

Russell, J.A. A circumplex model of affect. *Journal of Personality and Social Psychology*, volume 1, pages 49–80. Academic Press, New York, 1964.

9

BRAIN, SKIN AND COSMETICS: SENSORY ASPECTS OBJECTIVATED BY FUNCTIONAL MAGNETIC RESONANCE IMAGING

Bernard Querleux

Abstract   Cosmetic science is focused on the study of the hair and the healthy skin and the methods that can be used to preserve or modify their properties or appearance. However, we are also aware of the psychological and social benefits that enhanced attractiveness can provide for oneself and others.

For this reason it is important to find instrument-based procedures capable of characterizing objectively the reality of the sensorial criteria often used in relation to cosmetics: pleasure/displeasure, wellbeing, comfort/discomfort, pleasant/unpleasant, and so on.

We shall begin by presenting an investigation into the **comprehension of the sense of touch**, touching being a fundamental gesture in the cosmetics domain. We have analysed by fMRI the changes in brain activity maps observed when an individual touches artificial materials (smooth or rough) compared with touching the skin alone or the skin to which a cosmetic has been applied.

The second study relates to **sensitive skin**. We know through numerous epidemiological studies that approximately 50% of women say that they have sensitive skin and also that this percentage is found in many areas of the world. However, given the absence of any clinical signs under examination by a dermatologist or any clear discrimination based on local biophysical measurements, this skin type still suffers to some extent from a lack of recognition. This study enabled us to demonstrate a neural basis for sensitive skin for the first time *in vivo*.

1 Introduction

Humans possess various sensory organs making them responsive to stimulatory phenomena. These responses can be physiological, mental, behavioral or verbal. Today's cosmetic products are still designed with the same aims, i.e. to protect, to treat, or to prevent the effects of aging. The psychosocial benefits of preening, both for oneself and others, are generally recognized (Graham and Kligman, 1985; Moskowitz 1984). It remains necessary to elucidate the mechanisms by which stimuli are perceived, and this can be achieved by means of many objective methods.

101

J.H.D.M. Westerink et al. (eds.), Probing Experience, 101–108.
© 2008 *Springer*.

Most of the latter are based on psycho-sensory analysis of volunteers (Strigler, 1990). Such analyses can study both components of perception: the real component and the subjective component induced by the stimulus. Other methods are based on physiological and biological analyses that can be performed at the site of the stimulation to measure its direct effect. They may also take into account effects of the central nervous system, such as changes in the composition of body fluids (saliva or urine for instance; Kan and Kimura, 1994). The third approach consists of assessing stimuli with non invasive physical methods. Classical biophysical methods tend to measure the direct effect of the stimulus (Serup and Jemec, 1995). Emerging methods based on electrodermal and electrothermal techniques can be used to measure responses of the autonomic nervous system to a stimulus and aim to relate measurements to the subjective perception of the stimulus as assessed by psycho-sensory analysis (Collet et al., 1997). Finally, other biophysical methods are capable of mapping neuronal activity in the central nervous system in response to a stimulus. Functional magnetic resonance imaging (fMRI) is one of these functional brain imaging methods (Orrison et al., 1995), which are capable of showing the distribution of neuronal activity in different areas of the cortex induced by both components of a perception.

In a first study, we investigated the comprehension of the sense of touch, touching being a fundamental gesture in the cosmetics domain, by analysing with fMRI distributions of neuronal activity in response to passive tactile stimulation induced by artificial and natural textures.

The second study related to sensitive skin. We know through numerous epidemiological studies that approximately 50% of women say that they have sensitive skin and also that this percentage is found in many areas of the world (de Lacharrière et al., 1997; Distante et al., 2002; Jourdain et al., 2002; Willis et al., 2001). However, given the absence of any clinical signs under examination by a dermatologist or any clear discrimination based on local biophysical measurements, this skin type still suffers to some extent from a lack of recognition. We thus assessed brain activation in two groups of subjects classified as sensitive skin or non-sensitive skin during the standard lactic acid test (Frosch and Kligman, 1977), which could differentiate skin reactivity through the quotation of a global discomfort combining the sensations of stinging, burning and itching.

2   First study: Brain activation in response to a tactile stimulation (Querleux et al., 1999)

fMRI Protocol Magnetic resonance images were acquired on 21 females, after informed consent. A first paradigm consisted of passive tactile stimulation of the fingers of the dominant hand by 2 artificial textures, referred to by all subjects as rough or smooth, and one natural texture (the skin of an operator's fingers). The subjects were instructed not to move their hand while the operator was gently touching their fingers at a rate of about 1 Hz. The direction of the stimulation was frequently changed to avoid adaptation during the time allocated for each textured surface (1 min 45 sec). A second paradigm consisted of passive tactile stimulation of the fingers of the dominant hand with the skin of an operator's fingers, before and after the application of a cosmetic product. During the same examination the subjects were asked to imagine passive tactile stimulation of the fingers of their dominant hand by the skin of the operator's fingers. As usual in a brain functional imaging method, a period of rest was added to each paradigm to serve as a reference for non specific brain activation.

Cognitive analysis After each fMRI session the subjects underwent a semi-directive interview with a psychologist. The interview focused on the subjects' general state during the experiment, i.e. their perception of the difficulty of the task, their degree of emotion and boredom, the sensory and tactile images experienced, and the mental associations evoked. On the basis of the results we constructed an observations chart composed of 8 exhaustive and discriminatory descriptors of the subjects' state during the task (warm, pleasant, sensitive, concentrated, cool, imaginative, rational, and reactive). Each subject's general state was then described using the 8 descriptors, which were scored from 0 to 3 according to their intensity. This was used to define the subject's "mental profile".

Results and discussion Functional activity induced by each task was clearly recorded in the somatosensory cortex of all the subjects by means of fMRI (Figure 1). The extent and distribution of neuronal activity within 4 regions (the primary contralateral (PC), secondary contralateral (SC), primary ipsilateral (PI), and secondary ipsilateral (SI) regions) were modified differently by the various stimuli.

Activation was strong and correlated well in the PC with the different surfaces (rough, smooth and skin). Activation was less marked in the PI, but the correlation was still strong except for the "skin" versus "smooth" comparison. Interestingly, in most subjects, the skin stimulation caused more activation in PI than the artificial textures.

Figure 1.   Activation maps superimposed on coronal anatomical MR images in a right-handed volunteer in response to passive tactile stimulation. I: Ipsilateral, C: Contralateral.

As regards the skin versus skin + cream comparison, activation was marked and correlated well in PI, PC, and SC. We also noted a clear increase in PI during the skin + cream test. During the imagination test, activation was very weak and involved a restricted pixel range in both PC and SC in most subjects. Results in the ipsilateral areas were more subject-dependent. Nevertheless, there was a greater extension in PI and SI during the imagination task, than during the real stimulations.

A Partial Least Square analysis identified 3 significant axes that explained 71% of the variability in the fMRI data. The four cognitive variables with the highest values (rational, reactive, sensitive and imaginative) were those that mainly structured this information. The first axis (Figure 2) opposes the contralateral cortical regions, whatever the applied stimulus, to the ipsilateral cortical regions of the same stimulations. The primary and secondary contralateral regions therefore mainly correlate with high sensory reactivity and rationality. As regards the fMRI results, the second factorial axis opposes the secondary and primary areas (mainly ipsilateral). The primary ipsilateral cortical areas refer to a well-developed imagination and tactile sensations whereas the secondary ipsilateral cortical areas are less specific.

Conclusion fMRI and cognitive analysis allowed us to map the physical component of the tactile perception in the contralateral cortex. This study

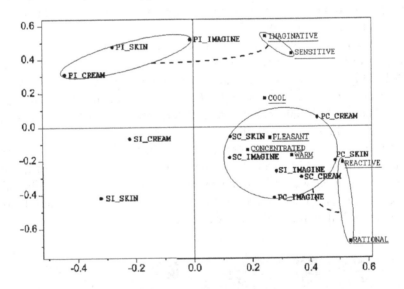

Figure 2. Simultaneous projection of the somatosensory cortical areas activated in response to different kinds of tactile stimulation, measured by fMRI, versus 4 principal psychological descriptors extracted from the cognitive analysis. Note the more extended activation in both contralateral areas for the most rational subjects, whereas the most imaginative subjects had stronger activation in the primary ipsilateral area.

also gave rise to a better understanding of the activation in ipsilateral areas, which was found to be mainly related to the subjective component of the stimulation.

3   Second study: Neural basis of sensitive skin

fMRI protocol Nine healthy young women classified as having sensitive skin and nine as having non-sensitive skin, based on their responses to a questionnaire, participated in this study after giving an informed consent. fMRI scans were acquired on a 1.5T MR scanner using an echo planar imaging sequence. Prior to the beginning of functional scans, test products, described as:"likely to induce discomfort", were applied on subjects' nasolabial folds in a single-blind manner: the provocative product (lactic acid) on the right side, and the vehicle (control neutral product, saline solution) on the left (Figure 3). Functional acquisitions consisted of a single run of 40 consecutive trials. At the beginning of each trial, an arrow pointing to the left or to the right was presented for 1.5 seconds (jittered) in the center of the visual screen, replacing the fixation cross. Subjects had to evaluate the degree of discomfort corresponding to the cumulative effect of stinging, burning and itching in their face side indicated by the arrow (i.e. in the right or left cheek), on a four-level scale: – 0: no or doubtful discomfort; – 1: slight discomfort; – 2: moderate discomfort; – 3: severe discomfort; and press the corresponding key with their right hand, using a four-key board placed on their abdomen. Presentation of left- and right-pointing arrows was counterbalanced (50% of each) and randomized over the run. Inter-stimuli interval was 16 seconds jittered.

The temporal dynamics of discomfort induced by lactic acid through the experiment was calculated for the two groups (Figure 4), in order to discriminate between periods of time when the degree of discomfort was low compared to periods of time when the degree of discomfort was high. These data were then used to analyze cerebral activity.

Results and discussion 3 of 18 involved subjects showed an important head motion during the functional scans and were excluded from the analysis. For the remaining 15 subjects (8 in the non-sensitive group and 7 in the sensitive group) the results of fixed-effect group analysis are reported. Statistical parametric maps obtained in either group for the specific activity associated with high discomfort induced by lactic acid are shown on Figure 5.

Brain activity was strikingly different between the two groups. In the non-sensitive skin group activity was mostly confined to the left primary sensorimotor area, contralateral to the discomfort site. This is in accordance with the classical role of the primary sensorimotor area, in each cerebral hemisphere, as the initial site for cortical processing of peripheral somatosensory information on the contralateral body parts. Some increase was also observed in

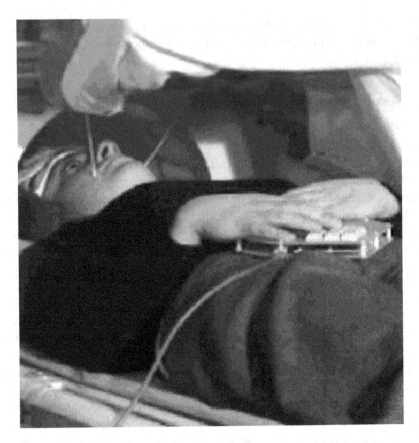

Figure 3. Installation and product application procedure. The subject is installed in the MR scanner, with his right hand placed on a response keyboard. The provocative product (lactic acid) and the vehicle (saline solution) are simultaneously applied to the nasolabial areas using a single-use cotton-wool bud. The keyboard is connected to a computer outside the MR imaging room so that during scanning, subjects' responses reflecting the perceived degree of discomfort will be registered simultaneously with the underlying cerebral activity.

the bilateral dorsal fronto-parietal network including the parietal cortex, prefrontal areas adjacent to the superior frontal sulcus, and the supplementary motor area. By contrast, in the sensitive skin group, the discomfort-related activity was found in the sensorimotor cortex in both hemispheres. Activity in the bilateral dorsal fronto-parietal regions was also much larger in the sensitive group than in the non-sensitive group. In addition, in the sensitive group only, specific discomfort-related activity was observed in the bilateral peri-insular regions classically considered as secondary somatosensory area. These results corroborate numerous imaging studies in which secondary somatosensory area was systematically activated in response to different

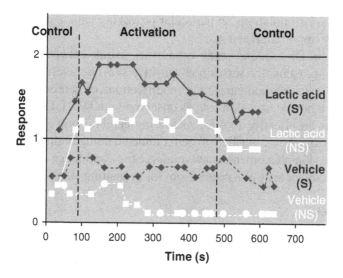

Figure 4. Temporal dynamics of discomfort reported by either group. Average responses, in group, to lactic acid and to the vehicle are plotted against time. Both groups steadily reported low discomfort on the left face side (vehicle), throughout the experiment. On the right side (lactic acid), both groups reported low discomfort during the initial period (0 to 96 seconds), increased discomfort during the medial period (between 112 and 496 seconds) and low discomfort again in the final period (512 to 640 seconds). This dynamics was used to build the fMRI contrasts: a neutral phase as the control phase, and a discomfort phase as the activation phase.

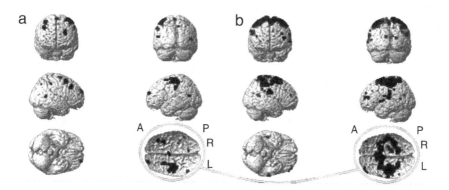

Figure 5. Brain activation maps obtained by fMRI, in response to the lactic acid stimulation as a provocative test. a: subjects with non-sensitive skin; b: subjects with sensitive skin. Non-specific activation was recorded in both groups in the primary contralateral sensory cortex, which can be considered as the first cortical pathway of this type of sensory perception. Bilateral extensions in the sensory cortex and the prefrontal cortex as well as in the cingulate cortex were specific to the sensitive skin group.

somatosensory stimulations, in particular provoking pain, emotion and other behaviorally important reactions.

Conclusion This second study establishes a link between the levels of skin sensitivity (sensitive versus non-sensitive skin) as determined by a self-assessment test (questionnaire), and modifications of cerebral activation in response to a provocative skin test, as observed with fMRI. Our results show that fMRI is an effective tool for measuring cerebral processes underlying skin sensitivity. They contribute to better understanding of the neural basis of the sensitive skin phenomenon, and reinforce the confidence in the reliability of self-assessment tests as a routine tool for evaluating skin sensitivity.

References

Collet, C., Vernet-Maury, E., Delhomme, G., Dittmar, A. Autonomic nervous system response patterns specificity to basic emotions. *J Autonom Nerv Syst* 62:45–57, 1997.

de Lacharrière O., Reiche L., Montastier C., Nicholson M., Courbière C., Willis C.M., Wilkinson J.D., Leclaire J. Skin reaction to capsaicin: a new way for the understanding of sensitive skin. *Australas J Dermatol* 38:3–313 (1997).

Distante F., Rigano L., D'Agostino R., Bonfigli A., Berardesca E. Intra- and inter-individual differences in sensitive skin. *Cosmet Toiletries* 117:39–46, 2002.

Frosch P.J., Kligman A.M. A method for appraising the stinging capacity of topically applied substances. *J Soc Cosmet Chem* 28:197–209, 1977.

Graham, J.A., Kligman, A.M., eds. *The Psychology of Cosmetics Treatments*, Praeger Publishers, 1985.

Jourdain R., de Lacharrière O., Bastien P., Maibach H.I. Ethnic variations in self-perceived sensitive skin: epidemiological survey. *Contact Dermatitis* 46:162–169, 2002.

Kan, C., Kimura, S. *Psychoimmunological Benefits of Cosmetics*. Proceeding of the IFSCC Meeting, Venise, 769–784, 1994.

Moskowitz, H.R., ed. *Cosmetic Product Testing: A Modern Psychophysical Approach*, Marcel Dekker, New York, 1984.

Orrison, W.W., Lewine, J.D., Sanders, J.A., Hartshorne, M.F., eds. *Functional Brain Imaging*, Mosby Press, 1995.

Querleux B., Gazano G., Mohen-Domenech O., Jacquin J., Burnod Y., Gaudion P., Jolivet O., Bittoun J., Benali H. Brain Activation in Response to a Tactile Stimulation: Functional Magnetic Resonance Imaging (fMRI) versus Cognitive Analysis. *Int J Cosmet Sci* 21:107–118, 1999.

Serup, J., Jemec, G.M.E., eds. *Handbook of non-invasive methods and the skin*, CRC Press, 1995.

Strigler, F., ed. *Evaluation Sensorielle: Manuel Méthodologique*, technique et documentation, Lavoisier, 1990.

Willis C.M., Shaw S., de Lacharriere O., Baverel M., Reiche L., Jourdain R., Bastien P., Wilkinson J.D. Sensitive skin: an epidemiological study. *Br J Dermatol* 145:258–263, 2001.

10

THE ASSESSMENT OF STRESS

Ad Vingerhoets

Abstract   In psychology, stress is defined as the state that ensues when there is a perceived imbalance between the demands of the environment and one's estimated capacity to deal adequately with these demands. This state may manifest itself at four levels: (1) at the subjective, emotional level; (2) at the cognitive level; (3) at the behavioural level; and (4) at the biological or somatic level. At the biological level, the focus can be on (electro-) physiological variables (cardiovascular, dermal), on endocrine measures, or on immune parameters. In this contribution, it will be demonstrated that measuring "stress" at the biological level is complex because the biological stress response may vary dramatically depending on (1) the nature of the psychological, emotional stress response; (2) the duration of the stressor; and (3) the sex of the respondent.

1   On defining stress

The term stress is currently so widely used by both lay people and professionals that one seldom wonders about the specific meaning of it. However, a critical evaluation of the use of this term both in the lay and the professional literature reveals that there is a serious lack of agreement with respect to the terminology. Two journalists once pithily summarized this disagreement and confusion by stating that stress "in addition to being itself, and the result of itself, is also the cause of itself" (Vingerhoets, 2004a).

Indeed, sometimes the term stress is used to refer to situations, stimuli, and conditions that may trigger emotional reactions and distress. For example, an exam, the loss of a close friend, marital problems, or a severe illness may all be considered examples of stress. However, in other texts, the term stress may be used to indicate the psychological and physiological reactions of a person to such stimuli or situations. Historically, this is the oldest meaning of the term stress, which was introduced by the endocrinologist Hans Selye (1956/ 1976). This author defined stress as "the non-specific (biologic) reaction of the body to any demand made upon it." Finally, there is a third type of definition which emphasizes that stress is a process, in which different components should be distinguished, including the antecedents and the consequences of stress.

J.H.D.M. Westerink et al. (eds.), Probing Experience, 109–117.

In this view stress refers to a state of an individual that occurs when an individual perceives the environmental demands as exceeding her/his appraised capabilities. In other words, stress is a condition that ensues when a person is aware that (s)he cannot deal adequately with the situation in which (s)he is involved. This state typically occurs when the person is exposed to taxing situations and it manifests itself in stress reactions.

In this contribution, the focus will be on this psychological stress model. First, each of the components of the model will be discussed briefly. These include the following concepts: stressors, appraisal, (short-term) stress reactions or strains, and long-term health outcomes. We conclude with a discussion of the measurement of "stress", in particular stress reactions (see also Vingerhoets, 2004a,b).

2   The psychological stress model

For the stress model presented in this contribution, the following three aspects can be discerned: (1) antecedents, (2) moderators, and (3) consequences (see Figure 1).

Antecedents of stress are indicated as stressors. A stressor can best be defined as any stimulus, situation, or circumstance with the potential to induce stress reactions. Whether such a situation indeed evokes a stress response, however, not only depends on the characteristics of the stressor, but in particular on the individual's appraisal of the situation and on several moderators including

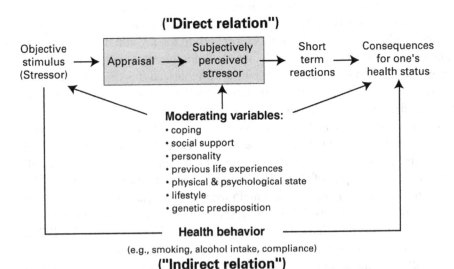

Figure 1.   Schematic representation of the psychological stress model described in this chapter.

the person's coping capabilities and social support. Appraisal, coping and social support are assumed to be determined by personality, psychological and physical state and previous life experiences. Stress reactions may occur at four levels: (1) the physiological level, (2) the subjective, emotional level, (3) the cognitive level, and (4) the behavioural level. In case of chronic exposure to stressful conditions, the enduring physiological stress responses may exhaust the body, decrease its resistance, and make it more vulnerable to all kinds of disease. These effects are also dependent on lifestyle (e.g., smoking, diet, exercising, etc.), physical shape, and genetic predispositions.

Each of these stress components will be discussed briefly in more detail below.

2.1 Stressors and appraisal

Stressors are situations or stimuli that have the potential to evoke stress reactions. Most important, however, is how the stressor is appraised. *Appraisal* is the core concept in psychological stress theory. Lazarus and Folkman (1984) distinguish primary and secondary appraisal, which refer to the questions "What is at stake?" and "What can I do about it?", respectively.

The former question may lead to the conclusion that the situation is not relevant for the individual or that it is relevant, but positive. Only if the situation is appraised as negative and harmful or a potential threat, rather than a challenge, a state of stress may be induced. However, also the secondary appraisal is relevant, because this process yields an answer to the question whether or not the individual expects that (s)he can cope with the stressor. For example, previous experience with a similar situation, reliance on a good social network that will provide support, or a high self esteem may contribute to the conviction that one is capable to deal adequately with that kind of challenging situation.

In this way, any objective situation is converted into a "subjective" situation, which may or may not have a special (negative or positive) meaning for the individual.

There are several ways to categorize stressors. Some investigators emphasize the importance of the duration or time dimension of the stressor and make a distinction between *acute* and *chronic* and, sometimes, *chronic intermittent* stressors (e.g., Burchfield, 1979; O'Keefe and Baum, 1990). This distinction is important because the biological stress responses show a development over time, implying that responses to acute and to chronic stressful conditions may vary considerably and in important ways.

Examples of acute stressors are exams, arguments, job loss (but not unemployment), painful medical procedures, or being involved in an accident. Marital problems, having a handicap or suffering from a chronic disease, and having a demanding job may be considered chronic stressors. Finally, situations and challenges that return with a certain regularity, e.g., demanding or emotional events in the work of service men, police officers, nurses, etc., are referred to as chronic intermittent stressors.

Other authors classify stressors according to life areas and make a distinction between family stressors, job stressors, disease-related stressors, natural disasters, etc. (e.g., Noshpitz and Coddington, 1990). In addition, there is a categorization which has its roots mainly in the history of stress measurement, where a distinction has been made between life changes or life events, daily hassles, chronic stressors, and role stressors (e.g., Hahn and Smith, 1999; Wethington, Almeida, Brown, Frank, and Kessler, 2001). There are many questionnaires available designed to inventory all these different kinds of stressors (see for an overview Wethington et al., 2001).

2.2 Moderators

The nature and intensity of the stress reactions is not only determined by the type and intensity of the stressor; other psychosocial factors including characteristics of the individual and his/her social environment play a role as well. Very important and best known are coping and social support, but certain personality factors, one's physical and psychological state, and previous life experiences are also relevant. In addition, genetic predispositions and lifestyle may interact with the short-term physiological stress responses and co-determine the long-term health effects of stressor exposure (see Vingerhoets, 2004a, and Rice, 1999, for a detailed discussion).

Coping has been defined as "the constantly changing cognitive and behavioural efforts to manage specific external and/or internal demands that are appraised as taxing or exceeding the resources of the person" (Lazarus and Folkman, 1984, p.141). There is a general consensus that at least two broad classes of coping behaviours can be distinguished: problem-focused coping and emotion-focused coping (Endler and Johnson, 2001; Myers, Newman, and Enomoto, 2004). Problem-focused coping refers to mental and behavioural efforts to neutralize or reduce the (intensity of) stressors whereas emotion-focused coping is aimed to reduce the emotional impact of the stressor exposure. Examples of the latter are seeking distraction, relaxation, engaging in sports, or taking drugs or alcohol. Occasionally, the focus is on additional coping dimensions such as avoidance, monitoring and blunting (Endler and Johnson, 2001) or repressive coping (Myers et al., 2004).

Social support is another important moderator of stress reactions (see Schwarzer et al., 2004; Van Sonderen and Sanderman, 2001). The availability of an adequate social network that offers adequate informational, instrumental, and emotional support is considered an important buffer against the possible negative health consequences of stressor exposure. However, it is clear that the effects of social support are not always positive, which may be related to the kind of support, who provides it and in what conditions.

Finally, certain *personality characteristics* have been proposed as making people more or less stress-resistant (Rice, 1999; Vingerhoets, 2004a). The best known of these are hardiness, sense of coherence, optimism, internal locus of control, and self-esteem. In addition, there is increasing evidence that, when confronted with stressful situations, people should not keep it secret, but should share it with others or write about it. There are strong indications that concealment and emotional inhibition may increase health risks (Nyklicek, Vingerhoets, and Denollet, 2002).

2.3 Stress reactions

If an individual appraises a situation as a potential threat, stress reactions may occur. These can occur at each of four different levels, which is why we speak of a multidimensional stress response. The following levels can be distinguished:

- *The physiological level.* Exposure to a threatening situation may induce the so-called fight-or-flight reaction, which is characterized by increased activation of the sympathetic system which results in increased heart rate, elevated blood pressure, redistribution of the blood from internal organs to muscles, and release of catecholamines (adrenaline and noradrenaline), which prepare the body for action. Less known is the so-called conservation-withdrawal reaction, although it may include Selye's GAS (General Adaptation Syndrome), which in many respects is a counterpart of the fight-or-flight reaction. In a conservation-withdrawal reaction, the individual feels helpless and hopeless and there is no tendency to act, but rather passivity and giving-up prevail. The heart rate slows down and there is no increased activation of the sympathetic nervous system but rather of the parasympathetic system and the pituitary-adrenal system (cf. Vingerhoets and Perski, 2000). The immune system also displays differential responses in these two reactions, activation versus depression (Bosch, De Geus, Kelderman, Veerman, Hoogstraten and Van Nieuw Amerongen, 2001). In addition recently, Taylor, Klein, Lewis, Gruenewald, Gurung, and Updegraff (2000) described what they consider to be specific female stress response, the "tend-and-befriend"- reaction. Tending refers to nurturing activities aimed at protecting the self and the offspring, while the term befriending describes establishing and maintaining social networks that may facilitate the former activities. It has been hypothesized that oxytocin, a hormone that also plays a major role in the onset of the delivery, is involved as the main specific psychobiologic substrate.

In conclusion, specific hormones or autonomic nervous system variables may behave very differently, depending on (a) the specific nature of the stressor (e.g., controllable vs. uncontrollable); (b) the duration of the stressor; and (c) the sex of the exposed individual. Note that this indicates that it is not possible to denote one specific physiological parameter as the objective "golden" standard for the determination of stress.

The assessment of physiological stress reactions may include cardiovascular activity (heart rate, heart rate variability, blood pressure), galvanic skin activity, (neuro)endocrine variables in plasma, urine or saliva (cortisol, catecholamines, oxytocin, etc.) and immune variables (numerical or functional variables, cytokines, etc.). For a detailed discussion of the methodology of measuring stress hormones or immune measures that may be relevant for stress research, the reader is referred to Hawk and Baum (2001) or Baum and Grunberg (1995) and Vedhara, Wang, Fox and Irwin (2001) or Kiecolt-Glaser and Glaser (1995), respectively.

- *The emotional level.* Stressful conditions may evoke feelings of helplessness, depression, frustration, anger, or anxiety. A wide variety of negative emotions and moods may be activated by stressor exposure. In case of more severe stressors, such as rape, sexual or physical abuse, disasters, or accidents, the victims are often additionally afflicted with feelings of intense guilt and/or shame. Remarkably, especially in the case of severe, traumatic stressors, there is also the possibility that these individuals become emotionally numb and lose their ability to experience and express emotions (Litz, 1992). A wide variety of questionnaires is available to assess stress symptoms, well-being, and specific mood states like anxiety or depression (cf. Furer, König-Zahn, and Tax, 2001; Stone, 1995).

- *The cognitive level.* During stressful episodes, people may worry and are not able to concentrate. They may become obsessively focused on certain thoughts and their memories may show problems with storage. Obtrusive thoughts, flashbacks, re-experiences of the events, and worrying are the most characteristic consequences of exposure to traumatic events. Thayer and Lane (2000) consider worry as the most important aspect of the stress response and speculate that it actually intensifies and prolongs the effects of stressors. Stress may also affect memory processes and other cognitive processes (Reason, 1988; Smith, 1990). There are specific tools for the assessment of rumination and worry (e.g., Penn State Worry Questionnaire and Worry Domains Questionnaire; see Rijsoort, Vervaeke, and Emmelkamp, 1997). In addition, there are examples of the application of concentration tasks such as proof reading (Fleming and Baum, 1986; see below), with the aim to determine to what extent the stressor exposure has affected the individual's capacity to concentrate him or herself on a specific task.

- *The behavioural level.* At this level, there is a wide variety of reactions, including crying, smoking, social withdrawal, use of alcohol or drugs, absenteeism, aggression, etc. It is important to be aware of these kinds of stress reactions, because many of these behaviours may have damaging effects on a person's physical well-being. Occasionally, stress may also have seemingly positive effects on work performance, for example, a man who fully concentrates on his work during his divorce proceedings in an attempt to find distraction. As described above, there are also examples of performance tests such as proofreading or reaction time tests being applied to measure the effects of stress (e.g., Fleming and Baum, 1986). Of course, much the same as for others stress assessment procedures, several other factors may influence performance, once more emphasizing the need to measure stress at different levels, including self-reported mood and physiological variables.

The major problem in determining whether or not a person is "under stress" is that the links between these four different levels of reactions are weak at best. An important and serious limitation in stress research is the lack of an objective standard to establish whether or not a person is in a state of stress. The heart rate may show either of two reactions – increase or slow down – and the same holds for many other physiological systems, including the catecholamines and cortisol, which may show enhanced release, but also decreased levels. In addition, immune parameters may demonstrate divergent reaction patterns. Whereas one person may feel well, but experiences difficulties with concentrating on work, another person may stay away from work and has elevated cortisol levels, while a third person may start smoking, feels bad, and withdraws socially, but at the physiological level shows hardly any reactions.

Note that, thus far, we have only discussed the short-term effects of stressor exposure. In many cases, the stressor is acute and its effects dissipate in due course. However, when the stressor is intense and becomes chronic, the person's well-being and health may be in jeopardy. In particular, chronic stressors are accompanied by psychobiological changes that increase the individual's susceptibility to disease. This is particularly the case when the physiological arousal, providing energy to support overt behaviour, exceeds the actual demands of the body or when the body becomes exhausted and no longer adequately supports the physiological need to adapt successfully to environmental challenges.

References

Baum, A., & Grunberg, N. (1995). Measurement of stress hormones. In S. Cohen, R.C. Kessler, & L., Underwood Gordon (Eds.), *Measuring Stress. A Guide for Health and Social Scientists* (pp. 175–192). New York: Oxford University Press.

Bosch, J.A., De Geus, E.J.C., Kelder, A., Veerman, E.C.I., Hoogstraten, J., & Van Nieuw Amerongen, A. (2001). Differential effects of active versus passive coping on secretory immunity. *Psychophysiology, 38*, 836–846.

Burchfield, S.R. (1979). The stress response: A new perspective. *Psychosomatic Medicine, 41*, 661–672.

Endler, N.S., & Johnson, J.M. (2001). Assessment of coping with health problems. In A.J.J.M. Vingerhoets (Ed.), *Assessment in Behavioral Medicine* (pp. 135–160). Hove, UK: Brunner-Routledge.

Fleming, I., & Baum, A. (1986). Stress: Psychobiological assessment. *Journal of Organizational Behaviour Management, 8*, 117–140.

Furer, J., König-Zahn, C., & Tax, B. (2001). Health status measurement. In A.J.J.M. Vingerhoets (Ed.), *Assessment in Behavioural Medicine* (pp. 330–352). Hove, UK: Brunner-Routledge.

Hahn, S.E., & Smith, C.S. (1999). Daily hassles and chronic stressors: Conceptual and measurement issues. *Stress Medicine, 15*, 89–101.

Hawk, L.W. Jr., & Baum, A. (2001). Endocrine assessment in behavioural medicine. In A.J.J.M. Vingerhoets (Ed.), *Assessment in Behavioural Medicine* (pp. 413–440). Hove UK: Brunner-Routledge.

Kiecolt-Glaser, J.K., & Glaser, R. (1995). Measurement of immune response. In S. Cohen, R.C. Kessler, & L., Underwood Gordon (Eds.), *Measuring Stress. A Guide for Health and Social Scientists* (pp. 213–230). New York: Oxford University Press.

Lazarus, R.S., & Folkman, S. (1984). *Stress, Appraisal, and Coping.* New York: Springer.

Litz, B.T. (1992). Emotional numbing in combat related post-traumatic stress disorder: A critical review and reformulation. *Clinical Psychology Review, 12*, 417–432.

Myers, L.B., Newman, S.P., & Enomoto, K. (2004). Coping. In A. Kaptein & J. Weinman (Eds.), *Health Psychology.* (pp. 141–157). Oxford, UK: BPS-Blackwell.

Noshpitz J.D., & Coddington R.D. (Eds.), (1990). *Stressors and the Adjustment Disorders.* New York: Wiley.

Nyklicek, I., Vingerhoets, A.J.J.M., & Denollet, J. (2002). Emotional (non)expression and health: Data, questions, and challenges. *Psychology and Health, 17*, 517–528.

O' Keefe, M.K., & Baum, A. (1990). Conceptual and methodological issues in the study of chronic stress. *Stress Medicine, 6*, 105–115.

Reason, J. (1988). Stress and cognitive failure. In: S. Fisher (Ed.), *Handbook of Life Stress, Cognition, and Health.* (pp. 405–421). Oxford: Wiley.

ŠRice, P.L. (1999). *Stress and Health.* Pacific Grove, CA: Brooks/Cole Publishing Co.

Rijsoort S., Vervaeke, G., & Emmelkamp, P. (1997). Kort instrumenteel: De Penn State Worry Questionnaire en de Worry Domains Questionnaire: eerste resultaten bij een normale Nederlandse populatie. *Gedragstherapie, 2*, 121–128.

Schwarzer, R., Knoll, N., & Rieckmann, N. (2004). Social support. In A. Kaptein & J. Weinman (Eds.), *Health Psychology.* (pp. 158–181). Oxford, UK: BPS-Blackwell.

Selye, H. (1956; 1976) *The Stress of Life.* New York: McGraw-Hill.

Smith, A. (1990). Stress and information processing. In: M. Johnston & L. Wallace (Eds.), *Stress and Medical Procedures* (pp. 58–79). Oxford: Oxford University Press.

Stone, A. (1995). Measurement of affective response. In S. Cohen, R.C. Kessler, L. Underwood Gordon (Eds.), *Measuring Stress. A Guide for Health and Social Scientists* (pp. 122–147). New York: Oxford University Press.

Taylor, S.E., Klein, L.C., Lewis, B.P., Gruenewald, T.L., Gurung, R.A.R., & Updegraff, J.A. (2000). Biobehavioural responses to stress in females: Tend-and-Befriend, not Fight-or-Flight. *Psychological Review, 107*, 411–429.

Thayer, J.F. & Lane, R.D. (2000). A model of neurovisceral integration, emotion regulation, and dysregulation. *Journal of Affective Disorders, 61*, 201–216.

Van Sonderen, E., & Sanderman, R. (2001). Social support: Conceptual issues and assessment strategies. In: A.J.J.M. Vingerhoets (Ed.), *Assessment in Behavioural Medicine* (pp. 161–178). Hove, UK: Brunner-Routledge.

Vedhara, K., Wang, E.C.Y., Fox, J.D., & Irwin, M. (2001). The measurement of stress-related immune dysfunction in humans: An introduction to psychoneuroimmunology. In A.J.J.M. Vingerhoets (Ed.), *Assessment in Behavioural Medicine* (pp. 441–480). Hove, UK: Brunner-Routledge.

Vingerhoets, A.J.J.M. (2004a). Stress. In A. Kaptein & J. Weinman (Eds.), *Health Psychology*. (pp. 113–140). Oxford, UK: BPS-Blackwell.

Vingerhoets, A.J.J.M. (2004b). Stressreacties en hoe deze te meten. In J.A.M. Winnubst (Ed.), *Stress, Ziekteverzuim en Reïntegratie. Deel 1: Individugerichte Benaderingen.* (pp. 61–76). Zaltbommel, the Netherlands: Thema.

Vingerhoets, A.J.J.M., & Perski, A. (2000). The psychobiology of stress. In: A.A. Kaptein, A.W.P.M. Appels, & K. Orth-Gomér (Eds.), *Psychology in Medicine*. (pp. 34–49). Houten: Wolters Kluwer International.

Wethington, E., Almeida, D., Brown, G.W., Frank, E., Kessler, R.C. (2001). The assessment of stressor exposure. In A.J.J.M. Vingerhoets (Ed), *Assessment in Behavioural Medicine* (pp. 113–134). Hove, UK: Brunner-Routledge.

11

DISCOVERY OF T-TEMPLATES
AND THEIR REAL-TIME INTERPRETATION
USING THEME

Magnus S. Magnusson

Abstract   The temporal structure of every-day human behavior and interactions is certainly a complex affaire rich in repeated patterns or translation symmetry. This paper concerns a view of the structure of real-time streams of behavior as repeated, temporal patterns of a particular kind called t-patterns. An instance of a pattern of this kind consists of a particular and possibly quite small set of primitives of behavioral significance (verbal, nonverbal and/or environmental) occurring significantly more often than chance expectation in a particular order and/or concurrently with characteristic intervals between them. The analogies thus exist with speech and writing where only a few letters or phonemes are combined to create hundreds of thousands of different words and common word combinations. While remaining statistically significant, the time structure of t-patterns is also flexible and thus accommodates that of, for example, words, phrases, melodies and musical themes, which may be performed with considerable variation between repetitions in speed and internal intervals.

T-patterns are thus hierarchical patterns of patterns etc. and as phrases, their interpretation and effects (meaning, function) depend on the particular words involved, the temporal aspects of their production (performance) and the general context in which they occur. Some t-patterns occur cyclically and this better known aspect is now also automatically detected by the software THEME, which has been specially developed for t-pattern detection. A typical characteristic that has caused much difficulty regarding the detection of behavioral "sequences" is that routines, ceremonies and verbal "t-frames" (such as if.. then.. else) is that other behavior may occur in various numbers and ways between the components of different instances of the same pattern. Profiling individuals, interactions and/or groups can be based on the existence of particular t-patterns and/or the absolute or relative frequencies of patterns.

The THEME software also detects various other phenomena derived from the so called critical interval relationship and the t-pattern type such as t-bursts, t-cycles, t-markers, t-paths, t-associates, t-frames, and t-packets. This is the primary task of Theme, but a considerable part of the software helps with the analysis and use of the detected patterns, which is done both through visual and statistical means.

J.H.D.M. Westerink et al. (eds.), Probing Experience, 119–126.
© 2008 *Springer.*

The software can thus automatically analyze a large number of datasets in a single run and automatically build a data base of detected patterns that can then be consulted in various ways. Highly significant effects of independent (experimental) variables on the frequency and complexity of detected t-patterns have often been found in studies where no significant effects were detected using the same initial data and standard statistical methods alone.

Real-time use of THEME for the interpretation of ongoing behavior seems feasible given some further development. Theme thus already automatically creates t-pattern templates (t-templates) on the basis of a detected pattern base – which can be updated off-line from time to time. Template matching being much faster than the preceding pattern discovery and template construction, t-templates could be matched real-time against incoming data. Higher speed could be obtained through parallel processing. THEME is currently developed in Delphi 2005 Professional and large parts have already been transferred to Linux using Kylix (for use in Bioinformatics) partly in preparation for a parallel processing version.

1   Introduction

Great leaps in scientific understanding have occurred when technological breakthroughs have made the invisible visible. The microscope and the telescope made visible some phenomena that were before our eyes but were invisible due to small size or great distance.

The same is true for things that are too complex to grasp through unaided observation. Every-day human behavior and interaction are certainly complex phenomena rich in repeated patterns. Those who focus on such phenomena also face the fundamental difficulty of invisibility as has been clearly stated:

"**Behavior** consists of **patterns in time**. Investigations of behavior deal with **sequences** that, in contrast to bodily characteristics, are **not always visible**." Opening words of Eibl-Eibesfeldt's book "Ethology: The Biology of Behavior", 1970, p. 1; {Emphasis added.}

This fact, however, is frequently overlooked and analysis of behavior and interactions proceeds by just recording the occurrences of directly visible/audible (detectable) behaviors and standard statistical analysis of the data. Moreover, the analysis is usually limited to the frequency and/or (average, total) durations of the coded behaviors. For example, the smiles of an individual are often just counted independently of their location within the behavioral stream neglecting their timing relative to other behavior of the same and/or other individuals. While such an approach would seem more or less unthinkable regarding verbal behavior it is commonly applied in the study of (non-verbal or mixed verbal/nonverbal) interactions within other behavioral sciences (such as psychology, psychiatry and ethology). This seems typically due to of lack of adequate methods and tools to deal with structural analysis rather than reflecting contentment with such oversimplification regarding the intricacies of human interactions where timing and context are known to play an essential role. Standard statistical sequential analysis methods (including, for example, Markov chain analysis) do little or no justice to such complex structures and easily lead to frustration and even abandoning of structural approaches. In any case, such structural approaches have been in minimal use within psychological research and a similar situation seems to prevail in related areas such as, for example, ethology and psychiatry:

"Only about 8% of all psychological research is based on any kind of observation. A fraction of that is programmatic research. And, a fraction of that is sequential in its thinking." (Bakeman and Gottman, 1997, p. 184).

2   The t-model: An evolving view of behavioral organization

The present work is the fruit of decades of R&D trying to create some models of temporal behavior organization as well as corresponding pattern detection algorithms that would allow the detection of patterns that otherwise are completely hidden to the naked eye/ear or at least "not always visible" (Anolli et al., 2005; Magnusson, 2000, 2003, 2004, 2005 and under "Publication" at www.hbl.hi.is).

Sometimes large numbers of patterns are detected and need to be analyzed and interpreted and summarizing their combined information into some kind of individual or situational profiles and/or "grammars" is one of the ultimate goals. Individuals and situations may thus be profiled in terms of their use of particular patterns. The inter-individual functions of particular behaviors or patterns may also be discovered or better understood.

The main theoretical result of this work is a view of the structure of real-time streams of behavior as repeated, temporal patterns of a particular kind called **t-patterns**. An instance of a pattern of this kind consists of a particular set of primitives of behavioral significance (verbal, nonverbal and/or environmental) occurring more often than chance expectation in a *particular order and with characteristic (significantly invariant) intervals* between them. Such patterns are assumed to be organized in a hierarchical fashion so that more complex patterns may be seen as patterns of simpler ones all the way down to the recorded primitives, which may be possible to detect using existing technology.

Examples of t-patterns are found in speech and writing where only a few letters or phonemes are combined to create hundreds of thousands of different words and common word combinations and temporal or spatial interval lengths are highly constrained. While remaining statistically significant, the time structure of t-patterns is flexible and thus also accommodates ceremonies, routines and rituals as well as melodies and musical themes, which may be repeated with varying distances between their primitives and higher order components (sub-patterns). With X_i standing for the ith primitive of a pattern and $\approx t_i$ for the approximate characteristic interval length between X_i and X_{i+1} when the pattern occurs, a t-pattern Q may be noted as:

$$Q = X_1 \approx t_1 X_2 \approx t_2 .. X_i \approx t_i X_{i+1} .. X_{m-1} \approx t_{m-1} X_m$$

Considering instead the variation intervals of $\approx t_i$ within a particular observation period (i.e., for a particular set of occurrences of Q) the following notation may be used:

$$Q = X_1 [d_1, d_2]_1 X_2 [d_1, d_2]_2 .. X_i [d_1, d_2]_i X_{i+1} .. X_{m-1} [d_1, d_2]_{m-1} X_m$$

Each t-pattern may be split into a left and right part, Q_{left} and Q_{right} related by a critical interval $[d_1, d_2]$, that is,

$$Q = Q_{left} [d_1, d_2] Q_{right}$$

And such binary splitting may be applied recursively to each side until the primitive (directly coded event-types) level is reached.

While patterns of this kind are often easily detected by unaided observers as the above examples indicate, in other cases human observers seem to have great difficulty detecting (seeing) them even under quite simple conditions as may be seen in Figures 1 to 3.

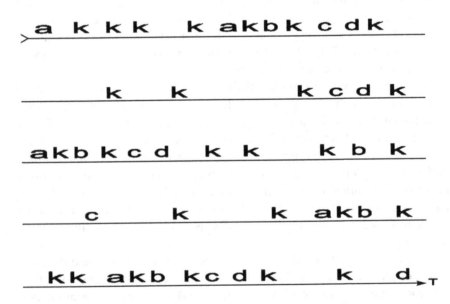

Figure 1.   T-patterns are here hidden by a little "noise", for example, some other behavior occurring in parallel.

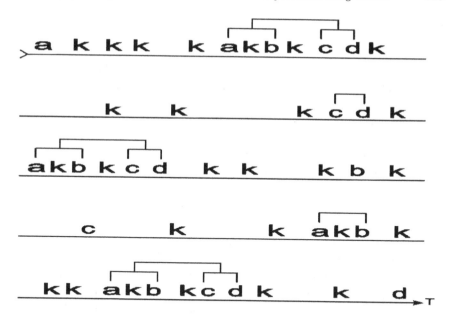

Figure 2. This figure is the same as Figure 1 but here the hidden t-patterns in Figure 1 are pointed out using a binary tree. The parallel behavior or "noise" is still present.

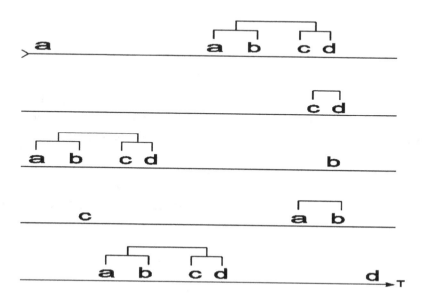

Figure 3. This figure is the same as Figure 2 except that the "noise" has been removed and the t-patterns appear clearly.

3   Detection

The detection algorithm reverses this recursive splitting procedure, starting with the primitives it searches for critical interval relationships and then connects primitives and/or eventually t-patterns of these to form/detect ever more complex patterns. The unavoidable combinatorial explosion problems due to redundant and partial detections are dealt with using an evolution approach (comparison, competition, elimination) where only the most complete versions of each pattern survive and constitute the result.

This ongoing R&D effort has resulted in software called THEME first presented in an AI workshop at the University of Uppsala, Sweden in 1982. It has since then been developed within various behavioral research contexts mostly at the Museum of Natural History in Paris, the University of Paris (V, VIII, XIII) and the University of Iceland in collaboration with researchers in Europe and the USA notably at the University of Chicago. It is hoped that Theme can be of use in research aimed at better understanding of human behavior and interactions, but for this increased automation of data collection and analysis seem necessary preconditions. – THEME is now developed by PatternVision Ltd, www.patternvision.com while international marketing and support is in the hands of NOLDUS IT; www.noldus.com.

4   From pattern detection to template matching and pattern bases

In each detected t-pattern all the parameters have been specified so that a template is formed:

$$Q = A\ [5, 11]\ B\ [2, 4]\ C\ [27, 35]D$$

Instead of being detected as above it can thus be matched against incoming data using much simpler and faster algorithms. To the extent raw data are automatically and more or less continually collected, t-pattern detection allows the building of data bases of such templates, t-template bases. Their matching with incoming data provides gradually improving statistics regarding their use, for example, by different individuals and families in different situations and times of day. Such information could constitute important input to ambient intelligence processes aimed at facilitating everyday life. As an important by-product knowledge would be acquired regarding everyday life and effects of, for example, aging, marital problems, handicaps and illness and possibly allowing better guidance, for example, by therapists and (social and educational) counselors. The ambient intelligence mechanisms could thus be continuously adapted to the inhabitants and their use of their space, tools and options in much the same way as some modern software adapts to the way it is used as, for example, when little used menu items being gradually removed (Magnusson, 2006).

5 Discussion

People are known to "get stuck" in unfortunate personal and interpersonal patterns of which they seem to be unconscious. In myriads of cases the consequences are serious and the work of therapists/counselors is often to become aware of this *as far as they can* and point out the patterns and their consequences. Unfortunate (but also fortunate) patterns may thus exist (at any time scale) that are unconscious to those performing them as well as to any observers. A multitude of such patterns are probably played out in the everyday lives of people in the millions of homes and households around the world where they are hidden from all systematic and scientific scrutiny partly due to the sanctity of individual privacy (much as the inner parts of human bodies used to be in earlier times), really and quite understandably a taboo matter. However, if better information and understanding could be obtained regarding ordinary life, large numbers of unfortunate patterns could probably be discovered or identified and hopefully eliminated, while more fortunate ones could be introduced.

The only hope for the necessary knowledge to be created seems to be through truly **anonymous** and **objective** observation and analysis and this would most likely involve behavioral research automation on a previously unthinkable scale. Technological and theoretical advances in this area thus seem to hold promise beyond imagination for the behavioral sciences and those parts of the world that would lead in this field might well find themselves in an enviable situation. Moreover, the likelihood such development will **not** happen in the near future seems small or tiny and ethical issues may increasingly relate as much to non-application as to application of new possibilities. – For the average citizen, the thought of one's elderly parent living in a completely non-intelligent apartment may eventually feel truly primitive and frightening.

References

Anolli, L., Duncan Jr., S., Magnusson, M. S., and Riva, G. (Eds.) (2005). *The Hidden Structure of Interaction: From Neurons to Culture Patterns*. Amsterdam: IOSPRESS (View/Download PDF version).

Bakeman, R. and Gotman, J. M. (1997). Observing interaction: An introduction to sequential analysis. Cambridge: Cambridge University Press.

Eibl-Eibesfeldt, I. (1970). Ethology: The Biology of Behavior". New York: Holt, Rinehart & Winston.

Magnusson, M. S. (2000). Discovering Hidden Time Patterns in Behavior: T-Patterns and their Detection. *Behavior Research Methods, Instruments and Computers*, 32(1): pp. 93–110. (View/Download PDF version).

Magnusson, M. S. (2003). Analyzing complex real-time streams of behavior: repeated patterns in behavior and DNA. *L'éthologie appliquée aujourd'hui*. (C. Baudoin, ed), Volume 3 – Ethologie humaine. Levallois-Perret, France: Editions ED. ISBN 2-7237-0025-9.

Magnusson, M. S. (2004). Repeated Patterns in Behavior and Other Biological Phenomena. In *Evolution of Communication Systems: A Comparative Approach* (Vienna Series in Theoretical

Biology). D. Kimbrough Oller (Editor), Ulrike Griebel (Editor). London: The MIT Press. ISBN: 0262151111 (View/Download PDF version).

Magnusson, M. S. (2005). Understanding Social Interaction: Discovering Hidden Structure with Model and Algorithms. In Anolli, L., S. Duncan Jr., M.S. Magnusson and G. Riva (Eds.) (2005). The Hidden Structure of Interaction: From Neurons to Culture Patterns. Amsterdam: IOSPRESS (View/Download PDF version).

Magnusson, M. S. (2006). Structure and Communication in Interactions. In G. Riva, M. T. Anguera, B. K. Wiederhold and F. Mantovani (Eds.) From Communication to Presence: Cognition, Emotions and Culture towards the Ultimate Communicative Experience. Festschrift in honor of Luigi Anolli. IOS Press, Amsterdam, 2006. (View/Download PDF version.)

Part II

PROBING IN ORDER TO FEED BACK

12

WHERE WILL THE USER "DRIVE" FUTURE TECHNOLOGY?

Antonio Maria Calvosa and Amedeo Visconti

Abstract   Both motivation and capabilities define a task and determine the result. When it comes to using a product, how can technology meet the user's needs at its best? Future human machine interfaces will need to strongly rely on assessing the human performances and benefits will be found into a reduced human workload and increased user's pleasure. How can we achieve this? What's the scenario in the automotive industry? Evidence shows that we are not too far from a new Renaissance.

1   Introduction

Achieving a goal by means of technology generally asks the user to make a selection of the best suited products and configurations. The accuracy of the interaction strongly relies on the user's knowledge of the product and many hours are usually spent on learning how to make a proficient usage. Simplifications of the learning curve are however taking place (see Figure 1). No further human input is, for example, needed to control the adherence of a vehicle during a ride on different road conditions: all the information on the environment is gathered and elaborated by a device and modifications are applied to the dynamic behaviour of the system. However, ways to assess the "positive" interaction of the user with the new systems are still under research. Today's scientists and engineers are trying to face this challenge and new applications – e.g. the intelligent room (Hirsh et al., 1999), the emotional learning and affective computer (Picard, 1995), the IBM emotional mouse (Ark et al., 1999) or the Wabian-2 robot (Waseda University of Tokyo, Japan & Scuola Superiore S. Anna of Pisa, Italy) – are starting to appear into the – consumer products – scene.

J.H.D.M. Westerink et al. (eds.), Probing Experience, 129–137.

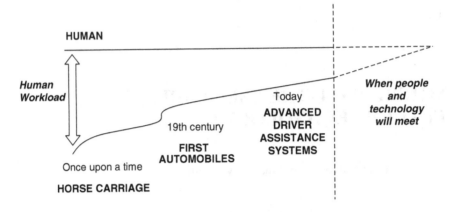

Figure 1.   Evolution of the user's effort to control a vehicle over the years.

2   Pleasure: the way for a "positive" interaction

Looking at mankind's evolution, it is possible to state that human behaviours and patterns have been suggested by pleasure (Tiger, 2000). Why should such an inherited mechanism not be applicable to user-product interaction? It does apply and pleasure plays a central role in contemporary product design (Patrick, 1998). However, feelings like frustration and irritation still affect the user's experience although they are generally accepted on the assumed not-human nature of technology. It follows that probing the user's experience, and instructing a "smarter" and collaborative technology to adhere to this vision, will bring a key differentiating benefit to the user and to the market of the future gamma products.

3   Human-Machine Interaction bottlenecks

Accomplishing a task or achieving a goal (see Figure 2) by means of technology requires the user to activate a series of relations with the chosen device. These relations are not only physical and are generally not limited to the two mentioned actors –i.e. user and device-. Due to the intentional – i.e. user's dictated – nature of these relations, the *physical, cognitive and emotive states* of the user come into play. A third actor, the environment, also is important with consequences depending on its capacity of undertaking similar intentional relations.

This scenario can be easily pictured considering a "driver-car" interaction capable of internal – human machine interface – and external – with other "driver-car" units – interactions.

It is the interplay between the user's states, the user's interaction with the external environment and the intrinsic capacity of the user's nervous system to elicit a peculiar user's behaviour.

One could argue that an obviously unpleasant feeling rises whenever the results expected from interaction don't meet the user's intentions. The degree

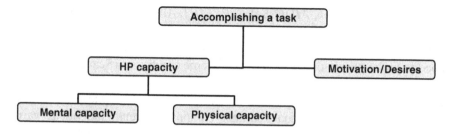

Figure 2. Human aspects that play a role in the human-machine interaction.

of difficulty for each of these interactions could hence be taken as a measure for (dis)pleasure.

Clearly, if the task becomes too long and/or complicated for the user's cognitive capacity, user's fatigue levels increase, bringing together emotive reactions such as frustration or anxiety.

Successfully probing the above mentioned states gives a feedback on the degree of positive interaction and constitutes the basis for a new generation of smarter technologies.

4 Human Performances Assessment (HPA): advantages and limitations of physiological signals

Over the last few years, a wide interdisciplinary interest has been devoted to find ways to probe and to understand the sensorial, the cognitive and the emotive states of a person. While a broad knowledge on how physical processes in humans take place has been reached, the cognitive and emotive processes are still under deep investigation (Andreassi, 2000; Cowie et al., 2005; Ekman et al., 1983). It is however possible to state that a foreseeable future technology will take advantage from physiological measurements, not only for medical or identification purposes but, and mainly, to probe and enhance the effectiveness of the interaction.

A widely acknowledged proof of concept for a biosensing-based human-machine interface indeed exists among the scientific community and several positive results assessing the emotional – e.g. sadness, happiness, anger, fear – and the cognitive state – e.g. mental stress, fatigue and effort, level of attention – have been claimed (Lisetti and Nasoz, 2004; Picard, 1995). Physiological signals, such as electrocardiogram, skin temperature and breathing rate, to name a few, are in fact innate and thus difficult to control and to mask voluntarily. They reflect the nervous system arousal and their quick onset, and distinctive appearance, brings up a good advantage with respect to more easily alterable vocal or facial recognition techniques (Bartlett et al., 2002; Kwon et al., 2003).

Nowadays, many technological advances – e.g. integration, power requirements and accuracy – have been achieved in a wide variety of research frameworks (*Sensation, AIDE, SAVE, PREDIT, AWAKE,* European Research Frameworks; Kahneman, 1973; Wylie et al., 1996). Taking advantage from the clinical experience, also innovative acoustic techniques have been developed to probe physiological signals in extreme conditions (Scanlon, 1998).

However, methodological challenges are still open due to the non specificity of the physiological markers, to the individual complexity and to the intra – among the same – individual and inter – among different – individuals variability. To associate a pattern to a physical, cognitive or emotional stimulus is indeed a hard task, not only for (today's state of) psycho-physiological research but also for humans, as our personal and interpersonal daily experience shows.

Multi-sensorial physiological measurements, with contextual probe on the user's activity, represent a common approach to bring more information into the system and an attempt to face specificity and intra-individual uncertainties. The effectiveness of this approach has been shown in today's health-care physiology-based products, such as the case of the "Armband" by Bodymedia Inc (Krause, 2003; Mignault et al., 2005) which correlates physiological data to movement sensors recordings. For the same product, the algorithms have also been tuned to match a fair amount of diverse physiological patterns, collected using various reliable and consolidated techniques, so as to overcome inter-individuals differences.

However, specificity and variability issues still foster the debate on the type of algorithms to be developed and on the classification dataset to be used to achieve the desirable accuracy. Basically, there is no "centre of pleasure" that can be assessed – yet – real-time to check the degree of "positive" interaction. It is also still very difficult to elicit and assess single emotions objectively, though several efforts in finding an international elicitation standard can be found in literature (Lang and Ohman, 1988).

Positive news comes from modern neuroimaging studies which try to investigate the functional neuroanatomy and identify peculiar activation centres (Phan et al., 2002). Physiology-based human performance assessment systems thus seem to follow the same development path of speech recognition systems with most of the early – current – versions relying on a single and restricted individual training set.

5 Automotive trends

Market demands in the automotive industry are due to pressures in several interconnected fields which range from the social, economical and environmental to the technological, political and infrastructural. In this framework, automotive technological trends can be identified and a roadmap can also be drawn (*Automotive Roadmap,* UK Foresight Vehicle, 2002). Besides the current well known issues – e.g. performance, safety, ergonomics, security, efficiency, emissions –, new drivers are also appearing to dominate the coming 20 years of technological development. They relate to performances in terms of human-vehicle and vehicle-infrastructure interaction, information management and user's predictability (*Automotive Roadmap,* UK Foresight Vehicle, 2002). These market demands will affect the business with a forecasted doubling in the automotive electronics which will account for the presence of adaptive cruise controls, biometrics systems, steering by wire and remote controls and other driving assistance devices.

Taking advantage from the developments in technology previously presented, car manufacturers and research institutions are moving along the above mentioned roadmap. A general and main interest is being devoted to driving assistance systems – e.g. Mercedes Distronic, Mercedes Brake Assist, Cadillac Night Vision System – whose effects will eventually turn into increased road safety, improved comfort and better regulated traffic.

However, to find the best level of automation to give to the user is still an open debate and the outcome strongly depends on the improvements that will be made on the state of the art of these technologies. The complex interplay between the reduction in the user's workload and the probability of failure of such electronic systems – and related unexpected consequences – should be carefully analysed before blindly pushing driving assistance to its frontiers (Bainbridge, 1983).

6 Physiology and automotive industry

A variety of automotive studies assessing drivers' performances through physiology have been recently performed. A research on electrocardiogram signals acquired during several Formula One races (Ceccarelli et al., 1996) proved that the physical and the emotional states are effectively correlated to the stimuli associated with the driving task. It is indeed possible, for example, to notice an increase in the heart activity at the beginning of the race – emotional reaction – and during dry, in contrast with wet, track conditions – change in physical commitment –. Physiological changes have also been shown to be more remarkable on less physically trained and more emotive drivers – inter individuals variability – and a need for a baseline signal – intra individual variability – has been evidenced. Similar results have been reported within research frameworks involving airline pilots (Ylönen, 1997), while studies on virtual and real city-drive activities confirm the possibility of physiological monitoring (Healey, 2000; Lisetti and Nasoz, 2004).

Also attention, as a limited resource to be shared during multi-tasking events (Kahneman, 1973), has been at the centre of recent automotive studies with current solutions relying on eye gaze/blinking, body movement detectors and electrooculogram (EOG) sensors (e.g. FaceLab system by Seeing Machines; Wylie et al., 1996). Mental fatigue, with relation to alertness and drowsiness, has further been investigated and relations with electroencephalogram (EEG) (Trejo et al., 2004) and electrocardiogram (ECG) (Rowe et al., 1998) spectra as well as facial electromiogram (EMG) analysis (Veldhuizen, et al., 2003) have been found.

These works have raised the interest of the automotive industrial community towards these new technologies. Several initiatives are hence being undertaken in order get a deeper insight in the opportunities that might derive from their successful application in the automotive context.

7 Innovation at Ferrari

Innovation represents a fundamental and key competitive advantage in the world of high-performance sports cars. When it comes to Ferrari, most of the innovation on road cars directly comes from the high-end Formula One (F1) know-how. Examples are the Electronic Differential for high-performance road holding – F430 model – or the F1 gear-shift integrated on the steering wheel. Also, the F1 genes of the single-seaters' steering wheel, demonstrating the degree of control at the drivers' finger tips, have recently been transferred into to the F430 and F599 models with the introduction of the so called "Manettino". Such a switch, integrated on the steering wheel, allows to change the car settings in order to suit the driver's preferences and goals for the ride, accounting for performance profiles, surface conditions and available grip.

But, how to close the loop? How to quantitatively sense the interaction between the user and the car? Physiology could come to the rescue.

At Ferrari, a multi-disciplinary team of engineers is indeed facing the challenge of assessing the feasibility of a project involving a new vehicle's interactive interface, capable of adapting to the physical, emotional and cognitive states of the driver (see Figure 3).

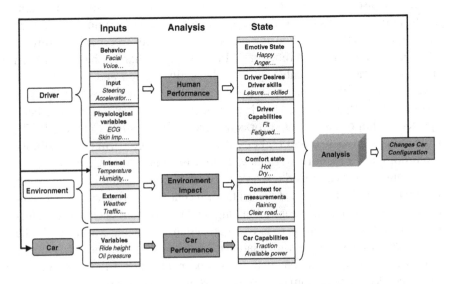

Figure 3.   Human Performance Assessment-based interface.

This study adheres to the vision that intra-individual variability affects the way we daily interact with our products to the point that a cutting edge experience cannot always be guaranteed. Finding out the bottlenecks in the car-driver interaction capacity, and consequently acting on the interface, will alleviate the users' "pain" and empower the user's relation with the system.

8 Technological challenges

Technological challenges are open and mainly relate to the state-of-the-art of physiology-based systems. Also, since a car represents a private environment, strict privacy and acceptability rules apply.

This fosters research in real-time algorithms that don't require long-term information storing – that might contain indications on the health status of a subject -, much like expert treadmills collect the heart-rate values of a runner to find the most opportune training.

Hardware requirements also play an important role. Non-contact, eventually remote, robust, reliable, low consuming, eventually self-powered, small sensors are needed not to interfere with the driving task, the car performances and the vehicle aesthetics. Advanced solutions are starting to appear into research and industrial labs – e.g. the seat embedded remote ECG monitoring systems (Harland et al., 2002) or the carbon nanotubes based sensors for ECG and EEG by Starlab Inc –.

Due to the very low intensity of the physiological signals – i.e. millivolt for ECG and microvolt for EEG through the scalp – and their low frequency significant components – i.e. below 1 KHz, but generally much more limited –, a high performing system is needed. Furthermore, remote sensing – i.e. without skin contact – suffers from two supplementary problems: the signal vs. noise degradation due to the source-transducer distance and the displacement field variations due to body movements – the body represents a large dielectric constant, mainly made of water –. Also, the system's wirings must be handled with extreme care to avoid false pick-ups from other car devices – e.g. ignition, telemetry, control signals – and external signals – e.g. radio communications –. Design solutions should hence be researched among current demanding applications such as the case of military devices. Some time will hence occur before affordable solutions will be accessible to a wider range of users. Sports cars could however be good candidates for the early-adoption of such systems provided that the technology will be mature enough to bring competitive benefits to the driver's-car interaction.

9 Conclusions

It is difficult to state that a fully working product, fitting the needs and capacities of the hypothetical user number "1371st-bis", will be on the market shortly. Many intermediate phases still have to occur. However, the user

"1371st-bis" should already be proud of being at the centre of the stage and of interacting so proficiently with the scientific community. A limited, arrogant and meticulous technology made this process happen thus paving the way for a richer, humbler and sympathetic personality of its own.

Acknowledgements

The author would like to acknowledge the members of the Innovation Team for the fruitful collaboration on the Human Performance Assessment project. Many thanks also to Prof. Carlo Perfetti for the deep insights into the theory of pleasure in the context of human-machine interaction.

References

AIDE. URL: http://www.aide-eu.org/ [Last accessed on October 25, 2007].

Andreassi, J. (2000) *Psychophysiology: human behaviour and physiological response*. New Jersey: Lawrence Erlbaum Associates.

Ark, W., Dryer, D. C., and Lu, D. J. (1999) The emotion mouse. *Proceedings of HCI International (the 8th International Conference on Human-Computer Interaction) on Human-Computer Interaction: Ergonomics and User Interfaces, Munich Germany* 818–823.

AWAKE. URL: http://www.awake-eu.org/ [Last accessed on October 25, 2007].

Bainbridge, L. (1983) Ironies of automation. *Automatica* 19 775–777.

Bartlett, M. S., Littlewort, G., Braathen, B., Sejnowski, T. J., and Movellan, J. R. (2002) A Prototype for Automatic Recognition of Spontaneous Facial Actions. *Advances in Neural Information Processing Systems* 15 1295–1302.

Bedini, R., Belardinelli, A., Palagi, G., Franchi, D., Ripoli, A., and Ceccarelli, R. (1996) Dynamic ECG analysis in drivers during a F1 championship. *Computers in Cardiology* September 645–648.

Cowie, R., Douglas-Cowie, E., Tsapatsoulis, N., Votsis, G., Kollias, S., Fellenz, W., and Taylor, J. G. (2001) Emotion recognition in human-computer interaction. *IEEE Signal Processing Magazine* 18 32–80.

Ekman, P., Levenson, R.W., and Friesen, W.V. (1983) Autonomic nervous system activity distinguishes among emotions. *Science* 221 1208–1210.

European Research Frameworks. URL: http://ec.europa.eu/research/index.cfm [Last accessed on October 25, 2007].

Harland, C. J., Clark, T. D., and Prance, R. J. (2002) New directions in the remote sensing of the human body. *Measurement Science and Technology* 13 163–169.

Healey, J. A. (2000) *Wearable and automotive systems for the recognition of affect from physiology*, PhD thesis, MIT Electrical Engineering department.

Hirsh, H., Coen, M., and Mozer, M. C. (1999) Room service, AI-style. *IEEE Intelligent Systems* 14 8–13.

Kahneman, D. (1973) *Attention and effort*. Englewood Cliffs, NJ: Prentice Hall.

Krause, A. (2003) *Unsupervised, Dynamic Identification of Physiological and Activity Context in Wearable Computing*. Engineering department, Munich University.

Kwon, O. W., Chan, K., Hao, J., and Lee, T. W. (2003) Emotion Recognition by Speech Signals. *EUROSPEECH-2003*, Geneva, Switzerland 125–128.

Lang, P. and Ohman, D. V. (1988) The *international affective picture system [photographic slides]*. Technical report, The Center for Research in Psychophysiology, University of Florida, Gainsville, FL.

Lisetti, C. L. and Nasoz, F. (2004) Using noninvasive wearable computers to recognize human emotions from physiological signals. *EURASIP Journal on Applied Signal Processing* 2004 1672–1687.

Mignault, D., St.-Onge, M., Karelis, A. D., Allison, D. B., and Rabasa-Lhoret, R. (2005) Evaluation of the portable Health Wear armband. *Diabetes Care* 28 225–227.

Patrick, J. W. (1998) *An introduction to usability.* London, UK: Taylor and Francis.

Phan, K. L., Wager, T., Taylor, S. F., and Liberzon, I. (2002) Functional neuroanatomy of emotion: a meta-analysis of emotion activation studies in PET and fMRI. *Neuroimage* 16 331–348.

Picard, R. W. (1995) *Affective computing.* MIT Press, Cambridge.

PREDIT. URL: http://www.predit.prd.fr/predit3/menu.fo?cmd=english Version [Last accessed on October 25, 2007].

Rowe, D. W., Sibert, J., and Irwin, D. (1998) Heart rate variability: indicator of user state as an aid to human-computer interaction. *Proceedings of the SIGCHI conference on Human factors in computing systems, April 18–23, 1998, Los Angeles, California, United States* 480–487.

SAVE. URL: http://www.save-u.org/ [Last accessed on October 25, 2007].

Scanlon, M. V. (1998) Acoustic Sensor for Health Status Monitoring. *Proceedings of IRIS acoustic and seismic sensing* 2 205–222.

Seeing Machines: FaceLab system. URL: http://www.seeingmachines.com/ [Last accessed on October 25, 2007].

SENSATION. URL: http://www.sensation-eu.org/ [Last accessed on October 25, 2007].

Tiger, L. (2000) *The pursuit of pleasure.* New Brunswick: Transaction Publishers.

Trejo, L. J., Kochavi, R., Kubitz, K., Montgomery, L. D., Rosipal, R., and Matthews, B. (2005) Measures and models for predicting cognitive fatigue. *Proceedings of SPIE* 5797 105–115.

UK Foresight Vehicle: *Automotive Roadmap* (2002). URL: http://www.foresightvehicle.org.uk/ [Last accessed on October 25, 2007].

Veldhuizen, I. J. T., Gaillard, A. W. K., and de Vries, J. (2003) The influence of mental fatigue on facial EMG activity during a simulated workday. *Biological Psychology* 63 59–78.

Waseda University of Tokyo (Japan) & Scuola Superiore S. Anna of Pisa (Italy). URL: http://www.robocasa.net/ [Last accessed on October 25, 2007].

Wylie, C. D., Shultz, T., Miller, J. C., Mitler, M. M., and Mackie, R. R. (1996) *Driver fatigue and analysis study: Commercial Motor Vehicle Driver Fatigue and Alertness Study. Executive Summary. Final rept.* PB98102346; Essex Corp., Goleta, CA; Federal Highway Administration, Washington, DC.

Ylönen, H., Lyytinen, H., Leino, T., Leppäluoto, J., and Kuronen, P. (1997) Heart rate responses to real and simulated BA Hawk MK 51 flight. *Aviation, Space and Environmental Medicine* 68 601–605.

13

A WEARABLE EMG MONITORING SYSTEM FOR EMOTIONS ASSESSMENT

Cecilia Vera-Munoz, Laura Pastor-Sanz, Guiseppe Fico,
Maria Teresa Arredondo, Francesca Benuzzi and Angel Blanco

Abstract   The automatic detection and study of human emotions has always been an area
of interest within the scientific community. The AUBADE European Union
funded project has addressed this problem by developing an innovative, intelligent, multi-sensor and wearable system for the assessment of the emotional
state of humans under special conditions (i.e. neurological diseases, stress, etc.).
The system recognizes the emotions after processing biomedical signals (electromyogram, electrocardiogram, respiration rate and galvanic skin response)
and can be applied in diverse areas. Currently, a health care sector scenario
has been considered and validated, primarily in the neurology and psychology
areas, in order to contribute to get precise diagnosis and treatment procedures
for patients.

1   Introduction

Emotions play an extremely important role in our life, conditioning all
aspects of our existence. Normally, there is a continuous interaction between
emotions, behaviour and thoughts, in such a way that they constantly influence each other. For that reason, the study of human emotions has aroused the
interest of researchers for decades (Goleman, 1995).

Darwin was probably the first to suggest the importance of emotions,
postulating in 1872 that human beings were able to recognise the expressions
instinctively, and they took their decisions based on the interpretations of the
gestures (Darwin, 1872). Later, in 1971, Ekman and Friesen (1971) defined
the existence of six primary emotions known as "basic" (sadness, anger, fear,
disgust, surprise and happiness). This set of emotions appeared to be universal, innate and applicable to all ethnic groups and cultures. Furthermore,
they established a relationship between these basic emotions and certain
facial expressions, and they defined a method for coding these expressions
by studying the movements of different regions of the face. Subsequently,
they proved that the majority of the emotions that a person experiences can

139

J.H.D.M. Westerink et al. (eds.), Probing Experience, 139–148.

be represented with a combination of the mentioned six basic emotions along with the neutral one (Ekman and Rosenberg, 1997). This meant that it was possible to identify almost any emotion by just studying the facial expressions of the individuals (Vera et al., 2005).

After these theories, there was a great effort in attempting to build systems that automatically detected human emotions. Most of them used advanced image processing techniques combined with the Facial Action Coding System (FACS) established by Ekman and Friesen (1978) in order to determine the facial expression of the subject and, consequently, his emotion. Nevertheless, there are certain situations where the traditional image analysis methods can not be applied. In these cases alternative techniques have to be used to conduct the study (Vera et al., 2005).

This paper presents a novel method for the recognition of emotions based on biosignals measurements. The system has been developed within the frame of the AUBADE project (IST 507605. European Commission Six Framework Programme), partially funded by the European Union under the Information Society Technologies (IST) area in the Six Framework Programme. The project main objective is the development of an intelligent, multisensorial wearable system that can ubiquitously monitor and classify the personal psychological condition of people under extreme stress or other special conditions (Vera et al., 2006). The core of the project is the development of a modular system that requires a combination of different innovation areas: wearable systems, biosensors, sensors management techniques, data fusion, medical decision support systems, 3-D animations, and telecommunications (Vera et al., 2005).

2   AUBADE system architecture

The AUBADE system relies on an open and flexible architecture design (Figure 1) that allows the adaptation to the different applications needs. The modules that compose the platform are: Wearable System, Data Acquisition Module, Communication Module, and the AUBADE application which manages the Feature Extraction, the Emotion Recognition and the Facial Animation Modules as well as the HL7-compliant HIS (Hospital Information System) data base.

The multi-sensorial wearable system measures various biomedical signals: electromyogram (EMG), electrocardiogram (ECG), respiration rate (RR) and galvanic skin response (GSR). The main component of this module is a kind of mask that includes the EMG and ECG sensors located in specific predefined zones of the subject under observation. A thin-film-multi-electrode grid, manufactured on a flexible carrier, has been chosen for the facial EMG as well as for the ECG. These sensors are small and, therefore, can be attached to the subject for long hours without causing any aggravation on the skin.

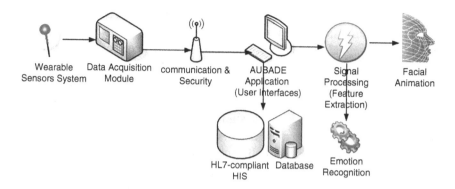

Figure 1.   AUBADE system architecture.

Additionally, these sensors have excellent signal quality and the electrical connections may withstand moisture as well as large tensile forces.

Sensors positioning for EMG was determined by a number of factors such as the orientation of muscle fibres, the depth of the muscular tissue and the anatomic points of reference. The design also considered the need to adapt each sensor to a specific muscle, taking into account the various anatomic characteristics of the different persons that utilise the system.

The respiration rate and galvanic skin response are measured with different types of sensors. For the respiration rate response, a sensor mounted on a simple Velcro band is used. The band is strapped around the subject's diaphragm, detecting the amount of expansion of the chest cavity as the person breathes in and out. Post-processing of the measured signal reveals the number of breaths per minute. The galvanic skin response is also measured using a Velcro strap that secures the sensor on a finger. The selected sensor is a high quality silver/silver chloride electrode that eliminates the polarization and movement artefacts common in conventional stainless steel GSR electrodes. The signals obtained are of high quality and virtually noise free.

Once acquired, the biomedical signal measurements are subjected to a conditioning process that includes amplification and digitalization in the Data Acquisition Module (DAM). The DAM of the AUBADE system is an electronic portable device that acquires the signals from the subjects, digitises and transmits them for further processing to a PC through a USB communication port. The DAM is powered by internal rechargeable batteries to provide full mobility and electrical safety. The power autonomy guarantees the continuous data acquisition during the monitoring time.

The Communication Module is responsible for the transmission of the acquired data between the DAM and the AUBADE Application (Central

Module). The transference is activated by an action of the health professional. Before the transmission, all data is checked for the correct format. Also, RR, GSR and ECG signals are down sampled, as they are acquired at a lower frequency with respect to the EMG sample rate.

The AUBADE central module applies processing and feature extraction techniques to obtain the necessary parameters to analyse the measured signals and to provide the output of the signal processing algorithms to the Intelligent Emotion Recognition and Facial Animation modules.

The system incorporates an intelligent module able to detect the emotional state of the individual observed in terms of basic emotions. For this purpose, a decision support system that applies intelligent techniques for the analysis, classification and knowledge extraction from the signals has been implemented. This information, along with the personal data of each subject, allows the system to determine the emotion that a user is experiencing at each precise moment.

The representation of the current emotional state is displayed in the application user interface. For each measurement, the system gives the emotion that the subject is experiencing as an output, with a percentage that represents the probability of feeling it. The user can also check the acquired signals in a graphical window as well as represent the corresponding facial expressions using the Facial Animation module. This element uses a generic 3D model developed from a deformable mesh of nodes arranged in three layers, representing the facial tissues structure. The model is fed with the measured EMG signals, reproducing the animation of each one of the facial movements shown by the subject.

The AUBADE Application is also able to be integrated with a healthcare institution's Information System (HIS) through an HL7 interface, so as to retrieve patient demographics and publish AUBADE results as an examination to the HIS.

3 AUBADE system validation

The clinical test and validation procedure of the AUBADE system has been performed in a hospital environment, using twenty-four healthy subjects (13 male and 11 female to consider any possible gender differentiation). From those tests, fifteen were used for training the Emotion Recognition Module, while the last nine were used for the validation and refinement of the mentioned module. All the subjects were recruited from the University of Modena- AUSL personnel and all tests were done in the presence of a psychologist.

AUBADE system intends to be applied to the diagnosis and following-up of two main progressive neurological disorders: Huntington' and Parkinson'

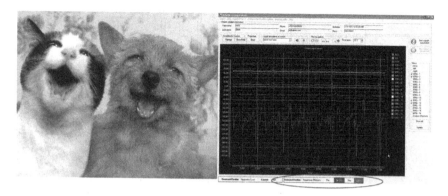

Figure 2. (Left) example of a happiness inducing picture. (Right) AUBADE system assessment.

diseases. The patients suffering these illnesses are defective in processing disgust and/or fear. Therefore, the tests made have only considered these mentioned basic emotions as well as a third one, happiness, which is used as control emotion. During the clinical tests, appropriate stimuli (especially selected to provoke fear, happiness and disgust) have been induced in order to evoke genuine emotions (Figure 2).

The resultant emotion that each subject is experiencing has been identified based on three different parameters: subjective experience (self assessment), physiological arousal (vegetative subject's reaction through the recorded biomedical signals) and behavioural expression (facial and vocal expressions).

In order to evoke the appropriate emotion, a new Emotions Inducing Test based on the International Affective Pictures System (IAPS; Lang et al., 1999) has been developed. The Emotions Inducing Test includes a set of 35 visual and sound stimuli that were presented to the subject, each one for a time of 4 seconds. The stimuli are colour photographs, randomly arranged in a Power Point presentation, with a 720×576 pixel dimension, that have been selected as follows: 10 fear inducing pictures (video clip including sound), 10 happiness inducing pictures, 10 disgust inducing pictures and 5 neutral pictures (to avoid any anticipation of the response for the fear inducing stimuli). In half of the cases, (5 out of 10), the fear inducing stimuli included a neutral picture (2 seconds) followed by a frightening picture combined with a sound (2 seconds).

For each stimulus, three different results were obtained. First the subject physiological response was acquired with the AUBADE system and stored in a local database. Additionally, the subject filled in the self-assessment test indicating the felt emotion. Finally, the psychologist assessed the emotion of the subject, based on his facial expression.

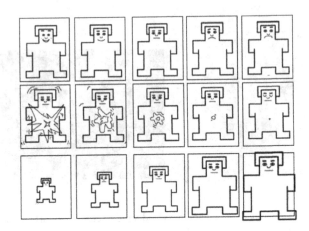

Figure 3. Self Assessment Manikin Test (SAM). From top to down: valence, arousal and dominance (Bradley & Lang, 1994).

To assess the subject's feeling we used the Self Assessment Manikin test (SAM; Bradley and Lang, 1994). The SAM test is a picture-oriented scale, assessing the tree main dimensions of emotions: valence, arousal and dominance. The main advantages with respect to verbal scales are the ease of administration (3 ratings instead of the 18 demanded by the Semantic Differential), a broader application scope (due to its non-verbal, pictorial character), and its high applicability in children and in patients studies, and finally, its highly correlation with different physiological measures (facial EMG, ECG, etc.; Bradley, 2001; Lang et al., 1993).

The test is divided into several modules, one for each stimulus presented to the subject. Each one of these modules is a three rows picture, as depicted in Figure 3, representing the three affective dimensions.

The first row represents the valence of the emotion. The emotion can be positive (smiling mouth on the left) or negative (sad mouth on the right). The second row represents the arousal or intensity of the emotion (very intense on the left, and little intense, on the right). The third and last row represents the dominance, the control of the subject over the emotion (little control on the left, big control, on the right).

As Figure 4 shows, SAM is a 9 point scale; for the clinical validation we considered three different levels (high, medium, low) for each one of the three affective dimensions (valence, arousal, dominance), and three different emotions, resulting in an emotional space with 9 different emotional classes: low, medium and high happiness, low, medium and high fear, low, medium and high disgust. For simplicity and convenience reasons, the AUBADE

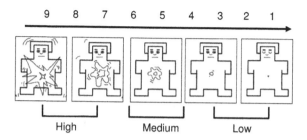

Figure 4. SAM test (Bradley & Lang, 1994). The subject will provide a level for each one of the three affective dimensions. Gradation from 1–3 will be considered as low level, 4–6, medium level, and 7–9, high level.

experiment only considered the self-assessed arousal dimension. Therefore, the algorithms from the Emotion Recognition Module were trained to recognise nine emotional classes.

The procedure for the validation tests was as follows. First of all, the sensors were placed on the subject's body as follows: 16 EMG sensors on the face, the ECG sensors on the shoulders, the respiration rate (RR) sensor on the chest, and the galvanic skin response sensor (GSR) in the fingers of one of the hands. This setup took around 40 minutes. Following, a psychologist explained to the subject the basics of the testing procedure and self-assessment test.

Then, the whole set of stimuli was presented to the subject while AUBADE system measured the physiological responses and the medical doctor assessed his emotions based on the facial expression. After receiving a stimulus he had 30–60 seconds for the self-assessment. First subject had to indicate by marking each row (either inside a picture or between two pictures) the level of each one of the mentioned dimensions (Figure 5).

In addition, subjects were also required to indicate whether the emotion they felt was most like happiness, fear, surprise, anger, disgust, or sadness indicating the appropriate labels that identified the feeling induced by the picture. All responses were registered by the experiment on a protocol were biographical data were also collected (name, age, gender, and handedness).

Once the biomedical signals were recorded and the subject provided his subjective experience through the test, the doctor validated the results, matching them with the subject's facial expression for each one of the presented stimuli. Whenever there was a disagreement between the doctor's assessment and the measurements, it was assumed that the doctor's opinion was the correct one. However, these records were discarded in order to avoid wrong measurements that could affect the accuracy of the system.

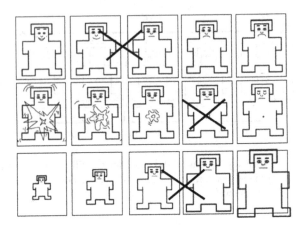

Figure 5.   SAM test (Bradley & Lang 1994), an example of the result after a happiness inducing stimulus.

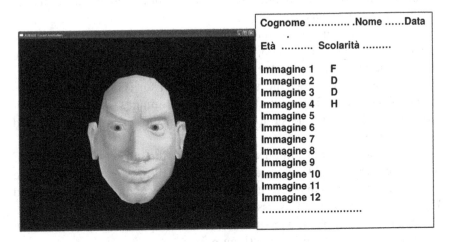

Figure 6.   (Left) Facial animation module in response to a happiness inducing picture. (Right) Doctor's assessment for the same stimulus.

After the conducted tests and validation process the system accuracy has found to be above 70% in all emotional classes classification except in one case (Katsis et al., 2006; Rigas et al., 2007). This exception was due to the lack of enough samples available during the training phase of the algorithms for this specific emotional class.

As an additional tool, the doctor could see the subject's facial expression using the AUBADE Facial Animation Module. This element was also a useful instrument to record the sessions and keep them as a backup for the neurologists' consultation (Figure 6).

4 Conclusions

The project presented in this paper has developed a system that recognizes the emotions of people under extreme conditions by utilising an innovative method: the analysis of biomedical signals. The final result of the project is a modular and multifunctional system to be used in diverse areas.

The current AUBADE system has been designed aiming mainly at health care professionals (neurologists, psychologists, etc.). In this sector, it is expected that the system contributes to improve the diagnosis and treatment of neurological diseases, as well as to open new research opportunities in the emotions recognition area. More specifically, the platform will be very useful for the diagnosis and follow up of two certain progressive neural diseases: Huntington's disease and Parkinson's disease. These illnesses are characterised by a deficit in emotional processing of fear and disgust and, thus, AUBADE system could be utilised to test the subject reaction/or absence of reaction to specific emotions, helping the health professionals to gain a better understanding of these disorders. On top of that, the system could be used to evaluate the patients' response to certain medicines and drugs.

Nevertheless, the platform has been designed to be scalable and improved. Therefore, it can be easily adapted to detect additional sets of emotions that could be of interest for other neurological disorders, other health care specialities and even additional sectors such as games industry, automotive, etc.

AUBADE project has developed the next generation of the remote emotion monitoring systems, providing health professionals with an innovative tool that will lead them to a deep study, analysis, understanding, and comprehension of human emotions.

5 Acknowledgements

We would like to thank the AUBADE Project Consortium for their valuable contributions for the realization of this work. This project is partially funded by the European Commission.

References

AUBADE project, IST 507605. European Commission Six Framework Programme.

Automatic analysis of facial expressions: The state of the art, IEEE Trans. *Pattern Anal. Machine Intell.* 22: 1424–1445, Dec. 2000.

Bisquerra, R. (2000). *Educación Emocional y Bienestar*. Barcelona: Praxis.

Bradley, M. M. and Lang, P. Measuring Emotions: The Self Assessment Manikin and the semantic Differential.J Behav. *Ther. Exp. Psy.* 25(1): 49–59, 1994.

Bradley M. M., Codispoti M., Cuthbert B. N., Lang P. J. Emotion and Motivation I: Defensive and Appetitive Reactions in Picture Processing. *Emotion* 1(3): 276–298, 2001.

Darwin C. *The Expression of the Emotions in Man and Animals*. J. Murray, London, 1872.

Ekman P. and Friesen W. V. Constants across cultures in the face and emotion. *Journal of Personality and Social Psychology* 17: 124–129, 1971.

Ekman P. Facial Expression and Emotion. *American Psychologist* 48(4): 384–392, April 1993.

Ekman, P. and Friesen. W. V. Facial action coding system: A technique for the measurement of facial movement. Palo Alto, CA: Consulting Psychologists Press, 1978.

Ekman, P. and Rosenberg, E. L. What the face reveals: Basic and applied studies of spontaneous expression using the facial action coding system (FACS), New York: Oxford University Press, 1997. Second expanded edition 2004.

Goleman, D. *Emotional Intelligence*, New York: Bantam Books, 1995.

Kan Y. et al. Recognition of emotion from facial, prosodic and written verbal stimuli in Parkinson's disease. *Cortex* 38(4): 623–30, 2002.

Katsis C. D., Ganiatsas G., and Fotiadis D. I. An integrated telemedicine platform for the assessment of affective physiological states. *Diagnostic Pathology* 1:16 doi:10.1186/1746-1596-1-16, August 2006.

Lang P. J. et al. The international affective pictures system (IAPS). *Technical Manual and Affective Ratings*. Gainsville, FL: University of Florida, 1999.

Lang P. J., Greenwald M. K., Bradley M. M. and Hamm A. O. Looking at pictures: affective, facial, visceral, and behavioral reactions. *Psychophysiology* 30(3):261–73, May 1993.

Pantic M. and Rothkrantz L. J. M. Facial Action Recognition for Facial Expression Analysis from Static Face Images. IEEE Transactions on Systems, Man, and Cybernetics – Part B, 34(3): 1449–1461, June 2004.

Rigas, G., Katsis, C., Ganiatsas, G. and Fotiadis, D. I.: IEEE Engineering in Medicine and Biology Society in conjunction with the biennial Conference of the French Society of Biological and Medical Engineering (SFGBM). August 23–26, 2007. Convention Center, Cité Internationale, Lyon, France.

Sprengelmeyer R. et al. Facial expression recognition in people with medicated and unmedicated Parkinson's disease. *Neuropsychologia* 41(8): 1047–57, 2003.

Vera, C. et al. Results of a wearable EMG monitoring system for neurological patients Telemedicine and Health Journal, Volume 12, Number 2, April 2006, pp 207 (ISSN 1530-5627), San Diego, California (USA).

Vera, C. et al. Wearable System for Automatic Emotion Detection in Extreme Conditions. Applied Technologies in Medicine and Neuroscience (Proceedings of the first international conference on Applied Technologies in Medicine and Neuroscience), pp 97–102 (ISBN: 3-85184-027-5), June 2005.

Vyzas E. and Picard R. W. Offline and Online Recognition of Emotion Expression from Physiological Data.Workshop on Emotion-Based Agent Architectures, Third International Conference on Autonomous Agents, Seattle, WA, 1999.

14

COMPUTING EMOTION AWARENESS THROUGH GALVANIC SKIN RESPONSE AND FACIAL ELECTROMYOGRAPHY*

Joyce H.D.M. Westerink, Egon L. van den Broek, Marleen H. Schut, Jan van Herk and Kees Tuinenbreijer

Abstract   To improve human-computer interaction (HCI), computers need to recognize and respond properly to their user's emotional state. This is a fundamental application of affective computing, which relates to, arises from, or deliberately influences emotion. As a first step to a system that recognizes emotions of individual users, this research focuses on how emotional experiences are expressed in six parameters (i.e., mean, absolute deviation, standard deviation, variance, skewness, and kurtosis) of not baseline-corrected physiological measurements of the galvanic skin response (GSR) and of three electromyography signals: frontalis (EMG1), corrugator supercilii (EMG2), and zygomaticus major (EMG3). The 24 participants were asked to watch film scenes of 120 seconds, which they rated afterward. These ratings enabled us to distinguish four categories of emotions: negative, positive, mixed, and neutral. The skewness and kurtosis of the GSR, the skewness of the EMG2, and four parameters of EMG3, discriminate between the four emotion categories. This, despite the coarse time windows that were used. Moreover, rapid processing of the signals proved to be possible. This enables tailored HCI facilitated by an emotional awareness of systems.

1   Introduction

Computers are experienced by their users as coldhearted; i.e., 'marked by lack of sympathy, interest, or sensitivity' (Merriam-Webster, 2007). However, 'during the past decade rapid advances in spoken language technology, natural language processing, dialog modeling, multi-modal interfaces, animated character design, and mobile applications all have stimulated interest in a new class of conversational interfaces' (Oviatt et al., 2004). The progress made in this broad

* This paper is an extended and updated version of Van den Broek et al. (2006), with kind permission of Springer Science and Business Media

149

range of research and technology enables the rapid computation and modeling of empathy for human-computer interaction (HCI) purposes. The latter is of importance since conversation is, apart from being an information exchange, a social activity, which is inherently enforcing (Oviatt et al., 2004). Futurists envision embodied, social artificial systems that interact in a natural manner with us. Such systems need to sense its user's emotional state.

Empathic artificial systems can, for example, prevent user frustration in HCI. Users feel frequently frustrated by various causes; e.g., error messages, timed out/dropped/refused connections, freezes, long download time, and missing/hard-to-find features (Ceaparu et al., 2004). Picard (1999) posed the prevention of user frustration as one of the main goals in HCI. When prevention is not sufficient, online detection and reduction of frustration is needed. Psychophysiological signals are expected to be useful in the detection of frustration (Picard, 1997). According to Hone, Akhtar, and Saffu (2003), an (embodied) affective agent, using techniques of active listening and empathy, could reduce user frustration.

The current paper discusses the emotions people can experience and their expression in and detection through psychophysiological measures, in Section 2 and Section 3. Next, in Section 4, affective wearables are introduced in which the proposed apparatus for the measurement of the psychophysiological signals can be embedded. In Section 5, we present an experiment into the appropriateness of various statistical measures derived from psychophysiological signals, followed by a reduction of the data in Section 6. The experimental results are described in Section 7. The paper ends with Section 8 in which the results are discussed, limitations are denoted, and future research is described.

2 Emotion

Despite the complexity of the concept of emotion, most researchers agree that emotions are acute affective states that exist in a relatively short period of time and are related to a particular event, object, or action (Ortony et al., 1988; Picard, 1997). In relation with physiology, emotions are predominantly described as points in a two-dimensional space of affective valence and arousal, in which valence represents overall pleasantness of emotional experiences ranging from negative to positive, while arousal represents the intensity level of emotion, ranging from calm to excited (Ball and Breese, 1999; Lang 1995). This allows us to tell the difference between four rough categories of emotions, when differentiated between both high and low valence and high and low arousal. Some researchers even differentiate between nine categories by including a neutral section on both the valence and arousal axis. However, an, in principle, infinite amount of other arbitrary number of categories can be defined, where the valence and arousal axes are not necessarily are divided with the same precision (Bosma and Andre, 2004).

The valence-arousal model, however, does not account for mixed emotions: positive and negative at the same moment. In order to be able to cope with mixed emotions, Larsen et al. (2003) and Konijn and Hoorn (2005) suggest that valence should be unipolar instead of bipolar. When valence is rated on two scales, one for the intensity of positive affect and one for the intensity of negative affect, mixed emotions, in the sense of both positive and negative emotions, will show. As an extension to the valence-arousal model, a unipolar valence axis, with separated positive and negative axes, might allow for a better discrimination between different emotions.

In the current research, solely the valence axis was explored. The reason is that the simplest differentiation of emotions is a differentiation between positive and negative emotions. In most cases of HCI, this is sufficient to improve the dialog between user and computer; e.g., when a user has a negative emotion, the computer can adapt its dialog to that, depending on the context.

3 Psychophysiological measures

The roots of psychophysiological aspects of emotions lay in Darwin's book 'The expression of emotions in man and animals', which he wrote in 1872. The overall assumption is that emotion arouses the autonomic nervous system (ANS), which alters the physiological state. This is expressed in various physiological measures, often stimulated through the ANS; e.g., heart rate, blood pressure, respiration rate, galvanic skin response, and muscle activity (Scerbo et al., 2001). The main advantage of using autonomic physiological measures is that autonomic variables are regulated by the ANS, which controls functions outside individual's conscious control (Scerbo et al., 2001).

In this research, we focused on how emotional experiences, rated to their positive and negative affect, are expressed in four physiological signals:

- Galvanic Skin Response (GSR), also often termed electrodermal activity (EDA; Boucsein, 1992), which is a measure of the conductivity of the skin: arousal of the ANS influences sweat glands to produce more sweat; consequently, skin conductivity increases. GSR was chosen because it is an autonomic variable; hence, it can not be controlled by the user.

- Three electromyography (EMG) signals: frontalis, corrugator supercilii, and zygomaticus major. EMG measures muscle activity of a certain muscle. Facial EMG is related to affective valence; however, the type of relation depends strongly on the muscle that is measured. The corrugator supercilii, which causes a frown when activated, increases linearly with a decrease in valence, while the zygomaticus major, which is responsible for smiling when activated, increases with an increase in valence (Lang et al., 1998). These measures were chosen because a great deal of emotional expression is located in the face (Larsen et al., 2003), as can be measured using facial EMG.

These measures have extensively proven their use to detect emotional experiences in laboratory settings, mostly in group-averaged, baseline-corrected paradigms. In order to make them useful for emotion-aware systems, three aspects will have to change:

- The measurements will have to be done in a less obtrusive manner,

- the interpretation of the signals will have to be meaningful on an individual (not a group-averaged) level,

- and robust signal interpretation algorithms will have to be developed that are baseline-free or incorporate automatic (non-manual) baseline correction.

The first issue is dealt with in the next paragraph, where we discuss the advent of unobtrusive affective wearables. Our focus for the remainder of the paper is on the search for robust signal interpretation algorithms that do not need a manual baseline correction.

4 Affective wearables

Using the GSR and EMG signals, a system will be able to determine the emotional state of its user, certainly if that system also possesses a user-profile. Affective wearables will facilitate such a system in monitoring the user in an unobtrusive manner. Direct physiological measures are often considered to be obtrusive to the user, but this is not necessarily true. In the field of affective computing, some efforts have been made to design unobtrusive measurement technology: affective wearables. Picard (1997) defines an affective wearable as "a wearable system equipped with sensors and tools which enables recognition of its wearer's affective patterns". Affective wearables become smaller in time, due to improved design and smaller technology components. Especially when hidden in daily used tools and objects, affective wearables could make a huge difference in user acceptance of direct physiological measures.

The acceptance of direct physiological measurements is of great importance since indirect physiological measurements are much more subject to noise. Indirect physiological measurements (e.g., through voice analysis; Van den Broek, 2004) have been applied in controlled settings such as telepsychiatry (Hilty et al., 2004) and evaluation of therapy effectiveness (Van den Broek, 2004).

However, outside such controlled conditions these measures have not proved to be reliable.

Measurement of physiological signals have already been embedded into wearable tools; e.g., Picard and Scheirer (2001) designed the 'Galvactivator', a glove that detects the skin conductivity and maps its values into a led display. In an overview of previous work of the Affective Computing Research Group at MIT, Picard (2000) describes several affective wearables. One affective wearable that is of interest in this research is the expression glasses. The expression glasses sense facial movements, which are recognized as affective patterns.

5 Experiment

5.1 Aim

The goal of the present experiment was to enable a search for robust (e.g. baseline-free) algorithms for use in future emotional awareness systems, which interpret positive or negative emotions from psychophysiological signals.

5.2 Subjects

24 Subjects (20 female) were invited from a volunteers database. They signed an informed consent form, and were awarded with a small incentive for their participation. They were aged between 27 and 59 years (average 43 years).

5.3 Materials

Sixteen film sequences were selected for their emotional content. Several of these sequences were described by Gross and Levenson (1995) for their capability of eliciting one unique emotion among various viewers. They were edited with Dutch subtitles, as is normal on Dutch TV and in Dutch cinemas. Since not enough material of Gross and Levenson (1995) was available with Dutch subtitles in acceptable quality, the set was completed with a number of similar sequences. The resulting video fragments each lasted between 9 seconds and 4 minutes[1]. If the fragment lasted less than 120 sec, a plain blue screen was added to make a total of 120 sec.

The video fragments were presented on a large 42″ 16:9 flat panel screen mounted on the wall of the room. Print-outs for significant scenes of each of the film fragments were used to jog the subjects memory of each film fragment after the viewing session.

---

[1] From Gross and Levenson (1995): Silence of the lambs (198 sec), When Harry met Sally (149 sec), The champ (153 sec), Sea of love (9 sec), Cry freedom (142 sec), The shining (80 sec), Pink Flamingoes (30 sec). Additional: Jackass the movie - paper-cut scene (51 sec), Static TV color bars (120 sec), The bear - intro (120 sec), Sweet home Alabama – wedding scene (121 sec), Tarzan - orchestra scene (133 sec), Abstract shapes – screen saver (120 sec), Lion King – dad's dead (117 sec); Nature documentary (120 sec), Final destination – side-walk café scene (52 sec).

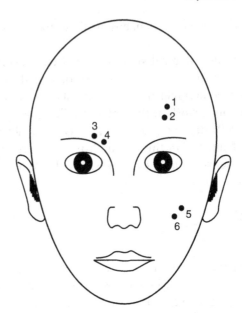

Figure 1. The points indicate the electrodes that were placed on the face of the participants to determine the EMG signals. The EMG signals of the frontalis, corrugator supercilii, and zygomaticus major were respectively measured through electrodes 1–2, 3–4, and 5–6.

The psychophysiological measurements were performed with a TMS International Porti5–16/ASD measurement system connected to a computer, in combination with TMS Portilab software. A ground electrode was attached to the right-hand lower chest area. Three EMG measurements were done: at the right-hand corrugator supercilii muscle, the left-hand zygomaticus major muscle, and the frontalis muscle above the left eye. At each site 2 electrodes were placed in the direction of the muscle (see Figure 1). These signals were first high pass filtered at 20 Hz and then the absolute difference of the two electrodes was average filtered with a time constant of 0.2 sec.

For the skin conductivity (GSR) measurements, two active electrodes were positioned on the distal phalanges of the index and ring finger of the right hand (see Figure 2). Skin conductivity was calculated from the measured signal with a time constant of about 2 sec, thus capturing GSR signal variations reliably in first order.

5.4 Procedure

At the beginning of the session, the subject was invited to take place in a comfortable chair and the electrodes were positioned: first at the fingers, then at the face. Then, the recording equipment was checked and aligned

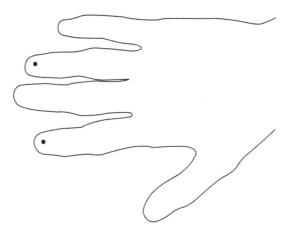

Figure 2. The points indicate the electrodes that were placed on the hands of the participants to determine the GSR signal.

when needed. A rest period of 5 minutes was taken into account. The subjects were presented with the 16 video fragments, each segment was presented only once.

A pseudo-random order of presentation was generated for the 16 video presentations. This order was designed to spread positive and negative scenes evenly over the session. It was presented to 12 subjects, each starting with a different scene in the list, but maintaining the same order. The reverse order was presented to the other 12 subjects, again each starting with a different scene while maintaining the same presentation order. In between two fragments, a plain blue screen was presented for 120 seconds.

After the measuring session, the electrodes were detached and the subject was requested to fill out a short questionnaire. In this questionnaire, representative pictures of the 16 video fragments were represented sequentially and the subject was requested to rate them according to two emotion-related axes: intensity of positive feelings and intensity of negative feelings, both on a 7-point Likert scale.

6 Data reduction

Average intensities for both positive and negative ratings were calculated for each of the film fragments, allowing for a classification of the fragments in 4 emotion categories: neutral, mixed, positive, negative. In each emotion category, the two fragments with a duration closest to 120 seconds were selected for further analysis (see Table 1).

The EMG data of 2 subjects appeared to be corrupt; therefore, these datasets were not analyzed. For the other subjects, the GSR signal and three EMG signals (of the frontalis, corrugator supercilii, and zygomaticus major) were

Table 1. The sixteen film scenes with the average ratings with the accompanying standard deviations (between brackets) given by the subjects (n=24) on both experienced negative and positive feelings. Based on the latter two dimensions, four emotion categories are founded: neutral, mixed, positive, and negative. The top eight film scenes were selected for further analysis.

Film scene	Positive	Negative	Emotion category
Color bars	1.60 (1.43)	2.20 (2.04)	neutral
Abstract figures	1.20 (0.70)	2.10 (1.94)	neutral
The bear	5.15 (1.50)	1.65 (0.88)	positive
Tarzan	5.10 (1.17)	1.50 (0.95)	positive
Final destination	3.11 (1.70)	4.32 (1.63)	mixed
Lion King	3.85 (2.21)	3.65 (1.93)	mixed
Cry freedom	1.95 (1.54)	6.25 (1.07)	negative
Pink flamingos	1.75 (1.20)	5.60 (1.54)	negative
Silence of the lambs	2.30 (1.38)	3.85 (1.73)	neutral
When Harry met Sally	4.60 (1.47)	1.80 (1.15)	positive
The champ	2.65 (1.46)	4.35 (1.05)	mixed
Jackass the movie	1.85 (1.57)	5.95 (1.47)	negative
Sea of love	2.15 (1.31)	3.90 (1.74)	neutral
Sweet home Alabama	4.35 (1.66)	1.70 (1.26)	positive
The shining	2.65 (1.39)	3.55 (1.47)	neutral
Nature documentary	4.50 (2.04)	1.45 (1.28)	positive

processed in order to determine their discriminating ability on the four emotion categories induced by the eight films. To determine the latter, six parameters (mean, absolute deviation, standard deviation, variance, skewness, and kurtosis) were derived from the four signals. Where the mean, standard deviation, and average deviation are well-known dimensional quantities (i.e., have the same units as the measured quantities x_j), the skewness and kurtosis are conventionally defined as non-dimensional quantities. Both skewness and kurtosis are less well known statistical measures and both are defined in several ways (Press et al., 1992; Weisstein, 2002). Therefore, we provide the definitions as adopted in the current research.

The skewness characterizes the degree of asymmetry of a distribution around its mean. It characterizes only the shape of the distribution. The usual definition is (Press et al., 1992; Weisstein, 2002):

$$Skewness(x_1 \ldots x_N) = \frac{1}{N} \sum_{j=1}^{N} \left[\frac{x_j - \bar{x}}{\sigma} \right]^3,$$

where $\sigma = \sigma(x_1 \ldots x_N)$ is the distribution's standard deviation. A positive value of skewness signifies a distribution with an asymmetric tail extending out towards more positive *x*; a negative value signifies a distribution whose tail extends out towards more negative *x*.

Kurtosis measures the relative peakedness or flatness of a distribution relative to a normal distribution. We applied kurtosis as (Press et al., 1992; Weisstein, 2002):

$$Kurtosis(x_1 \ldots x_N) = \left\{ \frac{1}{N} \sum_{j=1}^{N} \left[\frac{x_j - \bar{x}}{\sigma} \right]^4 \right\} - 3,$$

where the −3 term makes the value zero for a normal distribution.

7   Results

For each of the six statistical parameters, for each film fragment, and for each subject, the complete GSR and EMG signals were processed over the last 120 seconds of the film fragment. The duration of 120 seconds was chosen because it was available for the majority of the scenes. Two film fragments were shorter than that, and for them we included measurements taken during the blue screen following it in order to add up to a section of 120 seconds as well (see also Section 5.3). Note that we deliberately did not correct these values for their baseline, because – however useful in academic research – the baseline-correction procedure is not easily applicable in future emotionally aware systems.

Due to corrupted recordings during a few films with two of the subjects, the measurements of these two subjects were not taken into account. Moreover, for the same reason, the recordings of one subject, during the film scene of the "Pink flamingos", were skipped. For each parameter of each physiological measure, a repeated measures ANOVA was conducted, with the four emotions, each measured with two film scenes, as within-subject factors. So, a total of 24 (4 * 6) repeated measures ANOVAs were conducted.

The EMG of the frontalis did not provide a significant discrimination between the four emotion categories on any of the statistical parameters. Of all physiological measures, the zygomaticus major signal is the most discriminative physiological signal (see Table 2). The mean, absolute deviation, standard deviation and variance calculated over the zygomaticus major EMG signal showed strong significant effects of emotions. Significant effects did also show in the skewness and kurtosis of the GSR signal and the skewness of the corrugator supercilii EMG signal (Table 2). For the skewness of the zygomaticus EMG signal a trend is present (F(3,18) = 3.013, p = 0.057) over the four emotions.

Table 2. The discriminating statistical parameters for the galvanic skin response (GSR), EMG corrugator supercilii, and EMG zygomaticus signals. For each parameter, the average value for all four emotion categories is provided as well as the strength and significance of its discriminating ability.

Physiological measure	Statistic parameter	average value on				effect ($F(3,18)$)	
		neu-tral	posi-tive	mixed	nega-tive	strength	signifi-cance
GSR	skewness	0.46	0.01	−0.15	0.39	7.289	p = 0.002
	kurtosis	−0.66	−0.78	0.55	−0.19	3.812	p = 0.028
EMG corrugator supercilii	skewness	1.99	2.84	3.49	3.29	3.500	p = 0.037
EMG zygomaticus	mean	2.74	5.21	3.15	3.53	9.711	p < 0.001
	abs. dev.	1.64	3.77	2.10	2.42	8.369	p < 0.001
	SD	2.46	6.01	3.68	3.96	5.837	p = 0.006
	variance	7.23	63.82	18.69	23.21	4.064	p = 0.023

8 Discussion

8.1 Comparison with literature

Most 120 sec. averaged values of the physiological signals did not yield significant effects of emotion category, in contrast to what is generally reported in literature. One of the reasons might be that we chose not to correct our data for baseline values, as is common in psychophysiological literature. Another factor is that the present analysis was chosen to extend over a relatively long period of time including the beginning of the video fragment in which the targeted emotions were still in the process of getting elicited, which might have diminished the differences between categories of emotions.

For the zygomaticus major, we did find an effect for the average value, even when not corrected for baseline and averaged over 120 sec. This is in line with results of previous research of Larsen, Norris, and Cacioppo (2003), who concluded that valence influences both the corrugator supercilii and the zygomaticus major. They found that valence had a stronger effect on the corrugator supercilii than on the zygomaticus major in experiencing standardized affective pictures, sounds, and words, while our research shows a stronger effect of emotions on the mean zygomaticus major signal, than on the corrugator supercilii. In addition, the effect is present with four statistical parameters of the zygomaticus major, where it is only present in one statistical parameter (skewness) of the corrugator supercilii. The difference in strength of the effects found between the current research and that of Larsen, Norris, and Cacioppo (2003) can possibly be explained by the absence of a baseline correction in our procedure. Another difference between the two researches is the type of stimuli. Film scenes are dynamic and multi-modal, they induce emotions by both auditory and dynamic visual stimuli, as well as affective words, in some fragments. The dynamic and multi-modal characteristics of the film scenes also provide good means to build up emotions, or to create a shock effect. This is not possible with affective words, sounds or pictures of a static character. On the one hand, all these factors give film scenes a relatively high degree of ecological validity (Gross and Levenson, 1995). On the other hand, it can not be determined which modality influences the emotional state of the subjects to the highest extent.

For three of the four physiological signals the parameter skewness turned out to be important as a significant effect or as a trend. The skewness (and kurtosis) of EMG signals have been topic of previous research, although its use as discriminating descriptors is limited to only a few studies. In 1983, Cacioppo, Marshall-Goodell and Dorfman (1983) analyzed among a number of parameters, the skewness and kurtosis of skeletal muscle patterns, recorded through EMGs. Four years later, a paper of Cacioppo and Dorfman (1987) was published that discusses "waveform moment analysis in psychophysiological research" in general. In 1989, Hess et al. (1989) conducted research toward experiencing and showing happy feelings, also using video segments. Hess et al. (1989) recorded four facial EMG signals and extracted the mean, variance, skewness and kurtosis of these signals. The current research is distinct from that of Hess et al. (1989) since it distinguishes four emotion categories instead of the presence or absence of only one.

8.2   Use in products

Not all investigated parameters of all measures proved to be equally suited for sensing human's emotional state. This is no doubt due to the demanding analysis conditions we imposed: No baseline correction and averages over relatively long time intervals. Nevertheless, even under these demanding analysis conditions, still some of the measures succeed in distinguishing between the respective emotion categories.

For three of the four physiological signals used, the parameter skewness proved to be an interesting source of information. The skewness of the distributions of the data of two of the physiological signals differs significantly over the four emotions, where a trend is present for a third signal. The skewness characterizes the degree of asymmetry of a distribution around its mean. To inspect more distribution details of the signals, additional analyses could be conducted. Measures such as the slope of the signal and the peak density could be taken into account for further analysis.

In addition to adding more descriptors of the physiological signals, the time windows of measurement can be changed. In the current setup, the time window enclosed the complete length of the film scene. However, smaller time windows (e.g., 10 or 30 sec.) can be applied. Moreover, dynamic time windows can be applied that enclose the time directly after a critical event (if any) appeared in the film scene. The drawback of the latter approach is that it can not be applied in practice, while it can be expected to prove good results for data gathered through experimentation, as in the current research.

A more general notion that can have a significant impact on measurement of emotions is that the emotional state of people changes over time, due to various circumstances. Moreover, different persons have different emotional experiences during the same events, objects, or actions. The latter is determined by a person's personality. Personality traits correlate with affective states, especially with the personality traits extraversion and neuroticism, which have been linked both theoretically and empirically to the fundamental affective states of positive and negative affect, respectively (Matzler et al., 2005). Hence, to enable tailored communication strategies in HCI, not only the emotional state of a person should be determined but also his personality. When the system possesses a personality profile of its user, it will be able to react appropriately to its user's emotions by selecting a suitable communication strategy.

We conclude that the set of psychophysiological measures as introduced suits the vision of 'ambient emotion-aware intelligence', which is characterized as embedded, aware, natural, personalized, adaptive, and anticipatory. With the robust algorithms presented, the measurement of the psychophysiological signals can be embedded in wearables, can facilitate awareness for systems connected to it, can aim to mimic human empathy (i.e., is natural), can be connected to a user-profile, and can facilitate in utilizing knowledge to anticipate on people's mood and adapt its communication strategy.

References

Ball, G. and Breese, J.: Modeling the emotional state of computer users. In: Workshop on Attitude, Personality and Emotions in User-Adapted Interaction, Banff, Canada (1999).

Bosma, W. and Andre, E.: Exploiting emotions to disambiguate dialogue acts. In: Proceedings of the 9th International Conference on Intelligent User Interface, Funchal, Madeira, Portugal, ACM Press: New York, NY, USA (2004) 85–92.

Boucsein, W.: *Electrodermal Activity*, Plenum Press, NY, 1992.

Cacioppo, J.T. and Dorfman, D.D.: Waveform movement analysis in psychophysiological research. *Psychological Bulletin* 102 (1987) 421–438.

Cacioppo, J.T., Marshall-Goodell, B. and Dorfman, D.D.: Skeletal muscular patterning: Topographical analysis of the integrated electromyogram. *Psychophysiology* 20 (1983) 269–283.

Ceaparu, I., Lazar, J., Bessiere, K., Robinson, J. and Shneiderman, B.: Determining causes and severity of end-user frustration. *International Journal of Human-Computer Interaction* 17 (2004) 333–356.

Gross, J.J. and Levenson, R.W.: Emotion elicitation using films. *Cognition and Emotion* 9 (1995) 87–108.

Hess, U., Kappas, A., McHugo, G.J., Kleck, R.E. and Lanzetta, J.T.: Analysis of the encoding and decoding of spontaneous and posed smiles: The use of facial electromyography. *Journal of Nonverbal Behavior* 13 (1989) 121–137.

Hilty, D.M., Marks, S.L., Urness, D., Yellowlees, P.M. and Nesbitt, T.S.: Clinical and educational telepsychiatry applications: A review. *The Canadian Journal of Psychiatry* 49 (2004) 12–23.

Hone, K., Akhtar, F. and Saffu, M.: Affective agents to reduce user frustration: the role of agent embodiment. In: Proceedings of Human-Computer Interaction (HCI2003), Bath, UK (2003).

Konijn, E.A. and Hoorn, J.F.: Some like it bad. Testing a model for perceiving and experiencing fictional characters. *Media Psychology* 7 (2005) 107–144.

Lang, P.J.: The emotion probe: Studies of motivation and attention. *American Psychologist* 52 (1995) 372–385.

Lang, P.J., Bradley, M.M. and Cuthbert, B.N.: Emotion, motivation, and anxiety: Brain mechanisms and psychophysiology. *Biological Psychiatry* 44 (1998) 1248–1263.

Larsen, J.T., Norris, C.J. and Cacioppo, J.T.: Effects of positive and negative affect on electromyographic activity over zygomaticus major and corrugator supercilii. *Psychophysiology* 40 (2003) 776–785.

Matzler, K., Faullant, R., Renzl, B. and Leiter, V.: The relationship between personality traits (extraversion and neuroticism), emotions and customer self-satisfaction. *Innovative Marketing* 1 (2005) 32–39.

Merriam-Webster, Incorporated: Merriam-Webster Online. URL: http://www.m-w.com/ [Last accessed on February 27, 2007].

Ortony, A., Clore, G.L. and Collins, A.: *The Cognitive Structure of Emotions*. Cambridge, New York: Cambridge University Press (1988).

Oviatt, S.L., Darves, C. and Coulston, R.: Toward adaptive conversational interfaces: Modeling speech convergence with animated personas. *ACM Transactions on Computer-Human Interaction* 11 (2004) 300–328.

Picard, R.: Affective computing for HCI. In: Proceedings of HCI International (the 8th International Conference on Human-Computer Interaction) on Human-Computer Interaction: Ergonomics and User Interfaces. Volume 1, Lawrence Erlbaum Associates, Inc: Mahwah, NJ, USA (1999) 829–833.

Picard, R.: *Affective Computing*. Boston MA.: MIT Press (1997).

Picard, R.W.: Toward computers that recognize and respond to user emotion. *IBM Systems Journal* 39 (2000) 705–719.

Picard., R.W. and Scheirer, J.: The galvactivator: A glove that senses and communicates skin conductivity. In: Proceedings of the 9th International Conference on Human-Computer Interaction, New Orleans (2001).

Press, W.H., Flannery, B.P., Teukolsky, S.A. and Vetterling, W.T.: Numerical recipes in C: The art of scientific computing. 2nd edition. Cambridge, England: Cambridge University Press (1992).

Scerbo, M.W., Freeman, F.G., Mikulka, P.J., Parasuraman, R. and Di Nocero, F.: The efficacy of psychophysiological measures for implementing adaptive technology. Technical Report NASA/TP-2001–211018, NASA Center for AeroSpace Information (CASI) (2001).

Van den Broek, E.L.: Emotional Prosody Measurement (EPM): A voice-based evaluation method for psychological therapy effectiveness. *Studies in Health Technology and Informatics (Medical and Care Compunetics 1)* 103 (2004) 118–125.

Van den Broek, E.L., Schut, M.H., Westerink, J.H.D.M., Van Herk, J., and Tuinenbreijer, K., Computing Emotion Awareness Through Facial Electromyography, in: Thomas S. Huang, Nicu Sebe, Michael S. Lew, Vladimir Pavlovic, Mathias Kölsch, Aphrodite Galata, Branislav Kisacanin (Eds), Lecture Notes in Computer Science, Volume 3979/2006, ISBN: 3-540-34202-8, Computer Vision in Human-Computer Interaction: ECCV 2006 Workshop on HCI, Graz, Austria, May 13, 2006. Proceedings, pages 52–63

Weisstein, E.W.: CRC Concise Encyclopedia of Mathematics. 2nd edition. Chapman & Hall/ CRC: USA (2002).

15

UNOBTRUSIVE SENSING OF PSYCHOPHYSIOLOGICAL PARAMETERS

Some Examples of Non-Invasive Sensing Technologies

Martin Ouwerkerk, Frank Pasveer and Geert Langereis

Abstract   The quantification of the human perception of experiences can be achieved by the sensing of specific psychophysiological parameters. A growing interest develops for the daily life use of these quantification techniques by unobtrusive and unnoticeable data collection. Remote and non invasive sensing technologies are discussed for the sensing of the following psychophysiological parameters: heart rate variability, and muscle stress. A generic miniature platform for miniature wireless sensing applications is described as an important enabler for unobtrusive and unnoticeable sensing. The technology no longer seems to be a limiting factor for unobtrusive and unnoticeable sensing. Initially the sensors will be worn on the body, but ultimately implantable sensors will become widely accepted, allowing access to new parameters, such as hormone levels and body core temperature.

1 Introduction

Psychophysiological parameters, such as heart rate variability, galvanic skin response, breathing rhythm and muscle stress provide important information on the emotional and cognitive state of a person. Monitoring these parameters thus provides information on the perception of a person in daily life. For Philips the ability of probing the experiences of people is a long standing wish for a multitude of applications. In order to obtain unbiased and accurate sensor data the person under scrutiny needs to be unaware of the sensors. Above all it is important that the presence of the sensors is not disturbing or influencing the wearer.

The ultimate goal for supporting technology in the field of measuring experience is the availability of unnoticeable maintenance free sensors, wirelessly transmitting for example a person's emotional status in a real-time fashion. Clearly some steps are needed to achieve this, so in the short term researchers in the field have to make do with what is available now. This paper does not claim to present an overview of the current hardware capabilities for probing

163

J.H.D.M. Westerink et al. (eds.), Probing Experience, 163–193.
© 2008 *Springer.*

experience. It does however try to give the reader a flavour of what is currently being studied at Philips Research in terms of unnoticeable and unobtrusive sensing of psychophysiological parameters.

A distinction can be made between laboratory environment testing and field testing. Field testing requires wearable equipment often capable of maintenance free operation for days or even weeks, whereas laboratory experiments can be operator assisted, hardwired, recorded on video et cetera. In Figure 1 a cartoon shows an exaggerated representation of what the consequence is of the attempt to collect data simultaneously on a large number of parameters: the person under scrutiny clearly is influenced by the presence of the sensor equipment, leading to a distorted outcome of the experiments.

A valuable source of data for the interpretation of the experience of sensations is the measurement of electrical activity in the brain (Electro Encephalogram, EEG). Unfortunately the application of a multitude of EEG probes on the human skull is bound to influence the wearer significantly. Undistorted or minimally distorted sensor data can be obtained only when the sensors are not noticed by the wearer. In most cases this rules out equipment such as high resolution cameras for facial expression interpretation.

Figure 1. A typical example of obtrusive monitoring (cartoon by Wim Boost, http://nl.wikipedia.org/wiki/Wim_Boost).

An exception may be when the camera can be positioned in a place where the person under test is not capable of detecting its presence, for instance behind a semi transparent mirror.

Special emphasis will be given in this paper on the recording of psychophysiological information in a daily life setting in an unnoticeable and unobtrusive manner.

This paper endeavours to discuss in detail the work on three areas of unobtrusive sensing which are seen as interesting for Philips: heart rate variability sensing from a chair, muscle stress sensing from clothing and a platform for miniature wireless sensors.

2 Contactless sensors for electrophysiological signals

2.1 Electrophysiological signals

All living cells are surrounded by membranes. These membranes are selectively permeable for various ions and may actively transport them through the membrane resulting into a membrane potential. Nerve cells and muscle fibres are depolarised when activated by a certain threshold voltage. The result is the propagation of a depolarisation wave along the nerve and muscle fibre (Basmajian and Luca, 1985; Merletti and Parker, 2004). A depolarisation wave over the muscle fibre is the direct cause of muscular contraction and is subsequently followed by relaxation. The heart consists of muscle fibres which are synchronised when contracting. This results into a deterministic action potential over the heart tissue. For skeletal muscles, the quick combination of contraction and relaxation of a muscle fibre is referred to as "twitch". Since all muscle fibres in a muscle do not twitch simultaneously, the overall observed potential over a muscle is the random summation of multiple single fibre action potentials. For both the heart and skeletal muscles, the electrical waves in the muscle fibres are conducted to the surface of the skin. When measuring the potential on the human skin due to the depolarisation of the heart we speak of the electrocardiogram (ECG), for monitoring skeletal muscle activity on the surface of the skin we speak of surface electromyography (sEMG). In clinical environments, other methods of electromyography are used. For example, by placing metal needles as electrodes in the muscle tissue we obtain a high precision variant of EMG called needle EMG. For unobtrusive sensinf, the use of surface EMG is the most promising.

Figure 2 shows the depolarisation in a skeletal muscle and the conduction into a surface EMG signal. The muscle of the heart depolarises autonomically, but the transfer into skin surface potentials is similar.

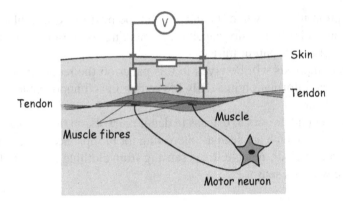

Figure 2. Schematic representation of the transfer of action potentials in a neuron to ionic currents in the muscle fibres and potential distributions on the skin.

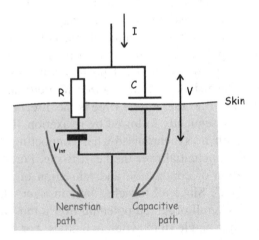

Figure 3. Electrode-tissue interface with components representing the ionic to electronic transition phenomena.

2.2 Contactless sensors

What sEMG and ECG have in common are the electrodes to pick up the skin potentials. A problem with such electrodes is that the interface potential between the skin and the solid electrode is a cause of noise and artefacts. In Figure 3, a closer view of the skin-electrode interface is drawn.

The electrical potentials in the human skin are induced by ionic currents, while electrical currents in the electrodes are the result of moving electrons.

This means that somewhere there is an ion-electron transition which results into a so-called overpotential (Webster, 1992).

There are two parallel paths by which the signal can be transferred from the skin to the electrode. First, there is the Nernstian path, characterised by a transfer resistance and an interface potential. The resistance is the result of dead cells in the stratum corneum and can therefore be reduced by sanding the skin or wetting the electrode. The interface potential is the result of an electrochemical transition described by the Nernst equation. Because the ionic strengths in the skin may differ in time and place, this interface potential is not stable. This is the reason that in conventional electrodes sometimes an AgCl load is included in the gel. This will form a well defined interface potential with the chloride ions in the skin.

So with conventional electrodes, wetting, sanding and AgCl loading is used to stabilise the Nernstian path. Another approach could be to benefit from the other path. This is the path in which signals are coupled directly from the skin to the electrode capacitively. To do this, we simply apply an insulating layer to the electrode surface and take care there is a nice parallel plate configuration of the electrode to the skin.

This was first demonstrated by Richardson of the US Airforce in 1967 (Richardson, 1967) and improved at the Case Western Reserve University in the early 1970's (Ko et al., 1970). It took over thirty years before some academic groups managed to employ modern semiconductor technology to realise small interface amplifiers. Groups structurally working on contactless ECG can be found at the University of Sussex (Harland et al., 2003) and the Seoul National University (Kim and Park, 2005). An American company Quantum Applied Science and Research Inc. (QUASAR) has developed contactless sensors for heart rate monitoring in 2001 as a DARPA project. The results are some patents in the field of capacitive sensors and electrical circuitry to stabilise the input signal (Quasar patents and patent applications).

2.3 Advantages and disadvantages of contactless sensors

The electrical consequence of a capacitive transducer is the high input impedance needed to track the ECG and sEMG signals which have components below 1 Hz. Due to this high impedance, the electrode acts as an antenna for environmental noise. To minimise the noise, active electronics is needed directly on top of the electrode. So complete textile integration will not be possible, there will always be a small module attached to the electrode. Design proposals for such a module are described in section 2.4. Such a module will hamper the options for washability of optional clothing with integrated contactless EMG/ECG electrodes.

Another disadvantage is that the capacitive transducer is more sensitive to motion artefacts than fixed electrodes. The electrical operation of a capacitor is described by the equation

$$i = C\frac{du}{dt} + u\frac{dC}{dt}$$

with i the current through the capacitor, u the voltage over the capacitor and C the instantaneous value of the capacitor. Because the capacitance C changes in time due to motions, the second term $u.cdC/dt$ is introduced. So the effect of motion dC/dt can electrically not be distinguished from heart and muscle signals dU/dt. To minimise this effect, we should take care of proper positioning of the sensor or introduce compensation of the change in the capacitor value.

Note that the problems with motion artefacts are fundamental, but can be solved in principle. Options can be found in digital signal processing techniques, which monitor the capacitance C and compensate for the fluctuations due to motion. So on the long term we expect even measurements with a clinical quality and robustness.

Nevertheless, a sensor which is not in galvanic contact to the skin has some essential advantages. It is uncomfortable to tape conventional contact electrodes onto the skin. The possibility to avoid direct skin contact reduces skin irritation problems. Contactless sensors can be implemented in the environment, for example a chair or wearable clothing. We can measure through clothes and hair and even measure on persons with burn wounds or irritated skin. In addition, the constraints with respect to safety are less critical when there is no galvanic contact.

So despite some concessions to robustness, contactless sensors may open options for new applications for monitoring electrophysiological signals. Especially monitoring over a long time in the natural environment is facilitated.

2.4   Contactless ECG

Figure 4 shows a photo of the capacitive sensors as developed at Philips Research. The size of the sensor is about 32 by 32 mm^2. The diameter of the capacitive coupling area is 14 mm, which is a trade-off between the signal strength (capacitance) and spatial resolution. In contrast to other capacitive sensors (Harland, 2003; Kim and Park, 2005; Ko et al., 1970; Quasar patent and patent applications; Richardson, 1967), care has been taken to realise an embodiment that is flexible. The rationale behind the flexible aspect of the sensor device is that enables unobtrusive measurements. The flexible

Figure 4. Philips Research flex foil capacitive sensor for electrophysiological signals.

foil is designed to be easily woven into fabric such that it is present in an unobtrusive way. Moreover, the flexing capability ensures that optimum capacitive coupling is maintained when the underlying human body surface has a curvature, which is often the case. A flex foil capacitive sensor e.g. woven into the clothing will then still continue to have good capacitive coupling with the body. A rigid shape would prevent flexing, so the curvatures of the human body will not be followed, leading to poor capacitive coupling, which deteriorates the signal strength.

The sensor can be fitted to regular EMG/ECG/EEG equipment without problems. The only difference is that the amplifier needs a small +7.5V/−7.5 V DC power supply. Presently this is because of portability insights provided by four flat rechargeable Li-polymer batteries.

An illustration of a controlled ECG measurement with the capacitive flex foil ECG sensors is shown in Figure 5. A comparison has been made between the conventional gel electrode attached to the skin and a flex foil sensor on top of a cotton shirt.

It can be observed that the flex foil sensors are capable of reproducing a signal comparable to the gel electrode measurements, however they are more prone to distortions. The latter effect is clearly seen between 69 and 70 seconds, where after 70 seconds the signal recovers to the gel electrode signal.

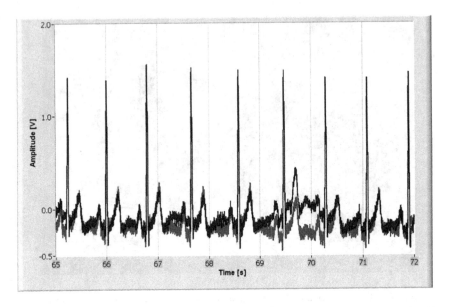

Figure 5. Comparison of a gel electrode measurement (red line) with sensors on the skin and the use of a capacitive flex foil sensor (blue line), where the sensors are put on top of a cotton shirt.

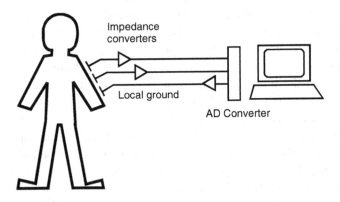

Figure 6. Set-up for contactless sensing of EMG signals.

2.5 Contactless sEMG

Figure 6 shows the bipolar set-up with two contactless electrodes with which the first EMG experiments are successfully performed. The electrodes are the same as used in the previous paragraph.

Figure 7 shows the measured EMG signal on the biceps while lifting a weight of 2.5 kg with a 90 degrees bended arm. The contactless sensors have

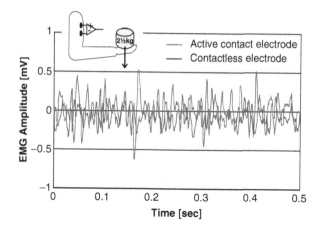

Figure 7. Recorded EMG signals with both an active- and contactless electrode.

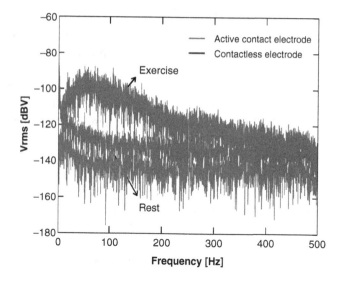

Figure 8. Spectra of the recorded EMG signals with both an active- and contactless electrode.

an electrode spacing of 37 mm and a gain of 11. It is compared to a commercial active sEMG electrode (B&L Engineering type BL-AE-N) having a spacing of 20.6 mm and a gain of 346. In Figure 7, the signals are normalised by the gains to give the skin surface voltage. Note that it is not possible to perform the two recordings simultaneously.

In Figure 8, the spectra are shown for the two measurement methods using the same data set as in Figure 7. As a reference, the spectra during rest are plotted as well. We can see that the contactless electrodes and the commercial active sEMG electrodes provide similar signal levels and shapes. Only the bottom noise during rest is a little bit higher. The bandwidth of the contactless electrode set-up is adequate and comparable to the reference measurement.

2.6   Conclusion

We have shown the feasibility of contactless sensors for monitoring surface EMG and ECG. Contactless sensors will open a whole new world of application areas because unobtrusive monitoring in our daily environment is enabled. In the next sections, we will see examples of applications.

3   Heart rate variability sensing from furniture: Sense chair

3.1   Heart rate variability sensing

The heart rate signal is known to not only give an indication of the physical state of the person, but also of his/her mental state. Well-being, attention and cognitive capabilities reside at least partially in the brain and from there they have an impact on the physiology of the body. Specifically, they influence the heart signal by varying the interval between the heart peaks in the ECG. In a study by Stephen H. Fairclough (2005), the authors monitored the EEG, ECG, EOG and respiration of thirty subjects over a learning period of 64 minutes. A multiple regression analysis revealed that specific psychophysiological variables predicted learning at different stages on the learning curve. The performance of two groups of children on a selective attention task was described in Althaus et al. (2005). EEG and cardiac activity were continuously recorded during the tasks. Decreases in specific spectra of heart rate variability were found to correlate with the degree of extraversion and task performance and with the children's temperament. It was observed that changes in attention are reflected in changes in the relative involvement of the sympathetic and the parasympathetic nervous systems on the heart. The sympathetic nervous system is known to increase heart rate, whereas the parasympathetic nervous system decreases heart rate. As a consequence, the R-R peak interval changes when the level of attention shifts. Attention is basic to and needed in many human activities. The results of the previously mentioned studies, however, were derived only after the collection and post-collection analysis of vast amounts of physiological data. It would be desirable to be able to produce indications of attention changes in real time and with minimal analytical complexity.

Probably the first application of a so-called Cepstrum technique to link with mental state is thought up by Dan Winter (http://www.soulinvitation.com/clinicalintro). He invented a real time measurement device called the Heart Tuner, which is said to measure and display moments of empathy and bliss.

The same technique could be used as a sensing algorithm capable of on-the-fly detection of attention shifts or lapses within two seconds of occurrence. By taking the Fourier transform of the last five-to-eight seconds output of ECG sensors a power spectrum can be obtained. A regular pattern of peaks occurs in this spectrum when a person has undivided attention (i.e. attention for just one subject) in this time period. Taking an inverse Fourier transform of the logarithm of the magnitude of the Fourier transform, often called Cepstrum (Bogert et al., 1963), yields in that case a strong peak at the R-R peak interval. Attention shifts or attention lapses break the short-term regularity of the R-R intervals, causing the "cepstrum peak" to (almost) disappear within two seconds.

3.2 Sense chair application

In the Ambient Intelligence (AmI) vision we anticipate a world in which technology is integrated into the fabric of everyday life (Aarts and Marzano, 2004). The present-day availability of powerful, low-energy sensors with small dimensions enables us to embed sensor networks into furniture. In this study we investigate concepts for the design of a smart chair for the purpose of sensing psychophysiological information, this information will be ultimately used to interact actively with changes in the environment.

3.2.1 Technology The aim of the Emotion-sensing Chair is to sense human physiological parameters, such as heart rate (ECG) or muscle strain (EMG) in a non-invasive manner. Small flat sensors on a flex foil have been developed which capture the ECG and EMG signals by means of capacitive coupling. The method of sensing ECG via capacitive coupling allows for non-skin contacted measurements and as such the sensors are placed behind the textile fabric of the upholstery of the chair. Capacitive coupling thus makes it possible to measure physiological parameters (e.g. ECG) in an unobtrusive and unnoticeable way. The flex foil capacitive sensors are invisibly present in the back of the chair. The high sensitivity of the sensors allows the measurement of the heart and muscle signals through both the textile of the chair and the clothing of the person. As soon as a person sits down, sensing is activated and heart and muscle activity data can be extracted and analyzed by appropriate algorithms. These algorithms e.g. link the heart rate via a wireless link to the light colour, illumination level, or the type of music that is playing.

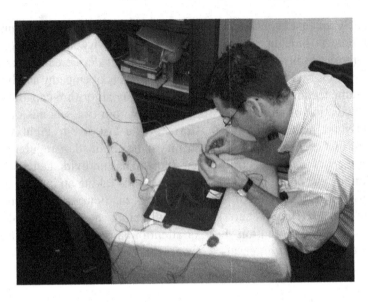

Figure 9. Preparing the sense chair. Amongst the sensor the capacitive groundplane is clearly visible.

3.2.2 Feasability A first prototype of the Emotion-sensing Chair was built using the Philips Research flexfoil capacitive sensors in a standard chair; see Figure 9. The chair contained sensors in the back and the bottom of the seat as well as in the armrests. A pad in the bottom was applied to ground the signals collected by the sensors.

The sensor output was collected using standard computer equipment. The idea is that this high sensitivity combined with smart noise reduction measures results in a high reliability in capturing the ECG and EMG signals.

A good example of obtained sensor data is shown in Figure 10, where the person is sitting in the chair wearing a cotton shirt with the sensors placed behind the upholstery of the chair. The peaks corresponding to the heart beat are clearly discovered in this graph, although the signal is only about 30–40 mV.

Additional digital signal processing can be used to obtain extra information. For instance, the onset of fatigue can be interpreted by analyzing muscle firing frequencies, or even emotional or mood changes can be derived from values such as the heart rate variability (HRV). The sensitivity of the HRV to emotional changes is obvious, but to ensure a correct and accurate interpretation requires careful study with users in a realistic context. A promising application domain for the Emotion sensing Chair is that of "Active Relaxation". By means of biofeedback, users can for instance be supported in achieving a more relaxed state.

One project demonstrator uses the capability of the chair to sense the heart rate of a person sitting in the chair and make the beating of the heart audible. Additionally, music is played with the same rhythm, as an alternative form of

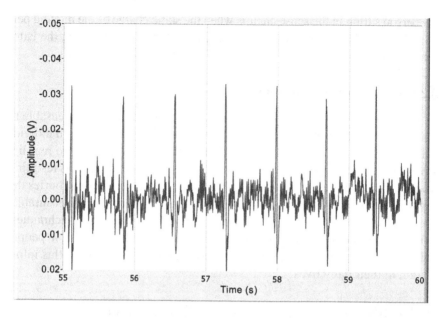

Figure 10. Sense chair sensor output with sensors behind heart and under lower right arm, using the capacitive ground plane below the legs.

biofeedback. It is envisioned that slowly decreasing the tempo of the music can help people to relax both physically and mentally. With the project demonstrator in Home Lab, the effectiveness of explicit and implicit biofeedback, such as music, can be investigated.

Feasibility studies in a realistic environment, as provided by Home Lab, showed that apart from the electrical signals emanating from the person sitting in the chair a multitude of other signals are detected by the system. The most prominent is the 50 Hz signal caused by the mains power lines. These signals are actually impinged onto the human body of the person sitting in the sense chair from elsewhere in the room, causing the sensors to couple into them through capacitors. Notch filtering eliminates most of this noise problem. A different problem that is much harder to tackle is interference from other people present in the same room. Motions of other persons cause charging and discharging effects in the person sitting in the chair, which in turn are picked up by the capacitive sensors. The resulting signals turned out to be of high amplitude and are almost impossible to filter out. As a result the signal quality of the ECG and EMG signals reduced severely. Another manifestation of the induced charging/discharging effects due to motion of people present in the same environment is that the signals could get so strong that the 50 Hz mains signal blocking notch filters were turned off-sync, because the signal went out o the operational range of the amplifier. The only way to solve the problem of induced charging/discharging of moving persons and objects in the vicinity of the person sitting in the sense chair is when the static charge of the moving persons is reduced by counter-measures, such as ion showers. However, the latter can be regarded as unacceptable from a user point of view.

3.3 Concluding remarks

The studies with the Emotion sensing Chair showed that it was feasable to build a chair that could remotely sense biometrical information of an individual, such as his ECG and EMG. However, putting the chair into the real-life environment of Home Lab, where there are many interfering signals resulting from the presence of electronic equipment as well as other persons, buries the captured body signals in noise to a degree that they become immeasurable. This calls for the development of sophisticated noise reduction techniques. After this problem has been resolved, the question will remain how people will react to the feedback given by the chair and how they will use this information in their daily lives.

4 Textile integration and the ConText project

An excellent embodiment of a health monitoring device is a wearable system, for example a health awareness system in cloths. Cloths are natural possessions and are part of the processes and routines in our daily life. The technological drive is to integrate sensors and electronics in textiles in such a way that the usage and advantages of cloths are maintained. A high level of textile integration has to be combined with aspects of reliability, comfort and wash resistance.

The ConText project (http://www.context-project.org/) was initiated to develop a wearable vest with sEMG sensors for constant monitoring of muscle activity. It is based on contactless sensors integrated into textile, hence the name "ConText". The vest measures muscle activity in order to derive the psychological stress level of a person. The first contactless sensors were the ones developed in the heart monitoring projects as described in section 2.4. By exploiting the research in a European project, we could benefit from the project partners to facilitate integration into textiles.

This chapter first describes the market of medical monitoring systems for home use. Next, a short introduction of the topic of stress is given after which the technical challenges of textile integration are summarised. The chapter ends with some measurements using textile integrated sEMG sensors.

4.1 Personalised health and musculoskeletal disorders

The healthcare market is currently subject to a structural change. Healthcare expenditures are currently focused on professional consultancy after an individual has become ill. This is an expensive system due to the high costs of medical examinations, interventions and hospital beds. One solution to reduce the healthcare costs is to put our efforts on the pre-intervention chain from health management, prevention, self-diagnosis to home monitoring. The technologies to enable this are gathered under the personalised health and electronic health monitoring concepts: pHealth and eHealth. The health monitoring tools are no longer solely prescribed by the professional but more and more the individual patient can buy health monitoring equipment in the shop. The World Health Organisation requires that every country develops a pHealth strategy within four years (Jean-Claude Healy eHealth technologies for the citizen centred health system).

A health monitoring tool like the ConText vest is an answer to this call. The initial class of diseases to be addressed are the musculoskeletal disorders (MSD). MSD occur when there is a mismatch between the physical requirements and the physical capacity of the human body. The term MSD refers to a group of disorders with similar characteristics like myalgia and tendonitis (Armstrong, 1993). MSD are caused by a combination of factors such as repetitive motion, force exertion, psychological and physiological stress, vibration and bad posture. For example, high physical and mental job demands can cause work-related musculoskeletal disorders (WMSD). WMSD have both personal consequences, such as discomfort, pain, malfunctioning and disability, and socio-economical consequences such as reduced productivity, reduced performance and absenteeism (http://wmsd.org). Over 40 million workers in all sectors are affected. The most common occurences are Repetitive Strain Injury (RSI) and lower back pain. They are responsible for forty to fifty percent of all work-related ill-health and lead to losses of 0.5 to 2% of GNP per year. The problem is noticed by the European Commission and reported in two memo's (European Commission press release IP/04/1358; http://agency.osha. eu.int/publications/reports/201/en/index.htm). The EU Advisory Committee on Safety, Hygiene and Health at work emphasizes that a number of measures should be taken to enable successful prevention of WMSD.

A tool to measure the pathomechanisms of MSD could be very useful. Wearable electronics can assist appropriate medical management by early diagnosis of symptoms and detection of MSD for enabling prompt treatment and proper rehabilitation.

4.2 Measuring stress

The scope of the ConText project is to investigate the influences of fatigue and stress on muscle activity. The human body is experiencing stress, whether this stress is pure physiological or psychophysiological, as a threatening situation. A strong hormonal reaction is provoked: the level of cortisol and norepinephrine in the body is augmented. This increase from the stress hormones brings the body in a condition with increased alertness where the surviving instinct of the body is augmented: increased heart rate, increased blood pressure, and increased muscle tension. This reaction is the so-called 'fight or flight'-reaction of the body. The secondary needs (emotions and thinking) are turned of by the body as they are not needed. Recent research did establish a relationship between stress and increase in muscle activity. It has been shown by Westgaard et al (1987) that an additional complex mental task to a postural load increases the muscle activity significantly in the M. Trapezius pars ascendens. Note that it is difficult to distinguish the muscle activity from postural load and the increased muscle activity from stress. Interpretation of the signals may be assisted by electrocardiography (ECG) signals and the output of and accelerometers.

The development of a stress algorithm would enable a bio-feedback signal that allows the reduction of stress at work or in other applications like sports, and revalidation specifically or WMSD in general.

4.3 Technical challenges

The textile industry in Europe sees electronic and functional textiles as a good opportunity for new growth, in view of the competition from the Far East. The textile industry is very focused on innovation as a means of increasing turnover and profit. However, one should realise that garment manufacturers are still very conservative. They are not interested in participating in the development process, although they are interested in incorporating the electronic devices once the development is completed and proven successful.

Apart from electronic textiles there is also a lot of development in passive, functional textiles. These textiles have special properties that give them extra functionality, for example textiles with antibacterial coatings that decrease the chance of infection in hospital or textiles with very high strength used in construction. A combination between active electronic components and passive functional textiles can be very interesting.

The link between personalised health and wearable electronics defines the technical requirements on electronic textiles. The most important are:

- Higher level of **textile integration**. Many products and demonstrators still contain metal wiring and big rigid blocks with the electronics. Further textile integration will make the devices more comfortable for the user and more "ambient intelligent".

- For wearable devices the **power supply** should be wireless and wearable. At the moment, batteries that are used are too heavy and too large. Flexible solar cells are an option, but are not so commonly available yet and are technically not good enough yet.

- **Connections** between flexible textile and rigid electronic components. Electronic textiles are now a combination of rigid ICs and other electronic components combined on a textile substrate. The connection between the two is one of the major points of failure. Consider the ConText project in which contactless electrical bio signal monitoring electrodes are used. A direct consequence of capacitive contactless sensors is that an electronic impedance converter must be placed as close as possible to the electrode. Therefore we must solve the interconnect problem because we can no longer put the active electronics in a removable box on the belt. The STELLA project focuses on technology for flexible substrates and stiff electronics.

- Overall robustness of the system, especially the **washability**. Mechanical stability upon stretching and flexing.

These technical challenges will in the end result into electronic functions integrated in our daily environment. These electronic functions, both sensing and actuating, will change our daily live by making professional medical and psychological guidance available. So, besides developing technology, it is extremely important to do structured research on what continuous and unobtrusive monitoring can do. An example of a project where the application development is balanced with technology research is described in the next paper.

4.4   Textile EMG sensors

The sensor as shown in Figure 11, was developed with the Fraunhofer Institute (IZM) from Berlin (Linz et al., 2007). It consists of an embroidered electrode on a woven substrate. The electrode is electrically shielded by a metal

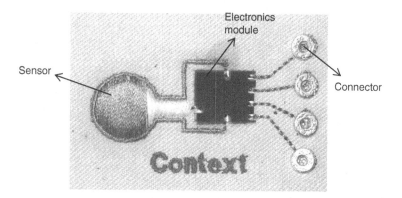

Figure 11.   Embroidered Sensor with interconnection to the electronic module and snap fasteners as interface to the computer (Fraunhofer IZM Berlin).

cup which is embroidered as well. The module with electronics is electrically connected in the same embroidery process.

To evaluate the embroidered capacitive transducers, without having the problems of motion artefacts and noise of the human body, an artificial muscle model was used. Figure 12 shows the hardware model. The muscle itself is emulated by a strip of moderately resistive paper. By two aluminium beams, an electrical current can be forced through this muscle. On top of the muscle, a leather chamois is used which mimics the human skin. On the chamois we can put several types of textile on which in its turn the sensor is placed. So, the model does imitate the

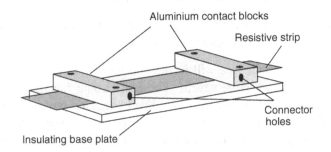

Figure 12.   Artificial muscle model.

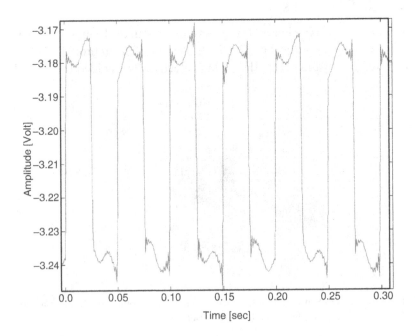

Figure 13.   Square wave recorded in capacitive manner.

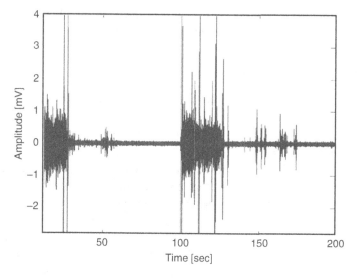

Figure 14.   Bipolar EMG on a human biceps recorded in a capacitive manner.

contactless behaviour and the distributed shape of a buried muscle, but does not include the human tissue volume conductor properties.

A waveform generator was connected to the artificial muscle. A square wave of 1 Volt peak to peak with a frequency of 20 Hz was generated. Figure 13 shows the recorded signal by using a single embroidered sensor on the artificial muscle. Note that the envelope of the recorded square wave shows a 50 Hz noise signal. This is the result of the single-sensor approach. By using a single sensor with respect to a grounded reference, we will see 50 Hz noise as picked up capacitively from the environment. This will be cancelled when using the set-up of Figure 6.

In Figure 14, the human EMG is measured on the biceps using two electrodes of the type of Figure 11. At t = 0 sec and t = 100 sec, a contraction of the biceps was applied. We can see that muscular activity is clearly detected by the textile embroidered sensors. Some motion artefacts are visible as spikes on the signal.

Further technology to be developed is a suitable method to integrate wiring for power and signal lines. Options can be found in the printing or weaving of conducting wires (Gimpel et al., 2003; Gimpel et al., 2004).

4.5   Conclusions

In the European project ConText, the expertise and skills of partners are combined to develop a muscle activity monitoring vest. The vest anticipates to a set of work related diseases, which are an increasing financial burden to our society. To exploit the natural usage of clothes, contactless EMG sensors are chosen. A direct consequence is that pre-amplifiers have to be mounted directly on the textile sensors. This results in the need for advanced interconnect technologies for textile integration.

5   Miniature wireless sensors

A typical way to achieve unobtrusive sensing is to make the sensor devices small, thin and wireless.

Research on the subject of small autonomous network devices at Philips Research finds its origin in a lecture on Ambient Intelligence (Aarts and Marzano, 2004) given by Emile Aarts for the Integrated Device Technologies group in March 2002. In this lecture a picture of ubiquitous computing was sketched with the example of swarms of embedded micro devices forming an electronics ambient, which senses people and reacts to people. The original thoughts on such a concept came from Mark Weiser from Xerox published in Scientific American (Weiser, 1991). The article starts with the sentence:

"The most profound technologies are those that disappear. They weave themselves into the fabric of everyday life until they are indistinguishable from it."

Although this reference is from 1991, the vision has until now not become reality. Miniature wireless sensor devices as small as a few cubic millimetres have been shown to be feasible, mass market introduction is still lacking. In general a severe reduction in size leads to a severe limitation in device functionality. In designing miniature wireless devices requirements such as fast reaction times, bi-directional wireless connectivity at medium data rates, long operational lifetimes, lead to relatively complex devices and moderate power levels. For instance most devices that are being commercialized use a wireless standard, such as 802.15.4, with security overhead and other features. Energy scavenging schemes, such as vibration energy scavenging, and thermal energy scavenging have been shown to have a poor power density and poor miniaturization possibilities, rendering them unsuitable for powering miniature wireless sensor devices except for some small exceptional niche applications. Photo voltaic energy scavenging is applicable in a wider range of applications, but miniaturized photo voltaic systems are still far from mature. In order to enable a long enough operational lifetime the battery volume needs to be sizeable. The energy density of Lithium rechargeable batteries (i.e. the batteries with the highest gravimetric energy density) determines in that case the size of the device. As an example the energy density of a LiR2430 80 mAh/3.6 V battery is 200 Wh/dm^3. Even if the battery volume is allowed to take 50% of the volume of the device, the volume reaches a value close to 3 cubic centimetres, far removed from several cubic millimetres.

In the literature several attempts have been made in order to have a sound comparison of the state-of-the-art wireless sensor systems (Anliker et al., 2004; Beutel, 2006; Hill, et al., 2004; Römer and Mattern, 2004). Various aspects have to be taken into account to make such a comparison, if possible at all. Aspects influencing the size of wireless sensor devices are the requirements and restrictions imposed by production. It can be concluded that if the manufacturability by present day production facilities is required the design needs to fulfil a host of requirements, almost all leading to size constraints.

As such one of the first problems in making a good comparison is the difference between packaged and unpackaged sensor devices. Many of the wireless sensor devices are offered in an unpackaged fashion, some even without battery holder or antenna. A product incorporating all these aspects as well as being small has yet to evolve. In Figure 15 we present an overview of some of the existing solutions for wireless sensor devices. The choice has been made to compare the Philips Research miniature wireless sensor device solution with three unpackaged solutions and three packaged versions that are commercially available and that are often cited in the wireless sensor devices community. The reason to take as well unpackaged solutions is because of the absence of a variety of packaged solutions let alone smaller. So benchmarking the level miniaturization and integration from electronics point of view should be done on the basis of comparison with unpackaged

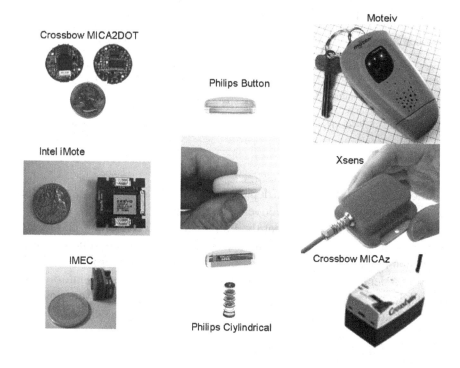

Figure 15. Comparison of the Philips solutions with different devices often cited in the wireless communications community.

Table 1. Clarification of the functionality of the sensor devices shown in Figure 15.

Philips Button	Philips Cylindrical
Processor CoolfluxDSP	Processor CoolfluxDSP/PCH7970
Wireless 2.4 GHz IEEE802.15.4	Wireless 2.4 GHz IEEE802.15.4
3D accelerometer, 3D magnetometer	3D accelerometer,
Antenna, battery, package included	Antenna, battery, package included
28 mm diameter, 10 mm height	14 mm diameter, 14 mm height
Intel iMote	**IMEC (1st generation)**
Processor ARM7TDMI	Processor MSP430F149
Wireless 2.4 GHz Bluetooth Sensors excluded	Wireless 2.4 GHZ, Nordic
Battery excluded	Temperature sensor
30×30 mm (W×L)	Battery included
	14×14×12 mm
Moteiv	**Xsens**
Processor MSP430F1611	wired system to wireless hub
Wireless 2.4 GHz IEEE802.15.4, Zigbee compliant	3D gyroscope, 3D accelerometer,
2D accelerometer, temperature sensor, light sensor,	3D magnetometer
microphone, loudspeaker battery included	No battery
50×94×22 mm (W×L×H)	58×58×22 mm (W×L×H)
Crossbow MICAz	**Crossbow MICA2DOT**
Processor Atmel Atmega 128 L	Processor Atmel Atmega 128 L
Wireless 2.4 GHz IEEE802.15.4, Zigbee compliant	Wireless 868/916, 433 MHz or
Light, temperature, sound, 2D accelerometer,	315 MHz
2D magnetometer	Temperature sensor
Battery included (W×L×H)	No battery/antenna included
	25 mm diameter, 10 mm height

solutions. The different devices depicted in Figure 15 are plotted such that the scale puts them in good perspective with each other.

From Figure 15 it is clear that the Philips devices offer a very good solution, especially because it also contains a package. The latter property makes it a valuable tool to allow for testing even in an outdoor environment. Obviously, in order to have a sound comparison we need the additional information about what is inside the package. In Table 1 we shortly list the functionality of the different devices in order to validate our current approach.

5.1 Design considerations

In designing a miniature wireless sensor device a number of parameters need to be considered. The application sets constraints and requirements for the device. Especially for wearable sensors the volume, shape and weight are important factors. These factors will be discussed in relation to a number of applications in the area of personal wearable wireless sensing in the next sections.

For a given application aimed at sensing psychophysiological parameters related to experiences the use case needs to be considered in terms of operational lifetime, duty cycle, accuracy and stability of sensor output. In operator assisted laboratory tests short operational lifetimes combined with full time sampling, high accuracy will prevail. In attempts to record these parameters in a daily life situation care must be taken to render the devices wearable. This use case dictates long operational lifetimes, small duty cycles and high sensor stability, sacrificing sampling rate and accuracy. The most challenging use case scenario is 24 hour round the clock monitoring, where even the incorporation of sensors into clothing may fall short of the goal (since some people like to sleep naked), and implanted or skin mounted devices are necessary.

Daily life monitoring falls within the scope of this paper, which is about unobtrusive and unnoticeable sensing. Incorporation of sensors into furniture, such as chairs and beds are an attractive option, but for full time monitoring they are obviously unusable. The authors are of the opinion that implantable devices have a level of invasiveness exceeding current mainstream acceptance. The necessity of skin worn devices or skin contacted devices is unavoidable in some cases, such as when measuring the galvanic skin response. The devices embedded into clothing certainly are the champions of unobtrusiveness, as long as weight, shape and volume stay within limits. These limitations are the subject of the following section.

5.1.1 Device volume In the device volume of the electronics, the package and the battery are the main contributors. Let's postulate a 5 cubic centimetre device volume as the maximum volume allowable for unobtrusive use. Relevant literature concerning this topic seems to be lacking. The volume of a modern (women's) watch is therefore seen as a reasonable assumption. The battery volume of such a hypothetical device is linked to the average power consumption and the desired operational life. In Figure 16 the relation of these parameters is shown for a 2 cubic centimetre rechargeable Li ion battery, taking up 40% of the available volume.

The average power to run the device for a day, week or year would be 15 mW, 2 mW or 40 μW respectively. Needless to say the choice of required operational life may pose severe restrictions on the choice of electronic components, sampling rate and duty cycle. With current state-of-the-art technology the collection of simple sensor data such as temperature or resistance may be feasible at reasonable sample rates to allow a device to be made to function for a year or even more. In a totally different field, such as automotive tire pressure monitoring such miniature wireless sensor devices are already a common product, operating up to 5 years (not continuously, because

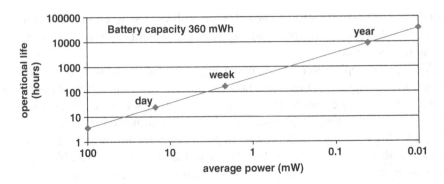

Figure 16. Operational lifetime as a function of average power for a 360 mWh battery capacity.

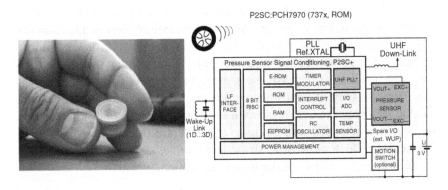

Figure 17. Miniature wireless temperature and pressure sensor based on NXP tire pressure sensor chip PCH7970.

a car is driven intermittently) on a single battery. Reuse of this hardware for body temperature and galvanic skin response monitoring is a distinct possibility. Philips Semiconductors (now NXP) developed a tire pressure monitoring product based on the microcontroller PCH7970 (http://www.nxp.com/acrobat_download/literature/9397/75015738.pdf). The block diagram of this chip is shown in Figure 17.

A tiny wireless temperature and pressure sensor for body sensing purposes has been made by Philips Research and is also shown in Figure 17 Since the pressure sensor as well as the high precision temperature sensor both are resistance monitors this device can be easily be used for galvanic skin response purposes.

The volume of the device is about 1 cubic centimetre and it runs continuously for 3 weeks at a sampling rate of 1 Hz on a simple 3 V Li CR1220 battery.

5.1.2 Shape considerations For miniature wireless sensor device which are to be worn on the body or in the clothing a number of shapes can be considered. Most desirable is a thin and highly flexible device, built nearly indistinguishable into the fabric of the clothing. The EMG devices discussed in the previous chapters are coming close to this form. A format which is mostly used for identification purposes is the smartcard. Already now electronics, displays and batteries are built into these cards (Chan et al., 2004). A possible next step is the incorporation of sensors. Activity and posture monitoring sensors and temperature sensors are candidates for this. The card may function as hub in a body area network, having a wireless link to other body worn sensors, fulfilling a function in data fusion, data processing and storage. Using a display it may even function as user interface. Other shapes to be considered are the button shape, the cylindrical shape and the pencil shape. Shapes with sharp edges, such as a box shape or a cube shape fail to meet the unobtrusiveness criterion due to the increased chance of being noticed by the wearer.

The pencil shape may double as a writing utensil, which most people tend to wear anyway. The high aspect ratio is a limiting factor for the capability of integrating electronically components. Some components, such as the antenna, or an AAA-type battery fit very well in such an elongated shape. The Button and cylindrical shapes have actually been made into prototypes and these will be discussed in more detail in the next section. In Figure 18 the considered shapes for unnoticeable and unobtrusive sensing of psychophysiological parameters for experience assessment are shown. The shapes are shown with the same volume, indicating aspect ratio differences.

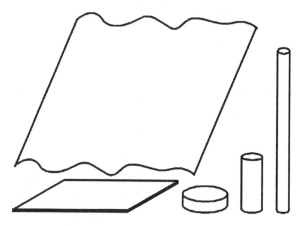

Figure 18.   Various shapes for miniature wireless sensor device embodiments: fabric, smartcard, button, cylinder and pencil shape. The shapes are shown with the same volume, indicating aspect ratio differences.

Table 2. Various shapes which are suitable for miniature wireless sensor devices compared with the same volume

Shape	Dimensions for a 5 cm³ volume
Fabric	0.2 mm × 160 mm × 160 mm
Smartcard	1.1 mm × 85 mm × 54 mm
Button	7.1 mm height × 30 mm diameter
Cylinder	34 mm height × 14 mm diameter
Pencil	100 mm height × 8 mm diameter

If a 5 cm² miniature wireless sensor device volume is taken as a starting point the aforementioned shapes can be translated into sizes that are tabulated in Table 2.

When taking a closer look to the values as given in Table 2 it can be argued that the different shapes all correspond to a particular use case. The size for *Fabric* is indeed such that it allows for unobtrusive use in clothing, the *Smartcard* dimension is identical to the currently used identification badges used by various companies and as such it has been proven to be an acceptable size. The *Button* shape is according to the authors suitable for application development testing of particular sensor combinations for 24–48 hours experiments in e.g. the medical and healthcare domain. The latter shape also corresponds nicely to the requirements for gaming applications. The *Cylinder* shape has the advantage that a specific electronics module can be used for each of the main components, but turns out to be the least wearable solution. For implantable and swallowable devices however the advantages are obvious. The *Pencil* shape may be easily integrated in writing utensil and the length could even be increased for this application. However, from an implantable and swallowable point of view the length is problematic, while the diameter is satisfactory.

5.1.3 Weight considerations As is the case with the optimal wearable volume without being obtrusive or noticeable, the optimal wearable weight of a miniature wireless sensor device is somewhat hard to define. Again looking at devices people tend to carry around without trouble, such as jewellery, timepieces, mobile phones the weight of a watch is seen as a reasonable criterion. Although watches may weigh as much as 100 grams a small sized (woman's) watch weighs about 10 grams. For unnoticeable and unobtrusive this is subsequently taken as the maximum allowable weight. In the case the devices are to be worn as jewellery there are deviating criteria.

The button shaped miniature wireless sensor device that recently have been realized within Philips is shown in Figure 19.

Figure 19. Button shaped miniature wireless sensor, showing top connector for additional modules or software upload/data download.

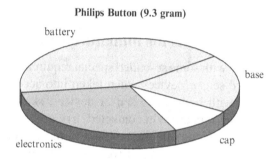

Figure 20. Weight Breakdown Phillips Button device with a diameter of 30 mm and a height of 9.7 mm.

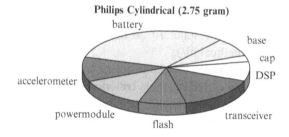

Figure 21. Weight breakdown for Philips Cylindrical device, with a diameter of 14 mm and a height of 20 mm.

In Figure 20 and Figure 21 a pie chart diagram is shown where a weight breakdown for the two unobtrusive miniature wireless sensor devices. From these figures it is clearly observed that indeed for both devices around 30% of the weight is taken by the batteries (even a bit more for the Philips Button device). Regarding the Philips Button solution, around 30% is taken by the package which is because the packaged of this device has been designed with a focus on robustness. For the Philips Cylindrical device (Figure 17) a larger part of the weight is taken by the electronics, due to an innovative stackable packaging concept.

For both the cylinder and the button device the electronics are the same in the weight breakdown comparison: in both cases the device is a motion sensor.

With respect to the impact of device weight on unnoticeability it can be remarked that due to inertia the maximum allowable weight will be less for parts of the human body that are prone to move at high accelerations. Also the ration of the device weight to the body part weight is important: Consider for example heart rate variability sensing using a photoplethysmograph: if the device is to be used as ear mounted jewelry this poses severe restrictions to the weight.

5.2   Special requirements for miniature wireless devices

This paragraph deals with some so-called special requirements that improve the quality of the final sensor devices when taken into account. Because of the fact that we deal with body worn sensor devices, skin contact is quite often the case. When sensors are skin contacted, irritation of the skin can be an unwanted result, or even an allergic reaction to the sensor devices. This is exactly one of the reasons why capacitive contactless ECG/EMG sensors have been developed. Another issue that strongly relates to sensing the ECG/EMG is the skin resistance, conductive gels are to be used in order to decrease the skin resistance and to have it a more or less constant value. Moreover the devices should be electrically safe, i.e. without problems regarding wireless emissions or external electrical fields. The devices should obey the rules regarding current IEC601–1 standard on human safety (Modi, 1997; http://www.tnocertificationmedical.nl/).

Another aspect is the battery, the choice for rechargeable batteries or primary batteries. The good thing of rechargeable batteries is the environmentally more friendly aspect. The battery is not immediately thrown away. This battery aspect is especially important when the considered sensor devices are only used for 24–48 hours experiments. However, when the application combines a long service life scenario and low power consumption simple primary coin cells such as the zinc-air type, offer a much larger energy density. These batteries are not capable of handling a high discharge rate. Recharging of the batteries is closely related to the so-called *Ease-of-Use* of the sensor devices. The word *Ease-of-Use* is used in the sense of a common denominator in what follows. One of the preferred ways of recharging the batteries is when the device is simply plugged on top of a connector. But this would mean that the device has an opening for the connector which out rules the use in water. The other option would be wireless recharging in a cradle, by means of induction coils, which is compatible with a completely closed package to be used in a watery environment as well.

The use in or close to a watery environment (i.e. the human body) in the sensing of psychophysiologal parameters offers an important requirement for the transceiver. The attenuation of electromagnetic radiation by water quickly rises when frequencies exceed several hundred megahertz. Especially for implantable miniature wireless sensors, or sensors which have to transmit through a human body, the choice of frequency is limited to bands below 1 GHz, such as the 402 MHz band for implantables, or for other devices the IST bands at 433, 868 and 916 MHz.

Another aspect regarding recharging of the batteries in close relation to *Ease-of-Use* is related to the topology of the wireless sensors network. Imagine the wireless sensors to be used in a large network. It is clear that the batteries should be rechargeable, and moreover, an energy scavenging option should be included because there is no possibility to change all the batteries one-by-one. Apart from the recharging options which influence the packaging of the devices the *Ease-Of-Use* also translates back in terms of possible out-door use. Regarding sensors that are integrated in the clothing *Ease-Of-Use* obviously means that washability is the key requirement, and when met, this would most probably mean that outdoor use of the particular clothing is possible as well.

Furthermore *Ease-Of-Use* regarding software upgrades in a large wireless sensor network it is a common understanding that the possibility of using a wireless link to achieve the software upgrade should be included. When the wireless sensors are not used in a large sensor network structure, but for application development, software upgrades could be realized via a connector which should easily accessible from the outside. An example of such a connector can be seen in Figure 19.

6 Concluding remarks

The research topics on psychophysiological sensing and miniature wireless sensor devices described in this paper show that within Philips there is a growing interest in the measurement of experiences, emotions and moods. The application areas suitable for such information are in the domain of wellness, motivation, persuasion, illness prevention and personal healthcare.

The interpreted sensor output can be used as such: offering information about oneself or relatives, friends. The value may be in how the information is conveyed or used: lighting or audio/video content may adapt to a person's mood or even attempt to improve upon it.

The technology no longer seems to be a limiting factor for unobtrusive and unnoticeable sensing. Initially the sensors will be worn on the body, but ultimately implantable sensors will become widely accepted, allowing access to new parameters, such as hormone levels and body core temperature.

The increased computing capabilities allow real time interpretation of complex data, such as facial expressions, data fusion of multi parameter sensor inputs.

The information on experiences, emotions, and moods will be used not only for a single person, but increasingly in interpersonal relationships. Ultimately hard to fathom aspects such as group feelings that occur in a highly coherent group may come into reach.

In interpersonal relationships uncertainties about how others react to you, how popular are you can be resolved, enabling feedback to improve in case of shortcomings.

Personal health indicators addressing issues such as chronic stress and mental health are becoming available for preventive healthcare in the case of 24 hours daily life monitoring of psychophysiological indicators.

All these fine future prospects have one major requirement: the obtaining of unbiased true psychophysiological sensor data relies on true unobtrusive and unnoticeable monitoring.

References

Aarts, E., and Marzano, S., The New Everyday, Views on Ambient Intelligence, Koninklijke Philips Electronics N.V. ISBN 90–6450–502–0.

Anliker, U., Beutel, J., Dyer, M., Enzler, R., Lukowicz, P., Thiele, L., and Tröster, G., A Systematic Approach to the Design of Distributed Wearable Systems. *IEEE Transactions on Computers* 53(8): 1017–1033, August 2004.

Armstrong, T.J., A conceptual model for work related neck and upper limb musculoskeletal disorders. *Scand J Work Environ Health* 19: 73–84, 1993.

Basmajian, J.V., and De Luca, J.C., Muscles Alive: their functions revealed by Electromoygraphy, Williams & Wilkins. ISBN- 068300414X. June 1985.

Beutel, J., Metrics for Sensor Network Platforms, Proc. ACM Workshop on Real-World Wireless Sensor Networks (REALWSN'06), ACM Press, New York, pages 26–30, June 2006

Bogert, B.P., Healy, M.J.R., and Tukey, J.W., The Quefrency Alanysis of Time Series for Echoes: Cepstrum, Pseudo-autocovariance, Cross-Cepstrum, and Saphe Cracking, Proc. Symposium Time Series Analysis, M. Rosenblatt, ed., John Wiley and Sons, New York, pp. 209–243, 1963.

Chan, P.K., Choy, C.S., Chan, C.F., Pun, K.P., Preparing smartcard for the future: from passive to active. *IEEE Transactions on Consumer Electronics*, 50(1): 245–250, Feb 2004.

ConText project webpage, http://www.context-poject.org/

European Commission press release IP/04/1358, Commision asks workers and employees what action should be taken to combat musculoskeletal disorders, Brussels 12 November 2004.

Gimpel, S., Möhring, U., Müller, H., Neudeck, A., Scheibner, W., The galvanic and electrochemical modification of textiles. *Band- und Flechtindustrie* 40: 115–120, 2003.

Gimpel, S. Möhring, U., Müller, H., Neudeck, A., Scheibner, W., Textile Based Electronic Substrate Technology. J. *Industrial Textiles* 33/3: 179–189, 2004.

Harland, D.J., Clark, T.D., Prance, R.J., High resolution ambulatory electrocardiographic monitoring using wrist-mounted electric potential sensors. *Measurement Science & Technology* 14(7): 923–928, July 2003.

Hill, J., Horton, M., Kling, R., and Krishnamurthy, L., The Platforms Enabling Wireless Sensor Networks. *Comm. of the ACM* 47(6): 41–46, June 2004.

http://nl.wikipedia.org/wiki/Wim_Boost

http://www.nxp.com/acrobat_download/literature/9397/75015738.pdf

http://www.soulinvitation.com/clinicalintro

IEC norm NEN 60101, http://www.tnocertificationmedical.nl/

Issue 201-Work-Related Neck and Upper Limb Musculoskeletal Disorders, European Agency for Safety and Health at Work, 15/11/1999, http://agency.osha.eu.int/publications/reports/201/en/index.htm

Jean-Claude Healy eHealth technologies for the citizen centred health system, International Workshop on Wearable Micro- and Nanosystems for Personalised Health, pHealth 2006, Luzern, Switzerland, January 30 – February 1, 2006.

Kim, K.K., Lim, Y.K., and Park, K. S., Common Mode Noise Cancellation for Electrically Non-Contact ECG Measurement System on a Chair, Proceeding of the IEEE 27th Annual Conference in Medicine and Biology, Shanghai, China, September 1–4, 2005.

Ko, W.H., Neuman, M.R., Wolfson, R.N., and Yon, E.T., Insulated Active Electrodes, IEEE Transactions on Industrial Electronic Control Instruments, IECI 17, pp. 195–197, 1970.

Linz, T., Gourmelon, L., and Langereis, G., Contactless EMG sensors embroidered onto textile, Procs. BSN 2007, 4th International Workshop on Wearable and Implantable Body Sensor Networks, 26–27 March 2007, Aachen University, Germany.

Modi, D., IEC 60-1–2 and its impact on medical device manufactures, Engineering in Medicine and Biology society, 1997. *Proceedings of the 19th. Annual International Conference of the IEEE* 6: 2531–2534, 30 Oct.-2 Nov 1997.

Monika, A. et al., Cortical and Autonomic Correlates of Visual Selective Attention in Introverted and Extraverted Children. *Journal of Psychophysiology* 19(1): 35–49, 2005.

Quasar patents and patent applications EP1366563A1, US2004070446A1, US6686800 and US20040254435A1.

Richardson, P.C., The insulated electrode: A pasteless electrocardiographic technique, Proc. Annu. Conf. Eng. Med. Biol., Proc. 20th ACEMB, 1967, paper 15.7.

Roberto, M., and Parker, P.A. (eds.), Electromyography, Physiology, Engineering and Noninvasive Applications, Wiley Interscience, 2004, ISBN 0–471–67580–6.

Römer, K. and Mattern, F., The Design Space of Wireless Sensor Networks. *IEEE Wireless Comm.* 11(6): 54–61, December 2004.

Stephen, H.F. et al., The influence of task demand and learning on the psychophysiological response. *International Journal of Psychophysiology* 56: 171–84, 2005.

The WMSD organisation http://wmsd.org

Webster, J.G. (Ed.), Medical Instrumentation, Application and Design, Second Edition, Houghton Mifflin Company, Boston 1992, ISBN 0–395–59492–8.

Weiser, M., The computer for the 21st century. *Scientific American* 265(3):94–104, September 1991.

Westgaard, R.H., and Bjørklund, R., Generation of muscle tension additional to postural muscle load. *Ergonomics* 30(6): 911–923, 1987.

16

IT'S HEART RHYTHM NOT RATE
THAT COUNTS

Heartmath Studies and Emwave PC Stress Relief System

Deborah Rozman, Rollin McCraty and Dana Tomasino

Abstract   Heart Rate Variability Coherence (HRV-C) biofeedback is exciting new technology that has broad-based applications for health and wellness and for performance enhancement. Based on research done at the Institute of HeartMath psychophysiology laboratory and at other institutions, heart rhythm coherence feedback training has proven to facilitate rapid, profound, and enduring improvements in a wide variety of conditions. An important reason this technology is effective in diverse applications is that it facilitates the maintenance of a highly efficient and regenerative internal state, characterized by reduced nervous system chaos and increased synchronization and harmony in human system-wide dynamics. This psychophysiological mode, termed *physiological coherence*, is conducive to healing, rehabilitation, emotional stability, learning and optimal performance. A heart rhythm coherence training and feedback system known as the emWave PC is now being used in a wide variety of settings for clinical, workplace, school, sports and fitness, and home applications.

...There are organism states in which the regulation of life processes becomes efficient, or even optimal, free-flowing and easy. This is a well established physiological fact. It is not a hypothesis. The feelings that usually accompany such physiologically conducive states are deemed "positive," characterized not just by absence of pain but by varieties of pleasure. There also are organism states in which life processes struggle for balance and can even be chaotically out of control. The feelings that usually accompany such states are deemed "negative," characterized not just by absence of pleasure but by varieties of pain.... The fact that we, sentient and sophisticated creatures, call certain feelings positive and other feelings negative is directly related to the fluidity or strain of the life process. Antonio Damasio, Looking for Spinoza (2003), page 131

J.H.D.M. Westerink et al. (eds.), Probing Experience, 195–204.
© 2008 *Springer.*

1 Heart Rate Variability Monitoring

Monitoring heart rate has become popular for exercise fitness, sports and relaxation training. Lowering heart rate increases parasympathetic nervous system activity and is helpful for relaxation. Higher heart rate (aroused sympathetic nervous system activity) is required to energize, feel more confident and perform at high speed. However, behavioral change and optimal performance often require a state that is both relaxed and energized.

Heart rate variability (HRV) is a measure of the beat-to-beat changes in heart rate. HRV monitoring displays the effect of the activity of both the sympathetic and parasympathetic branches of the autonomic nervous system, the interaction between them on the heart rhythm, and provides a window into the dynamics of the system as a whole. HRV can be derived either from the ECG (electrocardiogram using electrodes on the body or a chest strap) or from pulse wave recordings (using a plethysmographic optical sensor). ECG recordings have the advantage of producing fewer movement-related artifacts. However, pulse wave recording devices provide data suitable for most biofeedback applications.

2 Amount of HRV

The HRV signal can be analyzed by time domain or frequency domain (spectral) analysis, both of which can quantify the *amount of variability* in the heart rate in a given period. In general, being able to shift quickly between high heart rate and low heart rate indicates a high level of variability. The amount of variability is age-related. Young children show the most variability in heart rate and there is a natural decline as people age. Low HRV is associated with many disease states and with all-cause mortality. It is also predictive of sudden cardiac death (arrhythmias; Task Force of the European Society of Cardiology and North American Society of Pacing and Electrophysiology, 1996).

3 Heart Rhythm Pattern Analysis

Heart rhythm pattern analysis analyzes the varying shape of the HRV waveform, which is reflective of changes in emotional/psychological state, and thus is particularly powerful in applications where reducing stress, increasing emotional stability and behavioral change are critical. Heart rhythm pattern analysis has shown that stressful emotions, such as anxiety, irritation, frustration or depression, create an irregular and disordered heart rhythm pattern, indicating less synchronization in higher level control systems and in the activity occurring between the parasympathetic and sympathetic branches of the autonomic nervous system. On the other hand, positive emotions, such as love, care, appreciation or joy, create a highly ordered and harmonious heart

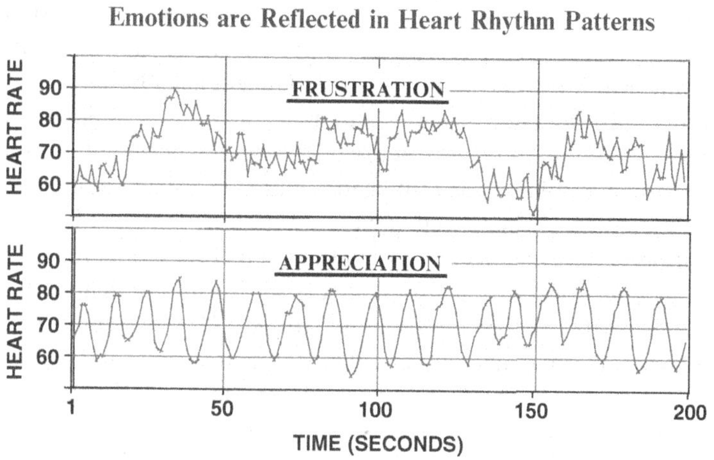

Emotions are Reflected in Heart Rhythm Patterns

Figure 1.   Emotions are reflected in Heart Rhythm Patterns.

rhythm pattern, reflecting greater synchronization between the two branches of the autonomic nervous system (McCraty et al., 1995; Tiller et al., 1996). The graphs in Figure 1 are of the same person, first recalling a feeling of frustration, then using a HeartMath coherence technique and shifting to a feeling of sincere appreciation.

Although the amount of variability (distance between high and low peaks) in the heart rhythm is related to heart rate, the heart rhythm pattern which reflects the individual's emotional state and performance is independent of heart rate. With heart rhythm pattern monitoring, people can learn to increase emotional flexibility and amount of variability. It's **rhythm, not rate** that reflects mental-emotional dynamics and performance ability.

4   Heart Rate Variability Coherence – HRV-C

With heart rhythm pattern monitoring, researchers at the Institute of HeartMath were able to identify and measure a distinct mode of physiological functioning that is associated with sustained positive emotion and high performance, called in sports "the zone" and in the workplace "flow." We termed this functional mode *psychophysiological coherence* (McCraty and Atkinson, 2003; McCraty and Childre, 2002). This mode of physiological coherence is reflected by a smooth, sine wave-like (coherent) pattern in the heart rhythms and a narrow-band, high-amplitude peak in the low frequency range of the heart rate variability power spectrum, at a frequency of about 0.1 hertz. Correlates of physiological coherence include: increased synchronization between the two branches of the autonomic nervous system, increased heart–brain synchronization (alpha rhythms become more synchronized to the ECG), increased vascular resonance, and entrainment among diverse physiological oscillatory systems (*i.e.*, heart rhythm patterns, respiratory, craniosacral, and blood pressure rhythms; McCraty and Atkinson, 2003; Tiller et al., 1996).

Physiological coherence provides a number of benefits in the human system: (1) resetting of baroreceptor sensitivity, which is involved in short-term blood pressure control and has also been found to be related to increased respiratory efficiency; (2) increased vagal afferent traffic, which is involved in the inhibition of pain signals and sympathetic outflow; (3) increased cardiac output in conjunction with increased efficiency in fluid exchange, filtration, and absorption between the capillaries and tissues; (4) increased ability of the cardiovascular system to adapt to circulatory requirements; and (5) increased temporal synchronization of cells throughout the body (Langhorst et al., 1984; Siegel et al., 1984). This results in increased system-wide energy efficiency and metabolic energy savings. The physiological coherence mode has also been associated with psychological benefits such as increased emotional stability and improved cognitive performance (McCraty, 2002; McCraty and Atkinson, 2003; McCraty et al., 1998; 1999).

The term "coherence" has a number of meanings, including being logically connected, harmonious, ordered and congruent. Coherence is a quality that emerges from the ordered relations among the parts of a system or among multiple systems. Efficient or optimal functioning is known to result from a harmonious organization of the interactions among elements of a system. A harmonious order in the pattern of heart rhythm activity signifies a coherent system, whose efficient or optimal function is directly related, in Damasio's terms, to the ease and "fluidity" of life processes. By contrast, an erratic, non-harmonious pattern of heart rhythm activity denotes incoherence or an incoherent system. The more incoherence in the heart rhythm pattern, the more it reflects the stress and "strain" of physiological processes.

5   Coherence-Building Techniques

Although physiological coherence is a natural state that can occur spontaneously, sustained episodes are generally rare. While rhythmic breathing methods can induce heart rhythm coherence for brief periods, cognitively-directed paced breathing gets boring and is difficult for most people to maintain or enjoy for extended time periods. Furthermore, breathing techniques alone do not necessarily shift the emotional state. For example, it is possible to breathe at a rate of six breaths per minute (a 10-second rhythm) and still be feeling anxiety or other feelings of unease. Research findings indicate that individuals can quickly enter and enjoyably maintain extended periods of physiological coherence by learning to self-generate a positive emotional state, such as sincere love, appreciation or care, while pretending to "breathe" this feeling through the area of the heart in a relaxed, smooth manner. After a few moments, they can forget their breathing rhythm and just continue to generate the positive feeling or attitude to sustain coherence. Using a positive emotion to drive the coherent mode appears to excite the system at its resonant frequency, so coherence emerges naturally, making it easy to sustain coherence for long periods without focusing on the breathing pattern.

Based on these findings and related research on the extensive interactions between the heart and brain, (McCraty, 2003) the Institute of HeartMath developed a set of positive emotion-focused techniques that foster physiological coherence. Collectively known as the HeartMath System, these positive emotion skill-building techniques utilize the heart as a point of access into the psychophysiological networks that underlie emotional experience (Childre and Martin, 1999; Childre and Rozman, 2002; McCraty and Childre, 2002). Heart rhythm coherence changes the pattern of afferent cardiac input sent to the cognitive and emotional centers in the brain which helps to synchronize and facilitate cortical functions. With practice of the HeartMath techniques, coherence patterns become increasingly familiar to the brain and nervous system, and eventually become established in the neural architecture as a new, stable baseline or norm. Coherence-driven repatterning facilitates behavioral changes that people have not been able to achieve before. Evidence from studies conducted across diverse populations suggests that coherence-driven repatterning can lead to both short-term and long-term improvements in key measures of physical and emotional health and performance. For example, individuals using the HeartMath coherence-building techniques have demonstrated significant reductions in stress, anxiety, and depression (McCraty et al., 1998; 1999; 2000; 2001; 2003; Luskin et al., 2002; Rozman et al., 1996; Barrios-Choplin et al., 1997; 1999); increases in positive affect and attitudes (McCraty et al., 1998; 1999; 2000; 2001; 2003; Luskin et al., 2002; Rozman et al., 1996; Barrios-Choplin et al., 1997; 1999); enhancement of humoral immunity (Rein et al., 1995; McCraty et al., 1996); and an increased DHEA/cortisol ratio (McCraty et al., 1998). As discussed further below, these interventions have also been shown to produce significant improvements in behavioral and health status in various clinical populations.

6   Heart Rhythm Coherence (HRV-C) Feedback: The Freeze-Framer Interactive Learning System

Heart rhythm coherence biofeedback is a powerful tool to quickly learn how to generate and increase physiological coherence at will, thereby reducing stress patterns, increasing emotional well-being, maintaining health, and improving health and performance outcomes. The HRV-C biofeedback system known as the emWave PC Stress Relief System was developed by Quantum

Intech, Inc., a spin-out company of the Institute of HeartMath in Boulder Creek, California. The emWave PC (formerly Freeze-Framer) incorporates a patented technology that enables physiological coherence to be objectively monitored and quantified on a PC. Using a fingertip or earlobe plethysmo-graphic sensor to detect the pulse wave, this interactive hardware/software system plots the changes in heart rate on a beat-to-beat basis and reveals the heart rhythm pattern. Both the heart rate tachogram and HRV power spectrum can be viewed in real time. The software also includes a tutorial that provides instruction in HeartMath coherence-building techniques. As users practice the HeartMath techniques, they can see and experience the changes in their heart rhythm patterns, which generally become less irregular, smoother, and more sine wave-like as they enter the coherent mode. This process enables adults and children ages eight and above to easily develop an internal reference for the shift into an emotionally balanced coherent state that they can go back to at anytime. The software also analyzes the heart rhythm patterns and calculates a coherence level for each session. The coherence level is fed back to the user as an accumulated score or "zone state." The coherence level is also used to drive game play in the colorful on-screen games which are designed to rein-force coherence-building skills. There are four challenge levels to help the user increase emotional regulation and coherence. Finally, the system includes a multi-user database to store results and track the users' progress.

Because the emWave PC technology uses a pulse wave monitor and involves no electrode hook-up, it is extremely versatile, time-efficient, cost effective and easy to use in a wide variety of settings to relieve stress, improve health, and opti-mize performance. The emWave PC is being used successfully by mental health professionals, physicians, executives, athletes, performing artists, educators and students. The emWave PC is also available with full functionality in a handheld, battery-operated device, called emWave Personal Stress Reliever.

6.1 Medical applications

Many health professionals have found heart rhythm coherence feedback to be an effective tool to support and facilitate a wide variety of therapies, both conventional and complementary. For example, the emWave PC technology is increasingly being used by neurofeedback practitioners to calm clients and stabilize the nervous system before sessions; this preparation often allows for a shorter and more effective session. Many clinicians have found HRV-C feedback to be an effective addition to treatment programs for chronic condi-tions that are associated with or exacerbated by emotional stress, including fibromyalgia, chronic fatigue, hypertension, asthma, environmental sensitiv-ity, sleep disorders, diabetes, and cardiac arrhythmias, among many others. The system has proven particularly effective in pain management and is used in burn clinics. It has also been demonstrated to be an effective intervention for facilitating brain surgery recovery. Finally, the emWave PC is employed in cardiac rehabilitation programs to help patients reduce stress and increase cardiovascular efficiency. Clinical studies have shown significant improvements in functional capacity in patients with congestive heart failure (Luskin et al., 2002) and significant blood pressure reductions in hypertensive individuals (McCraty et al., 2003) using the emWave PC in conjunction with HeartMath coherence-building techniques.

6.2   Mental health applications

Heart rhythm coherence feedback is also a powerful tool in mental health settings and has facilitated rapid and profound improvements in individuals with conditions as depression, anxiety, panic disorder, post-traumatic stress disorder, and attention-deficit hyperactivity disorder (ADHD). Many mental health specialists have commented that children appear to be particularly responsive to the emWave PC, as seeing their heart's rhythms and coherence-building through the games is often more tangible and engaging in comparison to EEG, GSR or other neurofeedback modalities they have used. The system is also frequently used to facilitate anger management and impulse control.

Because of the sensitivity of HRV patterns to changes in psychophysiological state, many psychologists utilize the emWave PC effectively as a "camera on the emotions." Continuous monitoring of clients' HRV throughout a therapy session is easily accomplished and can give both therapist and clients immediate insight into clients' emotional responses, often enabling a more efficient and effective session. HRV monitoring often proves helpful in identifying subconscious feelings, reactions, and emotional triggers that operate at a level below an individual's conscious awareness but are nevertheless reflected in the HRV pattern. The sensitivity of heart rhythm monitoring to psychological variables is clearly illustrated by the account of one psychologist who uses this technology with clients with multiple personality disorder. This clinician finds that he is able to reliably distinguish between the different personalities his clients manifest on the basis of distinct changes in their heart rhythm patterns.

6.3   Performance enhancement applications

In addition to improving physical and emotional health, heart rhythm coherence feedback is also used for optimizing performance in a wide variety of domains. By reducing performance-related anxiety and mental "noise," stabilizing nervous system dynamics, and creating system-wide coherence, this intervention helps individuals learn how to enter and sustain high-performance states at will. One application in which the emWave PC has proven particularly effective is helping students stabilize the nervous system to reduce anxiety and improve performance in high-stakes test-taking. Pilot studies with high school students have shown a 14% to 35% increase in standardized test scores in reading and math after 8 hours of training (over a 3-week period) with the emWave PC and HeartMath coherence-building techniques (Arguelles et al., 2003; McCraty et al., 2000).

Another rapidly growing application for heart rhythm coherence feedback is in the area of sports performance. Helping athletes learn how to consistently enter "the zone" through building their accumulated coherence scores, enables them to more consistently achieve a peak-performance state that maximizes emotional stability, focus, concentration, and physical coordination. The emWave PC has made a particularly notable impact in the professional golfing community for reducing the Yips and lowering handicaps (Managing Emotions-Golf's Next Frontier, Ground-Breaking Techniques for Health Performance).

7   The Future of HRV-C Biofeedback

In summary, HRV-C biofeedback is a versatile and cost-effective technology that has broad-based applications in clinical, workplace, home, sports, and academic settings for the enhancement of health and human performance. Because it can be easily used to promote a psychophysiological state conducive to behavior change, healing and regeneration, we foresee that HRV-C training will be increasingly incorporated in many types of disease prevention programs, as well as in the treatment of stress and emotional disorders of adults and children. In addition, using HRV-C biofeedback to learn to generate physiological coherence has innumerable potential applications for personal growth and performance improvement. In short, heart rhythm coherence biofeedback is a practical and powerful tool that can facilitate people in developing a greater awareness of the connection between their emotions, physiology, and behavior, and ultimately achieve greater mastery of their health and well-being.

HeartMath is a registered trademark of the Institute of HeartMath. Freeze-Framer, emWave and Personal Stress Reliever are registered trademarks of Quantum Intech, Inc. For more information on Institute of HeartMath research publications and programs for schools visit: http://www.heartmath. org. For more information on HeartMath corporate and health professional training programs or the emWave heart rhythm coherence feedback products visit http://www.heartmath.com For information on emWave technology licensing and OEM, visit http://www.quantumintech.com

Address for correspondence: Deborah Rozman, Ph.D., President and CEO, Quantum Intech, Inc., 14700 W. Park Ave., Boulder Creek, California, USA. Phone: (831) 338-8700, Fax: (831) 338-8704, Email: info@quantumintech.com

References

Arguelles, L., McCraty, R., Rees, R.A. The heart in holistic education. *Encounter: Education for Meaning and Social Justice* 2003;16(3):13–21.

Barrios-Choplin, B., McCraty, R., Cryer, B. An inner quality approach to reducing stress and improving physical and emotional wellbeing at work. *Stress Medicine* 1997;13(3):193–201.

Barrios-Choplin, B., McCraty, R., Sundram, J., Atkinson, M. The effect of employee self-management training on personal and organizational quality. Boulder Creek, CA: HeartMath Research Center, Institute of HeartMath, Publication No. 99–083, 1999.

Childre, D., Martin, H. *The HeartMath Solution.* San Francisco: HarperSanFrancisco, 1999.

Childre, D., Rozman, D. *Overcoming Emotional Chaos: Eliminate Anxiety, Lift Depression and Create Security in Your Life.* San Diego: Jodere Group, 2002.

Langhorst, P., Schulz, G., Lambertz, M. Oscillating neuronal network of the "common brainstem system". In: Miyakawa, K., Koepchen, H.P., Polosa, C., eds. *Mechanisms of Blood Pressure Waves.* Tokyo: Japan Scientific Societies Press, 1984: 257–275.

Luskin, F., Reitz, M., Newell, K., Quinn, T.G., Haskell, W. A controlled pilot study of stress management training of elderly patients with congestive heart failure. *Preventive Cardiology* 2002;5(4):168–172, 176.

Managing Emotions—Golf's Next Frontier: Ground-Breaking Techniques for High Performance. Boulder Creek, CA: HeartMath LLC, 2003.

McCraty, R. *Heart-brain neurodynamics: The making of emotions.* Boulder Creek, CA: HeartMath Research Center, Institute of HeartMath, Publication No. 03–015, 2003.

McCraty, R. Influence of cardiac afferent input on heart-brain synchronization and cognitive performance. *International Journal of Psychophysiology* 2002;45(1–2):72–73.

McCraty, R., Atkinson, M. *Psychophysiological coherence.* Boulder Creek, CA: HeartMath Research Center, Institute of HeartMath, Publication 03–016, 2003.

McCraty, R., Atkinson, M., Lipsenthal, L. Emotional self-regulation program enhances psychological health and quality of life in patients with diabetes. Boulder Creek, CA: HeartMath Research Center, Institute of HeartMath, Publication No. 00–006, 2000.

McCraty, R., Atkinson, M., Rein, G., Watkins, A.D. Music enhances the effect of positive emotional states on salivary IgA. *Stress Medicine* 1996;12(3):167–175.

McCraty, R., Atkinson, M., Tiller, W.A., Rein, G., Watkins, A.D. The effects of emotions on short-term heart rate variability using power spectrum analysis. *American Journal of Cardiology* 1995;76(14):1089–1093.

McCraty, R., Atkinson, M., Tomasino, D. Impact of a workplace stress reduction program on blood pressure and emotional health in hypertensive employees. *Journal of Alternative and Complementary Medicine* 2003;9(3):355–369.

McCraty, R., Atkinson, M., Tomasino, D. *Science of the Heart: Exploring the Role of the Heart in Human Performance.* Boulder Creek, CA: HeartMath Research Center; Institute of HeartMath, Publication No. 01–001, 2001.

McCraty, R., Atkinson, M., Tomasino, D., Goelitz, J., Mayrovitz, H.N. The impact of an emotional self-management skills course on psychosocial functioning and autonomic recovery to stress in middle school children. *Integrative Physiological and Behavioral Science* 1999;34(4):246–268.

McCraty, R., Barrios-Choplin, B., Rozman, D., Atkinson, M., Watkins, A.D. The impact of a new emotional self-management program on stress, emotions, heart rate variability, DHEA and cortisol. *Integrative Physiological and Behavioral Science* 1998;33(2):151–170.

McCraty, R., Childre, D. *The appreciative heart: The psychophysiology of positive emotions and optimal functioning.* Boulder Creek, CA: HeartMath Research Center, Institute of HeartMath, Publication No. 02–026, 2002.

McCraty, R., Tomasino, D., Atkinson, M., Aasen, P., Thurik, S.J. Improving test-taking skills and academic performance in high school students using HeartMath learning enhancement tools. Boulder Creek, CA: HeartMath Research Center, Institute of HeartMath, Publication No. 00–010, 2000.

Rein, G., Atkinson, M., McCraty, R. The physiological and psychological effects of compassion and anger. *Journal of Advancement in Medicine* 1995;8(2):87–105.

Rozman, D., Whitaker, R., Beckman, T., Jones, D. A pilot intervention program which reduces psychological symptomatology in individuals with human immunodeficiency virus. *Complementary Therapies in Medicine* 1996;4:226–232.

Siegel, G., Ebeling, B.J., Hofer, H.W., Nolte, J., Roedel, H., Klubendorf, D. Vascular smooth muscle rhythmicity. In: Miyakawa, K., Koepchen, H.P., Polosa, C., eds. *Mechanisms of Blood Pressure Waves.* Tokyo: Japan Scientific Societies Press, 1984: 319–338.

Task Force of the European Society of Cardiology and the North American Society of Pacing and Electrophysiology. Heart rate variability: Standards of measurement, physiological interpretation, and clinical use. *Circulation* 1996;93:1043–1065.

Tiller, W.A., McCraty, R., Atkinson, M. Cardiac coherence: A new, noninvasive measure of autonomic nervous system order. *Alternative Therapies in Health and Medicine* 1996;2(1):52–65.

17

TRANSFORMATIVE EXPERIENCE ON THE HOME COMPUTER

Lessons from the Wild Divine Project

Kurt R. Smith

Abstract   Healing Rhythms has the mission to deliver entertainment-based experiential transformation using biofeedback technology on the user's home computer. The truly compelling experience has three key stages – attraction, engagement and extension with six attributes at each stage – well-defined, fresh, immersive, accessible, significant and transformative. Following this definition the goal of our products is to create a compelling experience that has transformative extension into the user's life with focus on the achievement of a happy mind. In this paper, I will discuss the current and future methods we use to create such an experience and I will also discuss the impact our products have had on users.

1 Introduction

Healing Rhythms begin its mission over five years ago with the specific intent to deliver a disruptive self-care technology to the consumer. The meaning of 'disruptive' in this sense deserves some explanation. Dr. Clay Christensen (2000a) of Harvard Business School introduced disruptive innovation as an analytic and predictive phenomenon in numerous industries from rolled steel to microchips to healthcare. A disruptive innovation occurs within a marketplace when a less-skilled participant in the market can readily accomplish a service that has previously required a more highly skilled intermediate. Regarding the health care industry, Dr. Christensen (2000b) points out in his article that this industry may in fact find its cure through disruptive innovation and that one of the primary drivers for this innovation will be self care.

This notion seeded the mission of Healing Rhythms by motivating us to discover a self-care methodology that fit the 'disruptive' innovation paradigm. Biofeedback was selected as the disruptive technology in that it fits the constraint set – it is a well-known and tested care methodology that has been used successfully in the clinic for over thirty years for over 150 conditions and it was staged to be consumerized thereby defining itself as disruptive,

J.H.D.M. Westerink et al. (eds.), Probing Experience, 205–208.
© 2008 *Springer.*

i.e., the user could use biofeedback in the home and no longer needed to go to the clinic to take advantage of biofeedback as a care or wellness tool.

The use of biofeedback by the home user is highly motivated by a simple argument. The argument is bounded by a few simple facts:

- 66% of Americans are seeking help for stress

- AMA (American Medical Association) states that stress is the cause in 80 to 85 percent of all human illness

- 60–90% of primary care visits are stress/psychosocial related

Biofeedback is well accepted as a successful tool for teaching people how to cope with stress and counteract it. Obviously then, the adoption of biofeedback as an effective self-care tool for stress reduction could have enormous impact not only on the wellness of our society but also on the financial burden of health care.

Over the past five years Healing Rhythms has developed hardware and software that delivers biofeedback capability to the home user for under $200. In one sense you might say that we accomplished our mission and arguably technically we have but what now remains as a more important aspect of the mission is the delivering on the *promise* of biofeedback as a self-care method to the home user. This of course highlights the need to 'appeal' to the consumer in a such a way that they will adopt and comply with a regiment of self-care using biofeedback.

2 Probing Experience

Consumer 'appeal' is a broad and long-standing science which advertising agencies spend hundreds of millions of dollars on annually. However, we can view appeal in the sense of our interest as well of that of this book as *transformative experience*. After all, our mission cannot simply be to deliver the ingredients for the consumer to bake their own self-care biofeedback experience. Rather, it is our responsibility to provide for the consumer a transformative experience so that the value of biofeedback technology can actually extend into the user's life in a meaningful way. If we cannot provide a transformative experience, then our fancy technology and all the advertising budget in the world will not live up to the potential of biofeedback as a truly disruptive self-care opportunity.

Let us then probe experience and examine the elements that make an experience transformative. To frame the problem we refer to an insightful study performed by an innovation strategy firm in Chicago, IL, USA called the Doblin Group. The Doblin group examined experience and broke it down into **three stages**: attraction, engagement and extension with **six attributes**: defined, fresh, immersive, accessible, significant and transformative.

By using this framework as a language, we can really begin to probe experience in a descriptive way and importantly for us ask the question "when does an experience truly become transformative".

The Doblin group examines several experiences using this framework and it is instructive to review a few of them to gain a reference point.

Case Experience 1: School work, particularly working a problem on the board, has no attributes active in the attraction stage (thus can be viewed as unattractive). In the engagement stage the attributes that activate are defined, immersive, accessible and transformative and in the extension stage the primary attribute is significance. Thus, working out a problem on the school board has little attraction but is well-defined, immersive, accessible and transformative while it's happening and has a significant extension into user experience primarily in the area of building confidence in working in groups.

Case Experience 2: Attending a sports event on the other hand has accessible and significant attraction, activates all attributes at the engagement stage and has significant even transformative extension.

Case Experience 3: Learning to do your own taxes has a fresh and significant attraction, an immersive effect when engaged and extends into life in a significant and transformative way.

Given this framework for probing experience and a few reference points let us return to our central pursuit.

3   Biofeedback as an Experience

A strong argument can be made that the experience of biofeedback despite it's compelling reasons for adoption cannot extend into the user's life in a meaningful way unless the engagement with the user is significant and transformative. The reality into today's attention deficit world is that providing biofeedback to cope with stress as a technology tool alone falls short on what is required to achieve a transformative and thus extendible coping skill experience in the user's life. An example analogy for comparison may be eating well. We all recognize from health experts over decades that eating well is the best thing for us. However, until organic foods shopping becomes a 'hip' experience and more easily accessible for everyone will we really start eating well as a society. Exercise can also be viewed this way – I can do my push-ups and run in place at home but only through the 'hip' experience of a health club to I really engage in exercise in a significant and transformative way.

Biofeedback experience needs to be viewed in the light of these examples. The reality is that biofeedback delivered as a tool alone does not deliver on its promise as a disruptive self-care innovation. Let's examine biofeedback experience in the Doblin experience framework:

Biofeedback Experience – Reality: Offering biofeedback as a technology tool alone for coping with stress has *fresh* and *accessible* attributes in the attraction stage, arguably is *accessible* and well *defined* in the engagement and extension stages – we can tell the user exactly what they should do. However, the engagement stage suffers from *freshness* beyond the novelty period and has little immersive effect and practically no *significance* or *transformative* effect in the engagement stage despite having *significance* in the extension stage.

Biofeedback Experience – Goal: The ideal biofeedback experience such that the user has *significant* and *transformative* extension into life is to combine biofeedback technology as a tool with an engagement that is *immersive*, *significant* and *transformative*.

4   Achieving the Goal

Our mission as a company then can be easily framed – provide a biofeedback-based user experience that at engagement is immersive, significant and transformative – arguable the key attributes at the engagement stage in order to achieve transformative extension into the user's life and thus having sustainable impact on the user's ability to cope with stress.

We have tried to accomplish this goal in three key ways:

1   provide hardware to the user that has an everyday Lifestyle Technology feel, i.e. it's 'hip' to have and use;

2   provide a simple-to-use, well-founded multi-step training program that incorporates a highly compelling multimedia experience; and

3   provide the credibility of having well-known mentors in the training program.

Through these mechanisms we are confident that the user experience can achieve the goal of an immersive, significant and transformative engagement which provides extension into the user's life as they transfer the stress coping skills learned in the Healing Rhythms product into real life experience which after all is the only experience worth affecting.

References

Christensen, C. 2000a, "The Innovator's Dilemma", Harvard Business School Press, 2000.
Christensen, C. 2000b, "Will Disruptive Innovations Cure Health Care", Harvard Business Review, Sept–Oct. 2000.
Doblin Group, "Compelling Experience Dimensions", last retrieved from www.doblin.com on April 16th 2007.

18

THE EMOTIONAL COMPUTER ADAPTIVE
TO HUMAN EMOTION

Mincheol Whang

Abstract   Emotion provides an important context enabling people to understand each other, often hidden underneath their mind. Likewise, the computer needs to be more sympathetic to users' commands in the context of their emotion. A challenging attempt has been made to develop an emotional computer, which reads physiological signals and analyzes them with respect to human emotion. Sensors were attached to an emotional mouse to measure photoplethysmogram, electrodermal activity and skin temperature. These physiological signals were read into on-line chip processors and evaluated by a rule base into human emotions. A two-dimensional emotion model was adopted and several empirical studies were performed to find out valid physiological patterns and to map them onto nine categories of human emotions. This study showed the feasibility of constructing the emotional computer adaptive to user emotion. Further research is needed before the emotional computer may come to the market.

1   Introduction

Research in human computer interaction (HCI) has been directed towards cognitive aspects of the interaction between user and computer, such as its effectiveness and efficiency, easy-to-understand menus, and appropriate temporal structures (Shneiderman, 1998; Boucsein and Thum, 1997). However, emotion has been often observed to provide an important context in the communicative aspect of HCI (Picard, 1997). Nevertheless, the influence of emotion has not been thoroughly investigated in HCI. Positive emotions often result in faster, simpler and more flexible information processing strategies, while negative emotions may result in more systematic strategies but would also substantially slow down HCI (Norman, 2004; Forgas, 1999). The key for a satisfying HCI could be the development of an emotional computer. The emotional computer is defined as a system that analyzes the user's emotional state and responds appropriately to it. However, the emotional computer is not able to express its own emotion, since the emotional computer does not

J.H.D.M. Westerink et al. (eds.), Probing Experience, 209–219.

have any emotion. Strictly speaking, it has intelligence rather than emotion. The aim of the present study was to construct an emotional computer that provides good quality of computer working conditions and let the user stay in a state of positive emotion, helping him/her to work better.

2 Methods

2.1 Emotional model

A dimensional approach was used for defining human emotions. In general, the use of subjective measures into emotion research resulted in two- through four-dimensional solutions. The most common dimensions are valence (positive vs. negative) and arousal (excited vs. calm). The two-dimensional model of emotion suggested by Larsen and Diener (1992) was used in the present study. In this model, all emotions can be located on a circle (sometimes called a circumplex) in a two-dimensional space made up from valence and arousal. Emotions are classified in each of the four quadrants made up by the two axes: pleasantness vs. unpleasantness and arousal vs. relaxation as shown in Figure 1. The four quadrants were named after the combinations of the axes (U-A, P-A, U-R and P-R). In an earlier study, the present author and his colleagues successfully probed the usability of the two-dimensional system as shown in Figure 1 for monitoring four basic emotional states by means of psychophysiological measures (Whang, Lim, and Boucsein, 2003). The four basic emotional states (U-A, P-A, U-R and P-R) were induced by combinations

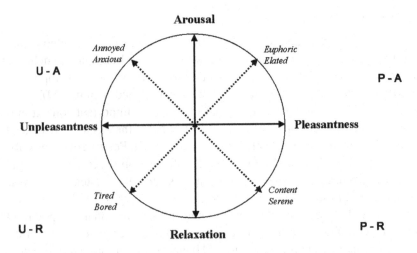

Figure 1. Two dimensional model of human emotion (Larsen and Diener, 1992, reprinted by permission of Sage Publications).

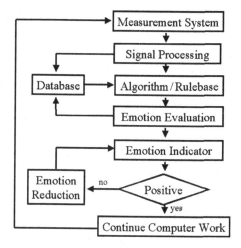

Figure 2. The systemic model for the emotional computer (Whang et al., 2003).

of olfactory and auditory stimuli. Four channels of electroencephalographic activity (EEG), electrocardiogram (ECG) and electrodermal activity (EDA) were recorded during stimulus presentation. As a result, multivariate combinations of physiological parameters figured out to be superior to any single measure.

2.2 General outline of the algorithm

The systemic model for the emotional computer is shown in Figure 2.

Sensors were designed to be wearable and comfortable with a minimal burden from their attachment, being able to continuously measure the user's physiological signals. The physiological signals were amplified, filtered, and digitized by a data acquisition system designed as small and light as possible. This system was constructed to be easy to embed in the computer main board or in a mobile computer system, PDA, web PAD, cell phone, etc. Wireless data communication between sensors and the data acquisition board will be introduced in a future step. Also, automatic noise detection and removal should be performed according to pre-defined specific algorithms in future solutions. The pre-treated signals were processed in order to extract appropriate physiological parameters that could be qualitatively normalized based on a defined state of emotional neutrality. These normalized data will be used in a special algorithm or rule base for evaluating the user's current emotional state. Both measured and processed data are stored in the database. Since the subjective report plays a central role in determining the qualitative aspects of any emotion, it is necessary to confirm the emotion evaluated by recording the user's subjective emotional state during a data acquisition phase and save it together with the physiological measures in the database. These confirmed data can be used to upgrade the database for the algorithm and/or the rule base. Furthermore, the system allows to be trained for an evaluation of an individual user during a learning process. An emotion indicator is used for presenting the user's emotion on the screen. In case of a negative emotion being detected, the program initiates a service of helping the user to develop a more positive emotion. In the present study, multimedia content is used to ease the intensity of the user's negative emotion.

2.3   Measures of emotion

To move from the laboratory setting to a real HCI, physiological measures have to be selected for an unobtrusive recording procedure which is impossible with EEG. Therefore, this study used autonomic nervous system variables. The measurement device called emotional mouse was specially constructed for recording three measures that cover the most salient aspects of autonomic activity: Electrodermal activity (EDA) as an indicator for sympathetic activity (Boucsein, 1992), skin temperature (SKT) as an indicator for parasympathetic activity and photoplethysmogram (PPG) as an indicator for arousal and orienting. EDA is a slowly changing signal and rising of its level means an increase of tension. SKT is also a slow signal, but rising means an increase in relaxation. PPG is a relatively fast signal with a peak about every 0.8 second, which is correlated with the heart beat. Thus, heart rate (HR) can be derived from PPG as an indicator for arousal vs. relaxation, and the modulation of the volume amplitude provides a measure of orienting.

2.4   Neutral band for reference

Since users are normally not experiencing pronouncing emotions during most of the time, the emotional state is predominantly neutral with respect to arousal and valence. The four quadrants defined by two-dimensional models as shown in Figure 1 are not able to explain a region for such a neutral state of emotion. However, this region of emotion is needed as a reference state that the non-neutral emotions should be defined from. Therefore, the emotional model was refined, augmented by a neutral band to the original emotions as shown in the left panel of Figure 3.

Taking such a neutral band into account for the boundary between each pair of quadrants and having an additional neutral-neutral field in the center increases the number of emotions from 4 to 9, as can be seen in the right panel of Figure 3.

The neutral band is defined separately for each physiological measure. Because the sensitivity of each measure can be different in different persons, neutral bands

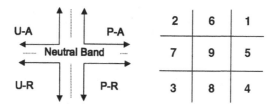

Figure 3. Neutral band of emotion.

are defined separately for each individual. A relatively narrow neutral band corresponds to high sensitivity but low accuracy of determining the emotion, and vice versa. During the system's adaptation process, subjective assessments of emotion are used to automatically adjust the neutral bands wider or narrower. Therefore, the neutral band is different in physiological signal within a user and among users at the same time.

2.5   Rule base for emotion determination

Once the neutral band is defined, any incoming physiological signal is calculated in percent variation from the neutral band as shown in Equation 1.

$$E = (C-N)/N \qquad (1)$$

E is expressed in percentages and equals the increase or decrease of each signal from the neutral state (N) to the current state (C). These normalized values of the physiological signals are used to set the rule base which used to determine emotions as shown in Figure 4.

The rule base uses three different entries for signal changes: an increase (+E) or decrease (−E) from the neutral band, or a zero value (0) in case of no deviation from the neutral band. Given these three entries (+E, −E, and 0) and three physiological measures (PPG, EDA, and SKT), this results in 27 different patterns. Six combinations (marked gray in Figure 4) can be eliminated because they should show an opposite direction for physiological reasons. The all-zero case is considered as reference and therefore also eliminated, so that 20 different combinations of physiological changes will remain for setting up the rule base. As a consequence, different patterns may result in the same emotion. Besides individual differences in the neutral band, there are also individual differences to be taken into account for the rule base. For example, a 5% increase of SKT, a 10% decrease of EDA and a 15% increase of PPT from the neutral band may indicate relaxation in one person, while 20% increase of SKT, a 5% decrease of EDA and a 10% increase of PPT may indicate relaxation in another person. Therefore, the values of the expression E are individualized for all nine emotions. The personal set of rule base is automatically updated by using the subjectively reported emotion.

Emotion	PPG	EDA	SKT
	+E	+E	+E
	+E	+E	0
	+E	+E	–E
	+E	0	+E
	+E	0	0
	+E	0	–E
	+E	–E	+E
	+E	–E	0
	+E	–E	–E
	0	+E	+E
	0	+E	0
	0	+E	–E
	0	0	+E
	0	0	0
	0	0	–E
	0	–E	+E
	0	–E	0
	0	–E	–E
	–E	+E	+E
	–E	+E	0
	–E	+E	–E
	–E	0	+E
	–E	0	0
	–E	0	–E
	–E	–E	+E
	–E	–E	0
	–E	–E	–E

Figure 4.   Rule base for emotion determination.

2.6   Subjective confirmation of emotion

In addition to the psychophysiological measures of emotion, subjective ratings of perceived arousal and valence are requested in regular intervals. A window is popping up on the screen, asking the subject to click on one of three buttons, representing relaxation, neutral arousal and high arousal state. Thereafter, another window enquires after unpleasant, neutral or pleasant feelings. To form a stable data base for each individual, a subjective evaluation is required every 2 minutes during the initial stage of emotion evaluation. If the incoming physiological signals are not in accordance with the subjectively reported emotion, the rule base is adjusted. After having reached a stable data base, subjective evaluation is required every 5 minutes or more.

2.7 Hardware and software development

An emotional mouse was customized to measure PPG, EDA and SKT. To establish a stable contact between sensors and skin, 10 design factors were considered. Its size (width 9–10 cm, length 18–19 cm) was determined by Korean anthropometric data of 20yr-aged in 1992.

Figure 5 shows the sensor location in the emotional mouse. The PPG sensor is contacting the thumb; the EDA electrodes make contact with the low part of the palm and the SKT sensor with the center of the palm. In the first version, there was no stable contact between sensors and skin. Therefore, a second version of the emotional mouse as shown in Figure 5 was developed, using three curvatures that reflect the natural form of the hand; the thenar-hypothenar curvature for EDA (Boucsein, 1992, Fig. 27), the curvature of the inner palm for SKT, and a special holder for the thumb was modeled for PPG, to prevent the thumb from moving up- and downward.

A customized integrated circuit board connecting the emotional mouse and the PC was constructed for acquiring, filtering, amplifying, and AD converting for PPG, EDA and SKT. It communicates with the PC via RS 232. Since data recording and processing lead to an excessive consumption of CPU, causing the computer to operate slowly, a client-server architecture was introduced as shown in Figure 6.

As suggested in Figure 6, the PC has only the functions of recording physiological signals and indicating the results of the emotion evaluation. The server performs the emotion analysis and its evaluation, and also the updating of both the rule base and the data base. The information of the subjective emotional state is sent to the server together with the physiological signal. The server sets and updates the neutral emotion band and the rule base, using new qualitative physiological data. The actual emotion is determined and sent to the PC for indicating. In addition, the PC indicates the results of emotion evaluation by a pop-up

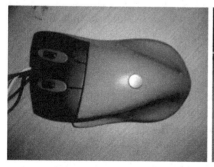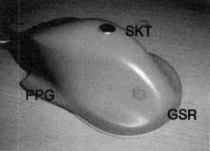

Figure 5. Emotional mouse.

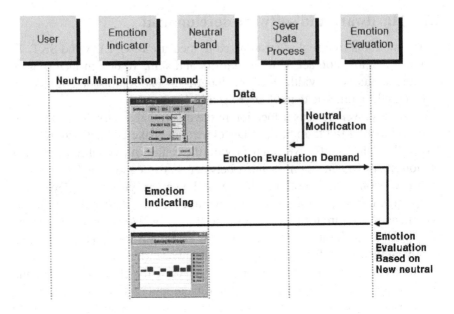

Figure 6.   Client-server architecture for the emotional computer.

emotion indicator, consisting of bars graphs, verbal explanations and a schematic face icon. For the icon, the mouth angles can be down neutral, and up, combined with three different orientations of the eyebrows, resulting in nine different icons that represent different emotions. The user can decide to see additional detailed information, given in numbers that represent results of physiological measures. The icon stays on the screen continuously until being updated.

The subject's confirmation is used to identify the current emotion. It is correlated with the incoming physiological data and also continuously used to re-evaluate the neutral emotion. During on-line processing, the data base is continuously developed and updated. It consists of the stored physiological parameters together with the E values for the 9 emotions. This data accumulation provides a continuously improving emotion evaluation that also takes personal characteristics into consideration.

2.8   Negative emotion recovery service

To keep the user in a positive emotional condition, the emotion computer is capable of providing a service for reducing the amount of negative emotion, once it is detected. This service is elicited by detecting the emotions 2 and 3 (see Figure 2). First, a pop-up window asks the subject to confirm accepting this service. If accepted, the subject's favorite multimedia data base is provided, offering his/her favorite music, video clips and the possibility to get rid of the negative emotion via playing a short video game. For this, the multimedia preference of the user is determined prior to using the emotional computer system.

2.9 Empirical system verification

For system verification, the consistency was tested between qualitative emotion as assessed by the emotional computer and subjective reports of emotion in 5 student subjects. The students rated their emotions 100 times for 3 days. Results show 70%–90% identification. Interestingly, the assessment was more accurate for arousal than for valence.

3 Discussion

The distinctive feature of an emotional computer is its adaptiveness of user interfaces, which is not the case in ordinary computers. The development of adaptive user interfaces is far from simple and requires interdisciplinary efforts. First of all, we need to know what provokes uneasy feelings of users, and determine the effect of emotion on computer work. Despite its importance, much research has focused on the technical aspects of user interfaces such as the customization of graphical interfaces and the design and behavior of interface objects (Preece et al., 1994; Shneiderman, 1998). Now the time has come to challenge the behavioral issues of emotion in the context of HCI. Most pertinent questions would be 'what influences does human emotion bear on the performance of computer tasks?' and 'what aids should be provided to let users stay with their comfortable feelings?' The present study proposed the theoretical framework of an emotional computer. It consists of three functional components of (1) physiological measurement, (2) pre-processing and (3) user interfaces. In relation to this theoretical framework, a number of research issues were raised. Firstly, the adaptive nature of emotional computers assumes their actions are in good tune with the subjective emotion of users. Such adaptability is to a great extent trusted to the signal processors of emotional computers. Thus, research should be initiated to determine under what conditions mathematical models perform robustly. Secondly, the apparatus to be affixed to the human body should be kept to a minimum and thus, unobtrusive to users. The device may include some sensors and transmission systems that are required to measure and transfer the physiological data. Lastly, the user interface should also be designed to provide appropriate action to alleviate the uncomfortable feeling of a user that may occur in the course of HCI. It should be noted that taking too much care of unstable emotion may lead to irritation. Thus, in addition to constant monitoring of physiological emotion, the subjective and behavioral state of emotion should be collected to keep track of the appropriateness of the adaptive behavior of user interfaces. Given the growing interests in emotion and its application into computing environments (Picard, 1997) and the principle of user-centered design in user interfaces, appropriate attention should be paid to research on emotional computers.

4 Conclusion

This study successfully developed an emotional computer. A specially-designed mouse for sensing the autonomic response of users enabled the evaluation of their emotion. Physiological recordings of PPG, GSR, and SKT were acquired and sent to a server being in charge of data processing. The emotion computer, taking back the results from the server, let the user know his/her emotion. The evaluation of user emotion was individualized according to updating the neutral band and the rule base using subjective confirmation. The emotional computer can provide a multimedia service for a user in negative emotion in order to make it more positive. The verification of the emotional computer obtained up to 70%–90% accuracy.

The emotional computer is capable of responding appropriately to any user emotion. The quality of communication between user and the emotional computer will be high, since it will act like a good friend. Also, a user will enjoy the emotional product manufactured by emotional computer technology.

A computer is going to be ubiquitous without irritating wires. The emotional computer will be continuously developed for a next version which is wireless, mobile and portable for future application in an ubiquitous computing environment.

References

Boucsein, W. (1992). *Electrodermal Activity*. New York: Plenum.

Boucsein, W., and Backs, R. W. (2000). Engineering psychophysiology as a discipline: Historical and theoretical aspects. In R. W. Backs, and W. Boucsein (Eds.), *Engineering Psychophysiology: Issues and Applications* (pp. 3–30). Mahwah, NJ: Lawrence Erlbaum Associates.

Boucsein, W., and Thum, M. (1997). Design of work/rest schedules for computer work based on psychophysiological recovery measures. International Journal of Industrial *Ergonomics, 20*, 51–57.

Forgas, J. P.(1999). Network theories and beyond. In T. Dalgleish & M. J. Power (Eds.). *Handbook of Cognition and Emotion* (pp. 591–611). New York: Wiley.

Larsen, R.J., and Diener, E. (1992). Promises and problems with the circumplex model of emotion. *Review of Personality and Social Psychology, 13*, 25–59.

Norman. D. A. (2004). *Emotional Design*. New York: Basic Books.

Picard, R. (1997). *Affective Computing*. Cambridge, MA: MIT Press.

Preece, J., Rogers, Y., Sharp, H., Benyon, D., Holland, S., and Carey, T. (1994). *Human-Computer Interaction*. Sydney: Addison-Wesley.

Shneiderman, B. (1998). *Designing the User Interface* (3rd Ed.). Sydney: Addison Wesley Longman, Inc.

Whang, M. C., Lim, J. S., and Boucsein, W. (2003). Preparing computers for affective communication: A psychophysiological concepts and preliminary results. *Human Factors, 45,* 623–634.

19

USING PHYSIOLOGICAL MEASURES FOR TASK ADAPTATION

Towards a Companion

Ben Mulder, Dick de Waard, Piet Hoogeboom, Lennart Quispel and Arjan Stuiver

Abstract Current Man Machine Interfaces (MMI) present information to the operator when it becomes available and when it is convenient to the computer; such automated systems do not act as a 'team player'. Computers lack insight in the actual status, intentions and occupations of the operator. An approach is presented (COMPANION) in which better co-operation between user and computer is stimulated. In this approach, information about the users' (physiological) state is used to adapt the MMI of the task at moments or in time periods where this is helpful for optimal task performance. Also task performance measures can be used in this feedback structure. COMPANION is about improving the Human Machine relation by: not interrupting the operator with non-urgent messages when he or she is completing an important task, and supporting the operator when task demands are high. In order to prevent specific solutions for each new task or for each additional information source an Operator Status Model (OSM) has been developed.

The approach is illustrated with a number of example studies, which show that several types of information can be used such as an eye lid closure sensor during car driving, as well as eye derived parameters, cardiovascular measures and a camera system that detect operators' mood changes. It is concluded that before this approach can be used in real practice several steps have to be taken that require experimental research at different levels. In particular, individual patterns of physiological state changes in relation to task performance need more attention. With respect to the 'probing experience' view, the COMPANION and OSM concepts could be helpful for development of products that may require adaptation of the tasks or environments in which users are working or living. Next to physiological signals, task performance indicators such as mouse actions could be useful in such situations.

J.H.D.M. Westerink et al. (eds.), Probing Experience, 221–234.
© 2008 *Springer.*

1 Introduction

One of the great challenges for system designers is to build systems that are enjoyable to work with and that do not provoke (too) much mental effort. There are several ways to approach such problems but the general experience is that in many complex systems goals are only partly met or only under restricted conditions. One of the most striking problems is that computer-controlled systems in general are not accounting for the needs and favors of the user. Current Man Machine Interfaces (MMI) present information to the operator when it becomes available and when it is convenient to the computer; such automated systems do not act as a 'team player'. Computers lack insight in the actual status, intentions and occupations of the operator. Especially during complex tasks this can be very disturbing; the operator may not be able to process the new information, and his current task may be adversely affected. A solution to this problem would be to make the automation aware of the (changes in) status of the user. This would result in an adaptive system that adapts itself to the operator's specific characteristics and actual status. The question is which type of information could be used to decide upon a possible change in the systems MMI or other specific task characteristics.

Research on this issue has indicated (Scerbo, 1999, Mulder et al., 2004; Fairclough and Venables, 2004) that physiological variables (e.g. EEG measures, cardiovascular state indicators such as heart rate and blood pressure) could give valuable information about the users' state, while task performance measures (e.g. reaction times, errors) could be indicative for task performance quality. Eye-derived information can be used as well for assessing the functional state of the user (Hoogeboom and Mulder, 2004). Is he or she free or busy with a task that cannot be interrupted? By interpreting eye scan data, blink rate or pupil diameter on a real-time basis, the automation might be able to decide that task adaptation is useful.

Adaptive systems have been in development for some time now, with varying degrees of success. The approach followed in developing such adaptive systems is often task specific, or has been tailored to specific users or tasks. This means that resulting systems are limited in their employability, and cannot be used for other software applications. Therefore, a more general approach is needed, which is based on generic operators' characteristics and behaviors and which is (almost) independent from specific task requirements. The aim of co-operative research of NLR and University of Groningen (Hoogeboom and Mulder, 2004) in this field is to develop an approach that does not have these drawbacks and restrictions. A generic 'Operator Status Model' (OSM) is under development that combines physiological information with task performance indicators to classify the actual user state. The resulting classification can be used by the automation to adapt the human-machine interface or other task characteristics with respect to aspects such as timing, location, contents and shape/modality of the presented information. Applications are developed in the field of Air Traffic Management and Pilot Workload Management by NLR and in the field of complex Ambulance Dispatch Work at University of Groningen. The aim of the present chapter is to show this approach and to illustrate this with some example studies.

2 Adapting to adaptation

Several levels of automation autonomy can be distinguished (Scerbo, 1999). 'Classical automation' for instance is directed at the allocation of (sub-)tasks to the computer in a direct fashion. Specific tasks are allocated to the computer and the user has to observe the behavior and monitor the correctness of the computer results. In this case the user has to adapt to the behavior of the computer. Only limited options to adapt the behavior of the computer exist in this situation; these consist mainly of starting/stopping the program and delaying necessary inputs.

One step further is the option to allow the user to select the preferred operating mode of the program: increases in computer performance allowed the introduction of more options in both data processing and the MMI. Consequently, users are given the option to adjust the software to suit their needs by (de-)selecting certain MMI options like window location and size as well as appearance of menu bars. This process of user selections of the available options of the software is commonly referred to as 'adaptable software'. Hence, with adaptable software the user remains in control of any change in the MMI. The last step in the software autonomy evolution is that the computer is allowed to modify its behavior itself, based for example on the perceived status of the user and/or task requirements. Hence, the computer program has become adaptive.

Endsley and co-workers discerned five different levels of automation: from full automation to manual control (Endsley and Kiris, 1995, Endsley, 1996):

1. full automation,

2. monitored AI,

3. consentual Artificial Intelligence (AI),

4. decision support,

5. no automation.

From 1. to 5. authority of the human operator increases, while the role of the system decreases. In 4. 'decision support' the system provides assistance, while in 'consentual AI' the system proposes actions which the operator can accept or reject. One level higher the operator can only veto actions initiated by the system while in full automation the operator cannot interact with the automated system at all. Obviously, research interest lies in levels 2. to 4. where there is interaction between man and automated system.

However, people themselves are also highly adaptive. This human adaptivity manifests itself in a couple of aspects.

- Firstly, most tasks can be performed in a variety of ways; these ways are called task strategies. An operator may employ a task strategy that is tailored to a certain interface, making extensive use of interface specific features. This interface might prevent him from performing optimally. However, a new interface not necessarily improves his performance. If the new interface doesn't support the operator's strategy (because it lacks crucial features), or guides him into another strategy, his performance may actually decrease, or he might stop using the system.

- Secondly, people learn. Learning is of course a special case of adaptation. Task performance of a novice operator will be different from task performance of an expert, and interfaces for both kinds of operators have different requirements. An adaptive system therefore needs to adapt itself not only to the operator, but also to the learning state of the operator.

- Thirdly, people adapt the way they perform a task to their situation. Some task strategies can be highly context specific. For example, air traffic controllers employ at least five strategies in handling air traffic. They change these strategies, based, among others, on the amount and complexity of traffic they encounter.

- Fourthly, people adapt their task strategies to their own state. A fatigued operator may not have the resources for an elaborate, very efficient strategy, and may favor to switch to a simple and easier to remember strategy.

Designing an adaptive system will only be successful if it supports or guides operator adaptation.

The focus of research has shifted from traditional to adaptive automation. In adaptive automation (e.g., Scerbo, 1996) the division of tasks between operator and system can be set by the operator, or can change dynamically. Level of automation as described above can be altered in real-time. Advantage is that the operator's role in the system remains active, he or she remains "in-the-loop". Temporary returning control to the operator has a favorable effect on the detection of automation failure during subsequent automatic control (Parasuraman et al., 1996). A positive effect is also counteracting the loss of skills. From aviation it is also known that many pilots worry about the loss of their flying skills and they consider manual flying a part of every trip important to maintain these skills (McClumpha et al., 1991). Adaptive automation is a step forwards in automation, however, if in adaptive automation operator needs and operator capability are not considered, then it may still suffer from the same problems as traditional automation (Parasuraman and Riley, 1997).

3 Companion

If you take care of operator needs, status, and capability, automation becomes a team player. It is exactly this idea that is central to the *COMPANION* concept. COMPANION is about improving the Human Machine relation by:

a. Not interrupting the operator with non-urgent messages when he or she is completing an important task, and

b. Supporting the operator when task demands are high.

COMPANION can be seen as an electronic pal. It evaluates what the task conditions are and whether the operator needs support or whether he or she can be interrupted or not. For this, system state and requirements are important input to COMPANION as well as information about the operator himself.

Making use of information about the operator's state and adapting the system on the basis of this information will create a co-operative system. The system responds adaptively based on the user's needs for type and amount of information presented. The basic idea is that by means of monitoring behavior, posture, eye movements, and physiology the operator's state can be inferred and if a higher risk state is detected the system responds. If the operator is assumed to be heavily loaded by high priority tasks this can result in lower priority information not to be presented when it becomes available, but postponing presentation to a more appropriate moment. It can also mean that an operator who is laying back because of low workload gets more tasks to perform to keep him or her 'in the loop'. As a result, there are not only consequences in terms of expected increased safety, but it will also make the whole process more efficient, and will increase involvement, job satisfaction and well-being of the user.

There are two types of state changes that should be detected:

1. Short-term changes (that take place in seconds to minutes) and

2. Long-term state changes (that take many minutes to hours).

Operator *status* is the relatively short term psychological and physiological situation where a concept such as high mental workload plays a major role. Operator *state* is a relatively long term psychological and physiological situation. Operator state is mainly about fatigue, long lasting stress and drowsiness. Since the boundary between *status* and *state* is relatively unclear and has led to considerable debate, this paper uses the term functional state. The functional state of a user is defined as the momentary state with parameters which may be reflecting behavior over multiple minutes, relaxing the formal definition of status a little to what is practically achievable and useful.

3.1 Operator Status Model (OSM)

Central in the COMPANION system is the Operator Status Model (OSM). In the OSM the operator's functional state is derived from physiological indicators such as heart rate or other physiological indices. This information is combined with information about task performance, which is taken from the active applications. Integrated measures of operator functional state are required that can recognize different operator states. The derived functional state can subsequently affect the Human Machine Interface (HMI) in such a way as to optimize the interface for the present functional state. Support can be offered with the aim to reduce operator workload. Modality of information can be altered, e.g. from visual to auditory, low priority messages can be postponed, important information can be made more salient or displayed at a location where the operation is focusing. The use of operator functional state as input to adaptive automation and adapting the interface on the basis of this information will in this way influence actual functional state. This is a closed (information) loop, depicted in Figure 1. The proposed COMPANION feedback structure is not task dependent but generic. Information from (sub) tasks is converted into a standard format that can be used at a higher end level. Consequently the COMPANION concept can be applied to new tasks or different application areas without much additional work.

For adaptive automation to be successful a high level of user awareness has to be maintained to allow judgment of the appropriate behavior of the automation (Parasuraman et al., 2002). First applications of adaptive automation were found in the military aviation domain. The idea is to present the right information in the right format at the right time. This is at the same time one of the risks of adaptive automation: a changing interface that can even be perceived as inconsistent (see also Hoogeboom and Mulder, 2004).

Figure 1 is simplified; Figure 2 is an extended version in which the multiple feedback loop structure is more evident. There may be multiple tasks to accomplish, and there is multiple input, both in terms of task performance parameters and physiological measures.

The task the operator has to perform in general is not a simple task, but is in general built up out of different sub tasks that are all dynamic, complex, and may have to be performed in parallel. Input to the OSM is the user's

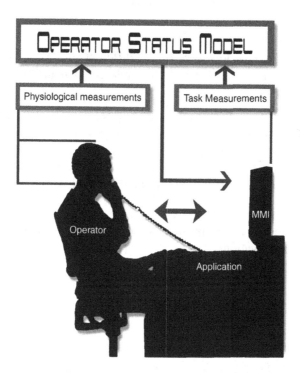

Figure 1. The Operator Status Model (OSM) concept. The OSM combines the operator's physiological information with task performance (taken from the active applications) and application states to derive the user's functional state, using generic dimensions like workload, visual task load and being occupied with a given task/application. The OSM information can subsequently be used by the applications to change their HMI to optimise the direct information exchange.

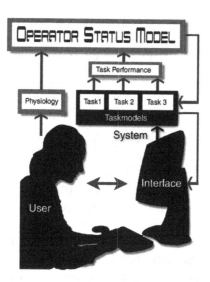

Figure 2. A more elaborated Operator Status Model. Multiple feedback loops for different subtasks, and different task models for different sub tasks.

physiology and task performance on the different sub-tasks. The OSM can adapt tasks and their interfaces. The separate components of the model are described below.

3.2 User

Performance of the **user** is affected by:

a. User knowledge of and experience with the system, and the user skills

b. Physiological status (present or not, occupied, waiting) and state (fatigue, motivation)

c. Available tools (hardware, software).

d. Context (climate, noise levels, et cetera)

3.3 Interface

The interface in general consists of (touch-)screen, mouse, and keyboard, although in other applications it might as well be a steering wheel, accelerator, a range of buttons, and voice or gesture input systems.

3.4 System

More than one task in the same domain can be performed simultaneously. Each task is modelled, its priority and the way it affects the interface is known. If the operator is occupied with Task 2 and Task 1 has to be performed with high priority the interface can be adapted. If Task 2 has higher priority Task 1 can be postponed.

3.5 Physiology

State and status need to be determined on the basis of physiology. For determination of operator state raw physiological data such as heart rate, blood pressure, and EEG, enter the physiology module. Both measurement and physiological artifacts need to be corrected on-line. After that, processed and analyzed data (filtered, FFT, etcetera) enter the OSM module. Based on the parameter status (e.g. moving averages) of the last couple of minutes state changes can be detected and inferences be made about the operator functional status. For detecting operator status, eye movement information and detection of present activities need to be pre-processed before these can enter the OSM. The pre-processing concerns calibration, filtering, determinations of area of interest and analysis of applied eye scanning strategy, et cetera.

3.6 Task performance

Task performance on the separate tasks in terms of speed, accuracy and applied work strategy are fed back into the OSM to be used as general level of performance.

3.7 OSM in the control loop

In the OSM, task performance, physiological data and context (work environment) come together and need to be interpreted to get an assessment of operator functional state. Workload demands, workload, scanning behavior (at areas of interest), fatigue, and perhaps mood need to be deduced from physiology and task performance. Criteria need to be set when the operator needs support, but also when support is not required or should be reduced. Support will also depend upon the state of the operator: an overloaded operator will need different support than a non-vigilant operator.

If an assessment of the operator's functional state is used to determine and affect the interface this is expected to influence operator state again resulting in a closed information loop. Important in the closed loop analogy is that:

1. The overall *loop-gain* should not be too high to avoid oscillation. The interface should be adapted with limited changes and low frequency. Changes like highlighting areas may be used whilst the basic information should remain the same. The operator should also have sufficient time to adapt to the new situation.

2. If the *delay* in the control loop becomes too large the user-machine co-operation may become instable. If the delay is long the interface's behavior is no longer linked to the triggering action and may become unexpected. Also many physiological analyses need a certain amount of data as input, for HRV frequency analyses, for example, at least 30 seconds of data are required.

3. Some hysteresis should be present in the system: not all operator functional state changes should result in a modified interface. Dead-bands in the action to be taken are therefore a necessity if users are to appreciate the system. A new situation has to exist for a little while before the interface is adapted to minimize continuous switching. However this last observation does not hold for all possible conditions. Safety and time-criticality are examples where dead-bands might be less appropriate.

An ideal system is stable, while at the same time it responds quickly enough to provide assistance if required. A distinction between continuous tasks and discontinuous operations may be useful. Continuous operations are best served by gradual changes in the interface, while events such as acute warnings can or should be more salient and attention-catching.

4 Implementing the OSM: where are we?

Before the OSM can be used at least three important steps have to be taken:

1. Designing and programming the OSM structure

2. Deciding which (physiological) variables are most adequate for detecting state changes

3. Selecting how to change the task at hand and at which moments

Although the first step requires some work, certainly with respect to keeping a general structure that can be used for several tasks under different conditions, this step proves to be the least problematic one. At the present a couple of example-OSMs at NLR and University of Groningen are implemented that can show the usefulness of the approach, without having realized the general structure completely. Steps 2 and 3 ask for more research before effective choices can be made. For example, in studies with ambulance dispatchers task-planning support was given to the operator, but it was not so easy to show that overall task performance was improved or that mental load decreased considerably during support conditions. Moreover, choices how to adapt a task effectively can only be made when enough insight in the task has been obtained, which requires at least adequate task analysis. Step 2, selecting the best set of (physiological) variables and deciding when a relevant state change has occurred proves to be the most difficult one. At least three aspects require different types of research than has been done in the past. In stead of finding significant effects of working conditions at a group level, state changes at an individual level have to be found. Secondly, in stead of finding differences between short-lasting (laboratory) tasks conditions, state changes as a function of time in (semi-)realistic working situations have to be searched for at an individual level. Thirdly, it has to be shown that when support (or other types of information) has been given to the operator this will evoke the desired state change. With respect of this latter aspect it has to be concluded that there are up to now rather few studies in which this approach has followed successfully (Pope et al., 1995).

5 Example studies in short

In order to show that several types of information sources are available that might be useful, our approach will be illustrated in short with a number of example studies.

In a study on driver state classification and correction an eye lid sensor was used to detect sleepiness of the operator (De Waard et al., 2004). The aim of the project was to develop an unobtrusive, reliable system that will monitor the driver and will detect hypo-vigilance in real-time and that has to work in all motorway scenarios. Next to the eye lid sensors, driving quality was monitored by measuring lateral position, speed and steering wheel actions. A 'traffic estimator' was implemented to value discrete risks and environmental factors. Drowsiness warnings were given to the participants in case such states were detected. Results of the first study indicated that the eye lid sensor worked adequately in about 60% of the rides. Subjects indicated that 63% of the given warnings were considered as correct, while 50% were exactly on time. On basis of the results of the study technical performance of the device could be improved and functioned better in later pilot studies.

Eye-derived measures, such as blinks, pupil diameter, fixations, dwell times, scanning behavior (entropy) were used in several studies at NLR and University of Groningen. In a study in a simulated ambulance dispatchers task participants were required to react as fast as possible on incoming '112' messages (urgent patient transport). However, most of the time (about 80%) was spent at planning of non-urgent transport of patient from home address to hospital and vice versa. Next to eye fixations and dwell times in specific regions of the computer screen an entropy measure was used, which indicated the degree of randomness of transitions between one area of interest to another (Kruizinga et al., 2006). When very busy time periods (about 15 minutes) were compared with more quiet ones, contrasting results were found in the urgent vs the non-urgent rides. Entropy was decreased in the busy time segments during the planning of the non-urgent rides, indicating a more systematic planning pattern when less time was available. During the planning of the urgent rides a less systematic eye scanning pattern was found in the busy periods. It was concluded that participants got disturbed by other on-going task elements in the busy time segments during the handling of the urgent 112 messages.

In a work load study in a small flight simulator pilots-in-training flew a flight scenario with increasing complexity during about 40 minutes. Heart rate increased during the flight with more than 20 beats/minute, while heart rate variability (HRV) decreased considerably already in the first phases of the flight. Eye fixation durations decreased from 500 ms in the first (easy) phase of the flight to 430 ms in the last (difficult) phases of the flight. There was a considerable correlation between heart rate and fixation times. More detailed analysis learned that fixation duration was not only dependent on task load, but also on task specific aspects, related to scanning behavior of the instruments in relation to transitions from stable task segments to new flying conditions (De Rivecourt et al., in review).

Cardiovascular research in the field of mental workload has a long history, especially with short lasting laboratory tasks. In general it is found that heart rate and blood pressure increase with increasing mental effort, while heart rate variability decreases. In the same task situation as already described with the ambulance dispatchers' simulation, participants worked for about 90 minutes; low work load task conditions (15 minutes) were followed by high task load conditions (also 15 minutes) and vice versa. The pattern of results showed a continuous increase of blood pressure in combination with a decrease of heart rate as a function of time. Heart rate variability showed an increase as a function of time, while indications were found for relatively decreased HRV in the most demanding task conditions. It was concluded that long lasting task performance induced a considerable cardiovascular state change, which was counteracted by more activity in short-lasting blood pressure control (baroreflex). This latter effect is responsible for the decrease in heart rate as well as the increase in HRV. However, more detailed analysis at an individual level, using a multiple regression model, learned that in 75% of the cases periods of high work load could be distinguished from low work load conditions (Mulder et al., 2004, De Waard and Mulder, 2006).

Recently, a pilot study was performed using a computer program to recognize human emotions, again in the already described ambulance dispatchers' simulation task. This time, emotions were evoked by incoming (urgent) telephone calls describing accident situations and patient states that should evoke emotional reactions to the operators. The emotions that could be distinguished were the 6 basic emotions (anger, disgust, fear, joy, sadness and surprise) according to (Ekman and Friesen, 1978); a neutral state was added (Van Kuilenburg et al., 2005). The computer program worked on-line, while off-line analysis afterwards allowed for more detailed descriptions of emotional state changes. The conclusion of this pilot study was that it is yet too early to use this approach in real experiments; first some technical improvements in the computer program as well as in the experimental set-up have to be made. However, the approach is promising.

6   Conclusions

The COMPANION approach as described offers good possibilities to realize a feedback structure that can be successfully applied in adaptive automation. However, before this can be realized in real practice several steps have to be taken that require experimental research at different levels. As a matter of fact, most of the research on mental work load that has been done in the last decades was directed strongly to laboratory situations, while paying not enough attention to the differences with real live working situation. Moreover, almost all research was directed to the group-level, thereby paying not enough attention to individual physiological patterns or state changes. Two other restrictions have to be mentioned. Many studies in the past were directed to only one field, e.g. cardiovascular or EEG measures, while not looking at other sources of information. In particular for state classification and related state changes, combinations of sources of information are extremely important. The reason that such combined studies were not performed is quite clear: it requires both theoretical knowledge and practical insight in each of the fields which were not available in many cases. The good news at the present is that gradually this knowledge comes available in a usable form, while technical and computational restrictions are becoming less relevant because of obtained technical progress. The discussed example studies above illustrate that several information sources are available to be used (on-line) to classify physiological state changes in combination with changes in task characteristics and/or task performance.

In relation to the 'Probing Experience' approach two remarks can be made. Firstly, in our experimental work we paid more attention to long term state changes (in particular cardiovascular) than to short term, while the latter probably are of more interest for situations in which the reactions of users on new products or new designs have to be estimated. Secondly, to our idea the COMPANION and OSM concepts as presented in this chapter in it self could be helpful for development of products that may require adaptation of the tasks or environments in which users are working or living. Next to physiological signals, task performance indicators such as mouse actions could be useful in such situations.

Acknowledgements

Parts of the presented work were facilitated by two research projects. One of them was the Companion project (Senter Novem IOP MMI 99002A&B), co-funded by the Dutch Ministry of Economic Affairs. The other was the HILAS Integrated Project (516181), which is funded by the Commission of the European Communities as part of the 6th Framework Programme.

The authors wish to thank the Technical Service Group (IDP) of the department of Psychology at the University of Groningen for their support.

References

De Waard, D., De Jong, C., Brookhuis, K., Brouwer, R., & Antonello, C. (2004). Detecting drowsiness on-the-road after a night shift. Report WP7, Pilot 16. AWAKE IST-2000-28062 Consortium. Groningen: TRAIL Research School, Experimental and Work Psychology.

De Waard, D. & Mulder, L.J.M. (2006). Can cardiovascular indices be used to adapt the ambulance dispatch worker's task? In S. Miyake and M. Trimmel (Eds.) Proceedings of the 6th International Conference on Psychophysiology in Ergonomics. PIE-IEA Maastricht 2006, pp 90–96.

De Rivecourt, M., Kuperus, M.N., Mulder, L.J.M., & Post, W.J. (in review). Heart rate and eye activity measures as indices for mental effort in aviation.

Ekman, P. & Friesen, W. (1978). *Facial Action Coding System: A Technique for the Measurement of Facial Movement*. Consulting Psychologists Press, Palo Alto, CA.

Endsley, M.R. (1996). Automation and Situation Awareness. In R. Parasuraman & M. Mouloua (Eds.) *Automation and Human Performance: Theory and Applications* (pp. 163–181). New Jersey: Lawrence Erlbaum Associates.

Endsley, M.R. & Kiris, E.O. (1995). The out-of-the-loop performance problem and level of control in automation. *Human Factors, 37*, 381–394.

Fairclough, S.H. & Venables, L. (2004). Psychophysiological candidates for biocybernetic control of adaptive automation. In D. de Waard, K.A. Brookhuis, and C.M Weikert (Eds.), *Human Factors in Design* (pp. 177–189). Maastricht, the Netherlands: Shaker Publishing.

Hoogeboom, P.J. & Mulder, L.J.M. (2004). Physiological indices for the estimation of momentary changes in cognitive workload and mental state. In D. de Waard, K.A. Brookhuis, and C.M Weikert (Eds.), *Human Factors in Design* (pp. 147–160). Maastricht, the Netherlands: Shaker Publishing.

Kruizinga, A., Mulder, B., & De Waard, D. (2006). Eye scan patterns in a simulated ambulance dispatcher's task. In: D. de Waard, K.A. Brookhuis & A. Toffetti (eds.). Developments in Human Factors and Transportation, Design and Evaluation. Maastricht, the Netherlands: Shaker Publishing (pp. 305–317).

McClumpha, A.J., James, M., Green, R.G., & Belyavin, A.J. (1991). Pilots' attitudes to cockpit automation. *Proceedings of the Human Factors Society 35th Annual Meeting* (pp. 107–111). Human Factors and Ergonomics Society: Santa Monica, Ca, U.S.A.

Mulder, B., Kruizinga, A., Stuiver, A., Venema, I., & Hoogeboom, P. (2004). Monitoring cardiovascular state changes in a simulated ambulance dispatch task for use in adaptive automation. In D. de Waard, K.A. Brookhuis, and C.M Weikert (Eds.), *Human Factors in Design* (pp. 161–175). Maastricht, the Netherlands: Shaker Publishing.

Parasuraman, R., Mouloua, M., & Molloy, R. (1996). Effects of adaptive task allocation on monitoring of automated systems. *Human Factors, 38*, 665–679.

Parasuraman, R. & Riley, V. (1997). Humans and Automation: Use, Misuse, Disuse, Abuse. *Human Factors, 39*, 230–253.

Parasuraman R., Sheridan, T.B., & Wickens C.D. (2002). A model for types and levels of Human Interaction with automation. *IEEE Transactins on Systems, Man, and Cybernetics – Part A: Systems and Humans.* Vol. 30, no 3, May 2000, p 286–297.

Pope, A.T., Bogart, E.H. & Bartolome, D. (1995). Biocybernetic system evaluates indices of operator engagement. *Biological Psychology, 40*, 187–196.

Scerbo, M.W. (1996). Theoretical perspectives on adaptive automation. In R. Parasuraman & M. Mouloua (Eds.) *Automation and Human Performance: Theory and Applications* (pp. 37–63). New Jersey: Lawrence Erlbaum Associates.

Scerbo, M.W. (1999). Adaptive automation: Working with a computer teammate. In L.J. Hettinger & M.W. Haas (eds.). Psychological issues in the design and use of virtual, adaptive environments. Mahwah, N.J.: Lawrence Erlbaum associates.

Van Kuilenburg, H., Wiering, M. & Den Uyl, M. (2005). A Model Based Method for Automatic Facial Expression Recognition, J. Gama et al. (Eds.): ECML 2005, *LNAI 3720, pp.* 194–205, Heidelberg: Springer-Verlag Berlin.

20

THE USABILITY OF CARDIOVASCULAR AND ELECTRODERMAL MEASURES FOR ADAPTIVE AUTOMATION

Florian Schaefer, Andrea Haarmann and Wolfram Boucsein

Abstract   In case of adaptive automation, a system automatically increases the operator's workload if there are signs of hypovigilance, reflected in psychophysiological arousal measures such as spontaneous electrodermal activity, and takes over more responsibility in case of workload becoming too high. Adaptive automation is currently discussed for long-term operations such as intercontinental flights according to instrumental flight rules. We constructed a closed-loop adaptive system for varying the strength of turbulence in a professional simulator. In the experimental condition, nine subjects flew thirty 60-s flight sections, keeping altitude and course while facing different turbulences. The number of nonspecific skin conductance responses was calculated every 60 s and was used for triggering the turbulence strength for the next 60 s, dependent on the set point of the individual subject. The other nine subjects belonged to the yoked control condition, flying the same sequence of turbulences as the corresponding experimental subject, however without adaptive automation. Our results indicate that the skin conductance responses of experimental subjects oscillated very close to the individual set point, indicating that the subjects maintained an optimal vigilance/workload level as a result of adaptive control in contrast to yoked control subjects.

1 Introduction

A certain degree of the operator's attention is a prerequisite for successfully operating complex man-machine systems. Increasing the degree of automation in a system may restrict the operator's role to one of a mere observer, thus considerably reducing his/her vigilance. Furthermore, complex systems may allow for multiple modes of automation. In case of an unexpected change in situational demands or a system failure requiring immediate operator actions, he/she may not be able to perform an appropriate response since he/she may have lost situational or mode awareness. Thus, there is a need for precautionary measures to prevent an operator from vigilance decrement in case of operating automated man-machine systems.

J.H.D.M. Westerink et al. (eds.), Probing Experience, 235–243.
© 2008 *Springer.*

Adaptive automation refers to the capability of a system to adjust its mode or increasing/reducing the degree of automation dynamically as a consequence of changes in the operator's vigilance (Byrne and Parasuraman, 1996; Pope et al., 1995). In case of hypovigilance, the system may alert the operator, thus increasing his/her attention. In turn, if the operator's workload is too high, the system may automatically take over more responsibility for the task in question.

Vigilance decrement as well as high workload may result in performance decrement and thus should be detectable by performance changes. However, in case of a fully automated system, no measure of the operator's performance will be available from the original task (Morrison and Gluckman, 1994). An introduction of secondary tasks would not only unnecessarily increase the operator's workload but also induce motivational problems. Since vigilance decrement is typically accompanied by a decline in psychophysiological arousal, it can be monitored by measures of central and autonomic nervous system (ANS) activity. Therefore, these measures may be used to continuously monitor the operator's attentional state. Increased workload is accompanied by an increase in arousal that is reflected in psychophysiological measures as well. Setting up an adaptive automated man-machine system will allow for both upward and downward adjustments in order to keep the operator in an optimal state for operating the system.

Arousal shifts are reflected in various psychophysiological systems such as spontaneous electroencephalography (EEG) or cardiovascular (ECG) and electrodermal activity (EDA). Physiological measures to be used in adaptive automation are required to be continuously monitored and on-line evaluated. They are not supposed to interfere with the task or impair the operator's well-being. First attempts to establish man-machine systems for adaptive automation in laboratory environments have used EEG derived indices (Pope et al., 1995; Prinzel et al., 2001; Prinzel et al., 2003), heart rate variability (Byrne and Parasuraman, 1996; Prinzel et al., 2003) or electrodermal activity (Yamamoto and Isshiki, 1992).

One important application for adaptive automation systems is conducting long-haul transport operations in an airplane. Today's commercial aircraft are flown by computer systems that allow for modes where the pilots remain almost passive during long periods of flight, a situation inherent to vigilance decrement. Endsley already discussed the *"out of the loop performance problem"* in system operators (Endsley, 1996), and Prinzel et al. (2001) referred to *"operator hazardous states of awareness"* in aviation. Because it is impracticable to record EEG from commercial pilots, attempts have been made to use autonomic nervous system measures to detect vigilance decrement in such pilots (Wright and McGown, 2001). The goal of our current research is to provide such a system, based on electrodermal and cardiovascular measures.

In a previous pilot study (Boucsein et al., 2005), we recorded electrodermal activity and heart rate from student subjects during four flight missions in a professional instrumental flight rule (IFR) simulator, varying the strength of turbulence in order to check the usability of ANS measures for adaptive automation. Increasing strength of turbulence resulted in an increment of nonspecific skin conductance responses (NS.SCRs) which can be interpreted as an indicator of increased workload. On the other hand, progression of flight missions was associated with habituation shown by a decreased frequency of NS.SCRs and reduced sum amplitude. The aim of the present study was to construct a closed-loop adaptive system, implementing NS.SCRs as adequate arousal indicator and control variable for adjusting the strength of turbulence onset during a flight task.

2 Method

2.1 Subjects

Eighteen student subjects (11 female, 7 male) aged 20 to 34 years (M = 26.39 years, SD = 4.5 years) took part in the study as part of a psychology course requirement. Five more subjects had to be excluded from the sample due to technical irregularities or electrodermal nonresponding.

2.2 Task and design

The subjects had to accomplish the following IFR flight missions:

1. Starting the plane and climbing to 2000 feet.

2. Flying straight and level northbound, controlling altitude, speed and course.

3. Turning 90 degrees eastward and keeping that course, controlling altitude and speed.

4. Keeping east course, controlling altitude and speed while facing turbulences (turbulence steps 0 and 2).

Before starting their task, subjects were familiarized with the flight simulator instruments during two practice trials without any turbulences and turbulence step 2. After having performed all four flight missions, subjects rested for stabilization (about 2 mins). Afterwards, two baseline recordings were made (60 s without turbulences as resting period, 60 s with turbulence step 2 as workload period). Next, the control computer calculated the subjects' individual set point for NS.SCRs, based on the arithmetic mean of the two baseline recordings. The subjects were divided into two groups:

1. In the experimental condition, nine subjects flew thirty 60-s flight sections, keeping altitude and course while facing different turbulences. The number of NS.SCRs was calculated every 60 s and was used for triggering the turbulence strength for the next 60 s, dependent on the set point of the individual subject.

2. The other nine subjects belonged to the yoked control condition, i. e. each yoked control subject received the same sequence of turbulences as the corresponding experimental subject, regardless of his/her own set point and hence without adaptive automation.

2.3 Apparatus

We used a professional IFR flight simulator software on a personal computer (LAS 5.0, made by Fahsig, Germany), extended by the feature of varying the strength of turbulence by means of external control. The cockpit instruments were displayed on a 17″ monitor placed 0.5 m in front of the subject. Controls for ailerons, elevator and throttle were provided, together with an electrical trim. A second computer was needed for the control of adaptive automation:

- triggering the automatic onset and offset of turbulences on the LAS computer according to the subjects' individual set point (comparator function)

- starting physiological data recording on a third computer

- receiving the on-line calculated NS.SCRs from the recording computer for adaptive regulation of the subjects' arousal.

Figure 1 gives an overview of the information flow between the subject and the various instruments.

2.4 Recording and data analysis

Recording of physiological data (EDA, ECG, respiration) was performed by means of a Nihon Kohden Neurofax EEG-8310 G polygraph, using a personal computer with a customized software package (*PSYCHOLAB,* ©Jörn Grabke, 1997). EDA was recorded thenar and hypothenar from the left hand with two Ag/AgCl electrodes (0.8 cm diameter), using isotonic electrode cream (Med Associates, Inc.), with a sampling rate of 20 Hz, a sensitivity of 0.001 µS, and a 0.3 Hz low pass filter. Frequency and sum amplitude of NS.SCRs were used as tonic EDA measures, calculated on-line by customized software (*EDR_PARA* and *EDR_SLCT,* ©Florian Schaefer, 2003), using an amplitude criterion of 0.01 µS. ECG was recorded by the Einthoven II-lead

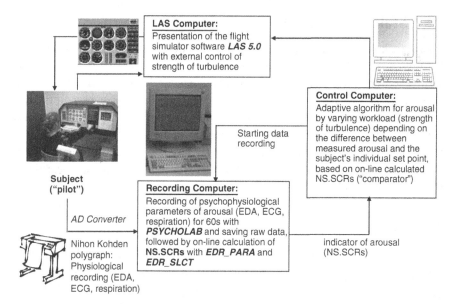

Figure 1.   Closed-loop adaptive system based on NS.SCRs.

(above the right wrist vs. above the left ankle) with two Ag/AgCl electrodes, filled with Hellige electrode cream, at a sampling rate of 200 Hz. A ground electrode was placed on the left forearm. The ECG signal was analyzed by customized software (*EKG_IBI, IBI_SCAN, IBI_PARA,* ©Florian Schaefer, 2003) calculating mean heart rate (see Equation 1) and heart rate variability (HRV) as square root of the mean square of successive differences (MSSD – see Equation 2).

$$\text{Mean heart rate} = \sum^{n} \frac{60000}{IBI} \bigg/ n \qquad (1)$$

$$\text{MSSD} = \sum_{i=2}^{n} \left(\frac{60000}{IBI_i} - \frac{60000}{IBI_{i-1}} \right)^2 \bigg/ n-1 \qquad (2)$$

whereby

$\dfrac{60000}{IBI_i}$ = time duration of interbeat interval *i*,

n = number of heartbeats observed.

For artifact control, a respiration belt containing a piezo element was fastened to the subject's thorax (sampling rate of 10 Hz).

2.5   Statistical analysis

For each pair of experimental and yoked control subjects the differences between nominal (set point) and actual NS.SCRs of thirty flight sections were calculated as absolute deviation values and compared with paired t-tests (one-sided). Such a procedure was necessary because each pair of subjects had a different sequence of turbulences, dependent on the experimental subject's electrodermal responses. Furthermore, the correlations between the frequency of NS.SCRs throughout the thirty flight sections and the resulting onset or offset of turbulences were calculated for each pair, using the Spearman's rho (ρ) coefficient.

3   Results

Figure 2 shows the physiological responses of two subjects dealing with the task to keep altitude and direction while facing turbulences during thirty flight sections. Subject 108 belonged to the experimental condition. Dependent on the individual set point, turbulences were turned on in case of low arousal (NS.SCRs $\leq$ 9) and turned off in case of high arousal (NS.SCRs > 9). An update of the electrodermal data was performed every 60 s. The same procedure was applied to subject 208 with the exception that he belonged to the yoked control condition, that is, he received the same sequence of turbulences as subject 108 regardless of his own set point (NS.SCRs = 8.5) and physiological responses. As can be inferred from Figure 2, the NS.SCRs of subject 108 oscillated very close to the individual set point of 9 per minute, indicating an optimal arousal level as a result of the adaptive control. In case of the yoked control subject 208, however, the NS.SCRs diverged from the set point as a consequence of the sequence forced upon him without an adaptive control being applied. A paired t-test revealed a significant mean difference between the two subjects shown in Figure 2 over thirty flight sections (mean deviation of 2.2 NS.SCRs [SD = 1.883] for subject 108 vs. 3.533 NS.SCRs [SD = 3.168] for subject 208, t(29) = 2.394, p<.05, see Table 1a). An analysis of sum amplitude values showed even more significant mean differences (p<.01, see Table 1a), although that parameter was not integrated in the closed-loop adaptive system. Overall, yoked control subjects had higher sum amplitude values than experimental subjects.

These data are supplemented by highly significant negative correlations between NS.SCRs and NS.SCR-induced turbulences (Spearman's rho [ρ] up to −.875, see Table 1b), indicating that the subjects in the experimental condition maintained an optimal vigilance/workload level as a result of adaptive control in contrast to the yoked control subjects.

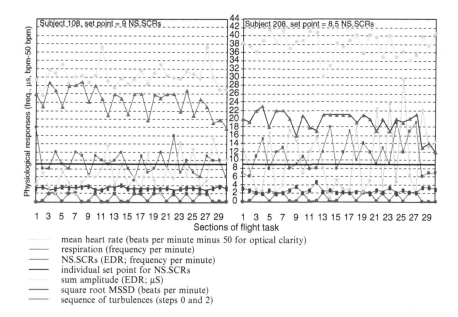

mean heart rate (beats per minute minus 50 for optical clarity)
respiration (frequency per minute)
NS.SCRs (EDR; frequency per minute)
individual set point for NS.SCRs
sum amplitude (EDR; μS)
square root MSSD (beats per minute)
sequence of turbulences (steps 0 and 2)

Figure 2. Comparison of an experimental subject (108) with a yoked control subject (208).

Table 1. (a) Mean deviation values (actual value minus set point value) and t-values for paired comparisons over 30 flight sections. (b) Correlations between EDA measures and resulting turbulences.

Subjects	a) NS.SCRs Mean deviation (SD)	t(29)	Sum amplitude Mean deviation (SD)	t(29)	b) Correlations ρ (NS. SCRs)	ρ (sum amplitude)
104	2.100 (1.768)	1.868	1.280 (0.405)	17.812**	−.741**	−.524**
204	2.700 (1.472)		9.341 (2.691)		−.014	−.073
106	3.033 (1.814)	1.057	0.957 (0.659)	3.215**	a	a
206	2.800 (2.351)		2.426 (2.966)		a	a
108	2.200 (1.883)	2.394*	3.230 (1.987)	3.462**	−.875**	.258
208	3.533 (3.168)		7.590 (7.555)		−.232	.273
109	1.967 (3.148)	.779	8.009 (5.765)	5.937**	−.874**	.268
209	1.867 (1.995)		1.931 (0.596)		−.190	−.288
110	2.533 (2.270)	1.249	3.919 (3.153)	6.845**	−.855**	−.039
210	2.167 (1.493)		0.123 (0.107)		.087	.071
111	3.567 (1.893)	4.238**	21.453 (6.082)	9.023**	−.439*	.201
211	5.433 (2.096)		9.930 (3.506)		−.244	−.077
112	2.767 (2.096)	1.899	5.715 (4.170)	1.182	−.873**	−.031
212	2.067 (1.552)		6.332 (3.283)		−.152	.232

Table 1 (contd).   (a)Mean deviation values (actual value minus set point value) and t-values for paired comparisons over 30 flight sections. (b)Correlations between EDA measures and resulting turbulences.

Subjects	a) NS.SCRs Mean deviation (SD)	t(29)	Sum amplitude Mean deviation (SD)	t(29)	b) Correlations ρ (NS. SCRs)	ρ (sum amplitude)
113	2.133 (1.525)	3.332**	8.471 (4.804)	1.091	−.600**	−.096
213	3.500 (1.576)		7.739 (5.869)		.198	−.181
114	2.467 (1.650)	2.603*	6.577 (0.372)	6.830**	−.864**	−.532**
214	1.600 (1.125)		15.149 (7.071)		.162	.214

* p<.05 ρ Spearman's rho
** p<.01   a not calculated (strength of turbulence did not change)

4   Discussion

The present study examined the adjustment of physiological arousal in a closed-loop adaptive system by means of NS.SCRs during a simulated flight mission task in a yoked control group design. In the experimental group, adaptive adjustment was performed by means of NS.SCRs according to the subjects' individual set point taken from two baseline recordings. In the yoked control group, subjects flew the sequence of flight missions of their experimental counterparts without an adaptive control, i. e. regardless of their individual set point. Results indicate that the experimental subjects were closer to their individual set point of arousal compared to yoked control subjects as a consequence of adaptive control.

The present results look promising for the usability of autonomic measures in adaptive automation. It is, however, rather unlikely that a single physiological system will have both sensitivity and diagnosticity to cover all aspects of vigilance decrement and arousal in man-machine systems. Instead, recording various physiological systems may be needed in order to gain a full picture of the different arousal and attentional systems (Boucsein and Backs, 2000). In an upcoming study, three major modifications will be made to the experimental setting:

Firstly, we shall compare different combinations of autonomic measures regarding quality of regulation (e.g. NS.SCRs combined with heart rate variability in an adaptive algorithm). Secondly, in order to obtain a more accurate calculation of the subjects' individual set point we shall take four instead of two baseline recordings (two without turbulences, two with turbulences). During baseline recordings in the present study, some subjects showed more NS.SCRs under resting than under workload conditions. Using a wider range of baseline recordings may adjust this problem. Thirdly, we shall consider extension of recording periods to 2 mins per flight section. In psychophysiological measurement, very short epochs may not detect slow changes in physiological measures. Very long epochs hold the problem of temporal effects occurring during long-term task performance, e.g. learning, adaptation and fatigue (Luczak and Göbel, 2000). Therefore, it is essential to determine recording periods which maintain effective and stable adjustment of arousal within an adaptive system.

References

Boucsein, W. and Backs, R.W. Engineering psychophysiology as a discipline: Historical and theoretical aspects. In: Backs, R.W. and Boucsein, W. (Eds.) Engineering Psychophysiology. Issues and applications. Lawrence Erlbaum Associates, Mahwah, NJ, (2000), pp 3–29.

Boucsein, W., Haarmann, A. and Schaefer, F. The usability of cardiovascular and electrodermal measures for adaptive automation during a simulated IFR flight mission. *Psychophysiology* 42 (2005) S26.

Byrne, E.A. and Parasuraman, R. Psychophysiology and adaptive automation. *Biol. Psychol.* 42 (1996) 249–268.

Endsley, M.R. Automation and situation awareness. In: Parasuraman R and Mouloua M (Eds.) Automation and human performance: Theory and applications. Lawrence Erlbaum Associates, Hillsdale, NJ, England, (1996), pp 163–181.

Luczak, H. and Göbel, M. Signal processing and analysis in application. In: Backs RW and Boucsein W (Eds.) Engineering psychophysiology. Issues and applications. Lawrence Erlbaum Associates, Mahwah, NJ, (2000), pp 79–110.

Morrison, J.G. and Gluckman, J.P. Definitions and prospective guidelines for the application of adaptive automation. In: Mouloua, M. and Parasuraman, R. (Eds.) Human performance in automated systems: Current research and trends. Lawrence Erlbaum Associates, Hillsdale, NJ, (1994), pp 256–263.

Pope, A.T., Bogart, E.H. and Barolome, D.S. Biocybernetic system evaluates indices of operator engagement in automated task. *Biol. Psychol.* 40 (1995) 187–195.

Prinzel, III L.J., Parasuraman, R., Freeman, F.G., Scerbo, M.W., Mikulka, P.J. and Pope, A.T. Three experiments examining the use of electroencephalogram, event-related potentials, and heart-rate variability for real-time human-centered adaptive automation design. NASA Langley Research Center, Hampton, Virginia, (2003), pp 1–62 (available via http://techreports.larc.nasa.gov/ltrs/PDF/2003/tp/NASA-2003-tp212442.pdf).

Prinzel, III L.J., Pope, A.T. and Freeman, F.G. Application of physiological self-regulation and adaptive task allocation techniques for controlling operator hazardous states of awareness. NASA Langley Research Center, Hampton, Virginia, (2001), pp 1–17 (available via http://techreports.larc.nasa.gov/ltrs/PDF/2001/tm/ NASA-2001-tm211015.pdf).

Wright, N. and McGown, A. Vigilance on the civil flight deck: Incidence of sleepiness and sleep during long-haul flights and associated changes in physiological parameters. *Ergonomics* 44 (2001) 82–116.

Yamamoto, Y. and Isshiki, H. Instrument for controlling drowsiness using galvanic skin reflex. *Med. Biol. Eng. Comput.* 30 (1992) 562–564.

Philips Research Book Series

1. H.J. Bergveld, W.S. Kruijt and P.H.L. Notten: *Battery Management Systems*. 2002
   ISBN 1-4020-0832-5
2. W. Verhaegh, E. Aarts and J. Korst (eds.): *Algorithms in Ambient Intelligence*. 2004
   ISBN 1-4020-1757-X
3. P. van der Stok (ed.): *Dynamic and Robust streaming in and between Connected Consumer-Electronic Devices*. 2005
   ISBN 1-4020-3453-9
4. E. Meinders, A.V. Mijritskii, L. van Pieterson and M. Wuttig: *Phase-Change Optical Recording Media*. 2006
   ISBN 1-4020-4216-7
5. S. Mukherjee, E. Aarts, R. Roovers, F. Widdershoven and M. Ouwerkerk (eds.): *AmIware*. Hardware Technology Drivers of Ambient Intelligence. 2006
   ISBN 1-4020-4197-7
6. G. Spekowius and T. Wendler (eds.): *Advances in Healthcare Technology*. Shaping the Future of Medical Care. 2006
   ISBN 1-4020-4383-X
7. W.F.J. Verhaegh, E. Aarts and J. Korst (eds.): *Intelligent Algorithms in Ambient and Biomedical Computing*. 2006
   ISBN 1-4020-4953-8
8. J.H.D.M. Westerink, M. Ouwerkerk, Th. Overbeek, F. Pasveer, and B. de Ruyter (Eds.): *Probing Experience: From Assessment of User Emotions and Behaviour to Development of Products*. 2008
   ISBN 978-1-4020-6592-7